Mark Lemon

Up and down the London streets

Mark Lemon

Up and down the London streets

ISBN/EAN: 9783743311121

Manufactured in Europe, USA, Canada, Australia, Japa

Cover: Foto ©Lupo / pixelio.de

Manufactured and distributed by brebook publishing software (www.brebook.com)

Mark Lemon

Up and down the London streets

AND DOWN THE LONDON ST

UP AND DOWN

THE LONDON STREETS.

BY

MARK LEMON.

TEMPLE GARDENS.

LONDON:

CHAPMAN AND HALL, 193, PICCADILLY.

1867.

As we had the honour to be born within the sound of Bow bells, a fellow-citizen of Sir Thomas More, John Milton, Alexander Pope, and Johnny Gilpin, we have, "e'en from our boyish days," taken pleasure to seek in books and odd places the story of Old London City; and having come to the belief that what has had for us so many attractions might possibly be made to interest others, we have COMPILED the following pages; and we desire it to be understood, that we only ask recognition for our industry, and not commendation for any original discoveries. We have freely gleaned from antiquaries, poets, historians, and compilers who have preceded us, thereby creating, mayhap, a desire for more knowledge of the old City, and which lies ready for the inquirer in other pages.* **Many** who loved the old City **well have** preserved in enduring printers' ink, chronicles **of its** ancient streets, their mansions and hostelries, and of many a haunted nook dear **to** the Cockney antiquary **and** historian. In their company **we** propose to walk " up and down the streets of London," chatting as we go, and occasionally detailing some of our own experiences—very small change to mix with the golden legends of the old City.

We do not present **ourselves as a** solemn antiquary, smothering you with **dust** of the **past.** No; we shall furbish up the old materials, **so that you** may see at a glance all that we **wish** to **show you;** nor shall we pause to test **the** truth **of all** we have to **tell.** **Y**ou must take us, if you please, as an arm-in-arm companion through some of the broadways and byways of London, recalling past times and their belongings, **and not** altogether forgetting new times and **their** improvements. We shall tell, doubtless, of much that you already know, of some things you **may** not care to hear

PRINCIPAL AUTHORITIES.—Fitzstephen (1191), Stow (1525—1605), Hall (1547), Camden (1551—1623), Hollingshed (1577), Clarendon (1608—1674), Strype (1643—1737), Pennant (1726—1798), Pepys, Evelyn, Speight, Maitland, Hughson, Charles Knight, Peter Cunningham, John Timbs, Burns, Morley, Saunders, Jesse, Weir, Smiles, and others, to whose works the curious in details are referred.

again, of many matters, we trust, which you may
be glad to recall, if they are not altogether new
to you, and we may perchance pass by subjects
which you may think should have been considered.
We shall therefore ask the great Shakespeare to
plead for us, as he once pleaded for himself :

"But pardon, gentles all,
The flat, unraised spirit that hath dared
On this unworthy scaffold to bring forth
So great an object . . . . . .
. . . . Jumping o'er times,
Turning the accomplishment of many years
Into an hour-glass.   Your humble patience pray,
Gently to hear—kindly to judge."

CHAPTER I.

LONDON was no doubt of British origin, and possibly the Trinobantum, which Cæsar in his Commentaries mentions as the chief city of the Trinobantes. It has been suggested (Hughson) that the word is easily convertible into *Tre-yn-y-bant*, which describes exactly the situation of the British *town in the valley*—the vale of London extending from Brentwood to Windsor one way, and from Hampstead to the Surrey hills another. As this appears to be a very probable derivation of the name we mention it; besides, it reads learned and antiquarian. There has been much speculation as to the derivation of the word "Cockney." It has been traced to "a cockered

B

or spoilt boy;" "a cock neiging;" and thus by inversion *incock, incoctus, i. e.* "unripe in countrymen's affairs." Could the terminal "*bantum*" have had anything to do with it? The suggestion is rather a wild one, but philologists do go it sometimes.

We propose, however, to keep to Roman London —Londonium, or, as it was called, Augusta, from its magnificence (Tacitus); and shall avail ourselves of the remarks of Mr. John Bagford, who wrote to his friend, Mr. Hearne, in 1714: "The Romans," he says, "landed at Dover, and then dividing their forces, approached London by different routes. They came along Kent Road to Stone Street, crossed the Thames, and landed at Dowgate, the river being much shallower and wider at that time, although free from the mud now defiling its banks. There were fords at many places besides Dowgate—as high up as Milford Lane and the Strand. The river was fordable at York House, where Inigo Jones's gate still stands. The Romans then made military ways—Old Street for one, and Watling Street, which extended from the Tower to Ludgate." Mr. Bagford will have it that the White Tower was built by the Romans, and we have no desire to dispute the point, though many learned antiquaries deny the assertion and assign the building to William the Conqueror.

The supposed site of the walls of Roman London has been determined by our knowledge of the positions in which various relics of Roman origin have been discovered at different times, and deposited *within* the old walls, whilst others of a sepulchral character have been found *without;* and as it was the wise custom of most nations of antiquity to inter their dead *without* their cities, the course of the Old London walls has been pretty clearly defined.

It is somewhat surprising that an opposite practice should have found favour in the eyes (or rather noses) of their suc-

THE OLDEST VIEW OF LONDON EXTANT. (With the Spire of Old St. Paul's, before 1569.)

cessors, and eight hundred and more years should
have passed by before their salutary and sanitary
custom was resumed. We have many other results
of the rule of those remarkable Romans, once the
world's enemies, but now only the schoolboy's.

We refer to Roman London principally to recall
the fact that the walls of London *proper* followed
the same course as their Roman predecessors, and
continued to do so until long after Elizabeth's
time, and because the subject-matter of our walk
will rarely emigrate beyond them.

At first there were but three gates in the City
walls, Aldgate or Oldgate, leading into the eastern
parts, as Essex, Suffolk, Norfolk, &c., Aldersgate,
leading to the northern parts, and Ledgate or
Ludgate, leading to the western roads, and to
which gate the Roman military road came direct
from the Tower. The other military road of the
Romans was Old Street; but the highway which
leads from Aldersgate to Islington is supposed to
have been made since the Conquest, and about the
time that the Carthusian monastery (the Charter
House) was built by Sir Walter de Mancy. The
walls were made of stone with layers of Roman
brick, and parts of them are still in existence.

As the railways above and under ground seem
likely to make a general terminus of the old City,

and sweep away all records of the past, **it** may be **as well to** recall the course of the ancient walls as traced and described by Dr. Hughson:—

" The walls commenced at the Tower of London, eastwardly, and passed between Poor Jury **Lane and** the Vineyard to Aldgate, **in** which extent between Wall's Court and Black Horse Alley was a bastion, and another opposite Weeden's Rents, a distance of eighty-two perches. From Aldgate, the wall formed a curve between Shoemaker Row, Bevis Marks, Camomile Street, and Houndsditch, fenced with three bastions, one opposite Harrow Alley, a second opposite Bowle Court, and a **third** between Hand Alley and Castle Yard, and abutted at Bishopsgate, a distance of eighty-six perches.

" Thence taking a westernly direction **through** Bishopsgate Churchyard, it continued **its** course behind Wormwood Street and Allhallows Church, **the back** of Bethlehem Hospital, where part of it **is still** standing, till it reached Moorgate, at the **end of Coleman** Street : continuing in a straight **direction, it** abutted at Cripplegate, at the distance **of one hundred and** sixty-two perches. Hence it continued westernly, **along the** back of Hart Street and the back of Cripplegate Churchyard, where, opposite Lamb's Chapel Court, was another bastion. From this place the wall took a southernly direction, between Castle Street and Monkwell Street, in which small distance were no less than three bastions at the back of Barber Surgeons' Hall: we pursue its course at the back of Noble Street, till we come to Dolphin Court, opposite Oat Lane,

BASTION OF LONDON WALL, CRIPPLEGATE, IN ITS PRESENT STATE.
(*From a Sketch by Percy Justyne.*)

where another bastion was erected; it then again proceeded westernly to Aldersgate, at the distance from Cripplegate of seventy-five perches. Keeping along the back of St. Botolph's Churchyard, it continued by the back of Christ's Hospital and the New Compter, where it again formed a curve to the south of Newgate, in which space were two bastions. The distance from Aldersgate to Newgate sixty-six perches. Keeping at the back of the present prison, the wall passed the ends of the College of Physicians, Warwick Square, the Oxford Arms Inn, Stationers' Hall, and the London Coffee-house, Ludgate Hill, where it abutted at Ludgate, the distance being forty-two perches. From Ludgate it continued by Cock Court to New Bridge Street, where remains of it are at present very perceptible, whence it proceeded along the Fleet Ditch to the east side of Chatham Square and to the Thames, at the distance of one hundred and thirty perches, making up a total of two miles and six hundred and eight feet in circuit." The City gates were pulled down with the bars, except Temple Bar, in 1760.

Two miles to the westward was the Royal Palace of Westminster, with bastions and breast-works, united to the City by the houses and river-gardens of the nobility and by the village of Charing, the Strand, and Fleet Street. To the east was Lollesworth (now Spitalfields), where a Roman burial-place was discovered in 1576, and away northward was the great Middlesex forest (until Henry III.'s reign), "full of stags, bucks, boars, and wild bulls.   Between **that** and London Wall was an open country **with** rivulets, brooks, and pools, cornfields, pastures, and delightful meadows, with many a mill whose clack was grateful to the ear."   We shall come again to these pleasant fields, to "loose a shaft," or play at football by-and-by. The bucks and bores are still in those parts—the stags went east, Capel Court way during the railway mania; **but we** don't know where the wild bulls **are**, unless—but possibly you may have heard that Irish insinuation before.

London received its first charter from William the Conqueror, and the original is still preserved in the City. The charter is written in English, in a beautiful Saxon character, on a slip of parchment six inches long and one inch broad. It is a good example of English shorthand, **and is** as follows :—

"William the King greeteth William the Bishop and Godfrey the Portreve, **and** all the Burgesses within London, friendly. And I acquaint you that I *will* that ye be all there law worthy as ye were **in** King Edward's days. And I *will* that every child be his father's heir after his father's days. And I will not suffer that any man do you wrong. God preserve you."

CHARTER OF WILLIAM THE CONQUEROR TO THE CITIZENS OF LONDON.

"William the King greeteth William the Bishop and Godfrey the Portreve, and all the Burgesses within London, friendly. And I acquaint you that I will that ye be all there law worthy as ye were in King Edward's days. And I will that every child be his father's heir after his father's days. And I will not suffer that any man do you wrong. God preserve you."

This charter of Three Points is one of the first granted to London; but it was not until Henry I.'s time that a real charter, one of any money value, existed. Henry granted Middlesex to the City, to farm at 300*l*. per annum (which must have puzzled some of the Cockney magnates, knowing what we do of cockney farming now-a-days), and to the citizens a free passage and exemption from tolls and customs all over England. It was something, then, you see, to be a Cockney.

Henry's charter gave the City its Corporation, confirmed by King John, " for a consideration," and he directed that the Mayor and Common Councilmen should be elected annually. London existed without aldermen till 1242, when some of the twenty-six wards received their names from their first aldermen. The present ward of Farringdon was bought by William Faryngdon, and remained in his family for upwards of eighty years: it was held by the tenure of presenting at Easter a gillyflower, then a great rarity.

Portsoken Ward implies, a soke or franchise at the gate.

Aldgate takes its name from the eastern gate of the City.

Lime Street, from (Stow says) making lime there, but another Dryasdust thinks it was named from the Saxon Lim—*dirty*—so the residents may take their choice.

Bishopsgate, from the gate constructed by Bishop Erkenwald, or more probably by Bishop William, the Norman, who had architectural proclivities.

Langbourne, from a brook which anciently ran through Fenchurch Street.

Billingsgate is said by some to be derived from King Belin—a sea king, engaged in the fish trade, we suppose, but nobody seems to know much about him. Dr. Hughson says if we look into *Junius's Etymologicum Anglicanum* we shall find under the word BELE—"*Scotis est signum igne datum è nave prætoriâ,*"—*i. e.,* being translated, "among the Scots, the Bele is a signal by fire, given from ships' cabins," and that Beling's gate was "where ships made signal by fire." What do *you* think? None of the ladies of the locality whom we have consulted can make up their minds upon the subject.

Candlewick Ward took its name from the candle-wrights in wax and tallow who resided there.

Walbrook was from a brook which passed through the City wall and emptied itself in the Thames at Dowgate : like the Fleet it is now a sewer.

Dowgate, from its descent to the river. The *trajectus* or ferry was at Dowgate.

The Vintry was where "the merchants of Bourdeaux craned their wines out of vessels and made sale of them." In the reign of Henry II., Fitzstephen writes, "there was a common cookery or cook's row," in the Vintry, the cooks selling only meat and the vintners selling only wine.

Cordwainers' Ward is from the Cordovan curriers and shoemakers who dwelt in Soper Lane.

Cheap Ward from Chepe, a market.

Cripplegate, from St. Giles, the abbot, who was a physician, and wrote a treatise on Palsy. Several religious foundations for lepers were dedicated to this saint, who was somewhat irreverently called "Hopping Giles." And—

Bread Street, from the bread market formerly held there.

It is as impossible to think of London aldermen apart from turtle, as to separate Christmas-time from plum-pudding ; but turtle came into England before aldermen ; for their fossils, three feet long— we mean the turtles—have been found in Tilgate Forest, Sussex. Edward III. (1328) granted a charter, and Charles II. (1680) confirmed all existing charters, but seized them in 1682, under a writ of *quo warranto*, because the citizens petitioned against the prorogation of Parliament—a thing we never hear of citizens or westenders doing now-a-days.

James II. returned all the charters, however, in 1690, and George II. confirmed them.

The first Lord Mayor of London was elected in 1189. His name was Henry Fitzalwhyn, and he occupied the civic chair twenty-four years, thus beating Dick Whittington (who did all the story-books say he did, despite the modern antiquaries) by twenty-one years.*

The Lord Mayor is King of the City, and, within his own domain, takes precedence of the Prince of Wales. His court consists of a Recorder, Chamberlain, Common Serjeant, Comptroller, City Remembrancer, Town Clerk, Swordbearer, Mace-bearer—the funny men who look out of the windows of the Lord Mayor's state coach, like peeping Toms—and other officers. The city regalia is very curious, and consists of the mace (sometimes called the sceptre), and four swords of state—their bright blades long since, we fancy, converted into carving-knives. There is the *Common* sword, to go to the Sessions and Courts of Aldermen and Common Council; the *Pearl* sword for evening parties; the Sunday sword, and the Black sword, once used on

* Sir Richard Whittington, citizen and mercer, served the office of Lord Mayor three times—the last in 1419. He founded his college dedicated to the Holy Ghost and the Virgin Mary in 1424, and his almshouses at Highgate in 1429, near the spot where he heard Bow Bells call him back to wealth and greatness.

Good Friday and all **fast** days, on the 30th of January, and the anniversary of the **Fire of** London, when the **Lord Mayor** *ought* to go to St. Paul's, but does not. When the mace was repaired some few years ago, the metal of the crown was found to be an alloy not used in art manufacture since the time of the Conquest—so said **Rundell and** Bridge.

When the late **Sir P—— L——** was Lord Mayor, an old friend called at the **Mansion** House and reminded him of the following circumstance. Sir P—— had been **one** of those fortunate youths who **come to London with** half a crown in their pockets, and make, very properly, large fortunes. Half a crown seems **to be** the necessary capital for that purpose. **When Sir** P—— was only **plain P.,** he was **concerned in some** private theatricals, and played the Lord Mayor in Richard the Third. Being of " frugal mind," he dressed his lordship in an old duffel dressing-gown and a coachman's wig, little thinking he should ever enact Lord Mayor at the Mansion House.

The oldest object in London is " London **Stone,**" formerly placed in the centre of the City, and is now embedded in the wall of St. Swithin's **Church,** Cannon Street, to be out of the way **of** further mutilation or displacement. It formerly stood on the opposite side of the way (1742), and when Wren, after the great fire, dug about it, he discovered the remains of a very considerable monument.

Camden supposed London Stone to be similar to the Milliarium in the Forum at Rome, and the English Milestone, whence the British high-roads radiated all over the island, and the distances were measured before the erection of the Standard in Cornhill. It was a landmark in the time of Athelstane, who reigned from 925 to 941, and had a remarkably short way with thieves, if they were over twelve years of age,—in point of fact, he hanged them : he lived in Addle Street, close by.

And now, striking our walking-sticks on London Stone, in imitation of Jack Cade—

" Now is Mortimer lord of this city "—

let us walk eastward and visit London Bridge, not as it is now-a-days, with its quadruple rows of vehicles and its mud-bespattered policemen—poor fellows ! placed there no doubt in penance for some weakness incidental to policemen nature, but on the original bridge of timber, due to the pious legacy of a ferryman's daughter.

The ferryman who plied where Dowgate now stands, died and left his stock and goodwill to his daughter Mary. She finding no "jolly young waterman," we presume, to her liking, took to building, and **erected** "an house of **sisters**" **in** Southwark, giving thereto the profits of the said "ferry." But in course of time the house of sisters being converted into a "college of **priests**"—the process of transmutation is not explained—"the priests builded a bridge of timber (to save themselves the labour of ferrying, we suppose), until, by **the** aid of the citizens and others, one was builded of stone." Here is a **capital theme** for some budding poet,—**fine old ferryman—silver** Thames— **blighted Mary (must** have been blighted to **have** builded **a house of** sisters), and though it may be difficult to adduce proofs of the truth of this legend, it is really as good as real.

The timber bridge, mentioned in **the** charter of the Conqueror to Westminster Abbey, **was** partly burned in 1136 (by a fire which began **at** London Stone), and afterwards repaired.

The first stone bridge was begun **in** Henry II.'s **time,** and completed in **King** John's. The architect was Peter of Cole church, St. Mary's, Conyhoop Lane (now Grocers' Alley), in the Poultry **and** St. Mary's was the chapel where Thomas à Becket was baptized. The bridge consisted of twenty **arches,** supported on nineteen piers; the road was 926 feet in length, 40 feet wide, and 60 feet in height from the river. The building was paid for principally by a tax upon wool ; hence the saying that London Bridge had been built upon woolpacks.

Over the central pier was a chapel dedicated to à Becket ; and so anxious were the ministering priests to observe *fast* days, that they made a fishpond in their particular starling of the bridge, and which was discovered in 1832.

About fifty years after its commencement, the bridge contained "innumerable people dwelling upon it ;" so many indeed that, when the bridge took fire at both ends in 1212, 3000 persons are said to have perished, including those who were sunk in the vessels when attempting to assist those on the bridge—but we fancy we must make large allowance for the mediæval penny-a liner's arithmetic in this statement.

The eleventh arch, Southwark end, was a drawbridge (for the passage of large vessels), and connected with a tower, on which were placed the heads of persons executed for high treason, until the erection of a singular edifice, called "Nonsuche House," made in Holland, and brought over in pieces. The heads were removed in 1577 to the Tower, called afterwards Traitors' Gate, at the Southwark end of the bridge.

Although the old bridge remained unchanged in

C

a great part until its demolition **in 1832, yet** it must have been modified and rebuilt considerably, owing to its rude treatment by fire and storm. In 1212 we have said it caught fire at both ends. In 1281, five of the arches were carried away by ice or **a swell** of the river. The Great Stone Gate, Southwark end, fell down in 1437, and in 1633 a **fire** broke out "in the house of one Briggs," by the carelessness "of a maid-servant placing hot coals **under** a pair of stairs." So our very greatest grandmothers were not exempt from domestic plagues any more than we are. Then the great fire in 1666 burnt across the bridge until it came to a vacant place. Again, in 1725, **another** careless servant set it on fire. It is not **said that** it was a *maid*-servant this time, so we **will give the** sex the benefit of the doubt, and say *man*-servant; and that was the last.

Among the illustrious traitors whose heads have "grinned horrible" from those bridge towers, were the patriot Wallace, in 1305; old Northumberland, father of the gallant Hotspur (1408); Sir Thomas **More and** Bishop Fisher, both beheaded for denying Henry VIII.'s supremacy (1535). Fisher was first executed, **and** "his head was retained," says Hall, his biographer, "to be shown to Anna Boleyn" (poor lady!). The next day, "the head

being parboiled was prict upon a pole, and set on
high on London Bridge ; but after it had stood up
the space of fourteen days, it could not be perceived
to waste or consume, but grew daily fresher and
fresher, so that in his lifetime he never looked so
well for (from) his cheeks being beautified by a
comely red."

In consequence of this strange sight, the traffic
of the bridge was stopped by gazers, and the executioner being commanded to throw down the head
during the night into the river, Sir Thomas More's
was set up in its place. But the miracle continued,
and Sir Thomas More's head, when subsequently
bought by his daughter Margaret, was found " to
have retained its lively favour and his grey hair
turned to a reddish or yellow colour."

These ghastly expositions continued until the
breaking out of the civil war in Charles I.'s
time, and after the Restoration the heads of some
of the regicides were set upon London Bridge ; so
there were blots and blurs on the face of Merrye
England. We question if she were ever more
comely than at present.

And many a brave sight had the old bridge
seen since the citizens of London presented
Richard II. and his good Queen Anne, on their
way from Richmond, " with two fair white steeds

trapped in cloth of gold, pailed of red and white, and hanged full of silver bells," and so they had music wherever they went. Four years after Richard had a new queen, Isabella of France, and passed over the bridge again, on his way to keep state in the Tower. In less than four years more Richard was dethroned and murdered.

Henry V. on his return from Agincourt crossed this civic highway. Doubtless a gross fat man, one Falstaff, fat as butter, was in the crowd, crying aloud—

"My king, my love, I speak to thee my heart."

to the admiration of Justice Shallow and the exemplary Pistol,—admiration that may have been a little damped by the king's ungentlemanly observation—

"My Lord Chief Justice, speak to that vain man."

About nine years later Henry's funeral procession on its way from conquered France passed over. "His effigy, made of boiled leather nigh to the semblance of him as could be devised, robed and jewelled, with royal sceptre, a ball of gold, covered with red silk beaten with gold, laid on a chariot, and drawn by four great horses." So Madame Tussaud is only a plagiarist after all.

Here, in 1831, had Wat Tyler forced a passage

over; and in 1430 the commonalty of London threw open the bridge to Jack Cade, he who was to make " it felony to drink small beer."

Here gentle Sir David Lindsay, in 1390, did battle in single combat with Lord Wells for England, to prove the comparative valour of the two nations. Lord Wells was unhorsed and hurt sorely, and Sir David embraced him tenderly, to show that they fought " with no hatred, but only for the glory of victory." But the days of chivalry are gone—quite gone, passed away with Sir Thomas de Sayers. Sir Richard Mayne has thrown down the truncheon, and the lists are broken through.

Henry VI. (1445) and the she-wolf of France, Margaret of Anjou, were received here by " Mayor and Aldermen, and pageant of Peace and Plenty, and Noah's ship." Margaret in her days of sorrow again passed over to her prison in the Tower. Falconbridge, in a last attempt for Henry, was driven over London Bridge into Southwark, the houses to the drawbridge all in flames. In a month his royal master was murdered in the Tower.

Katherine of Arragon came over in great state to her marriage with Prince Arthur ; and Wolsey, the worst enemy Katherine had, took his departure hence for France.

Needle-making is a considerable article of commerce, and the first made in England were manufactured by a negro from Spain, living in Cheapside, in Mary's time. He died without imparting
the secret of tempering them, and the art was not
recovered until 1560, in the reign of Elizabeth,
when one Elias Growse, a German, taught the
English how to make needles.

The persons on the bridge (according to Pennant) who occupied shops were pin and needle-
makers, and haberdashers of small wares; but
other traders found patronage; for in the fire
occasioned by Mr. Briggs's maid-servant there
were burnt out twenty-seven other traders, and
the curate and clerk of St. Magnus. "The Blue
Boar" was luckily empty, as that was roasted also
with another house.

In the 16th century the booksellers mustered in
strong force on the bridge, and some of their signs
—such as the "Sugar Loaf," the "Angel,"
"Lion," "Bear," "Black Boy,"—are found on
the titlepages of works of that time. "In those
days," says a writer in Knight's "London," "a
shopkeeper's sign was the most ponderous and sub-
stantive of realities, projecting or swinging over
his door, and all the Sugar Loaves, Angels, Lions,
Bears, Bibles, Black Boys and Breeches, dangling

and creaking away, must have made wild work
enough among them, on London Bridge especially,
when the wind was
at all high." The
waters roaring be-
low must have
added not a little
to both the noise
and the terror of
the thoroughfare,
and made a hurly-
burly, enough to
have wakened the
seven sleepers. Yet
we are all creatures
of habit, more or
less; for it is re-
lated of a Mr. Yeld-
wyn, who lived in
Chapel House on
the bridge (and who
found there, by-the-
by, Peter of Cony-
hoop's monument
under a staircase, in
1737), that he (Mr.
Y.) being ordered

BANKSIDE, SOUTHWARK. (From an old Print.)

into the country for change of air, could not sleep
for want of the roaring lullaby of the river beneath
him. Something like the lady whose husband
being a sleeper of a noisy character—perhaps a
native of the Essex village called Great Snoring—
could never close her eyes during his absence
unless a coffee-mill was turned at her bedside.

There are few records of persons living on
London Bridge. But Holbein lived there; and
Walpole relates an anecdote of the father of the
Lord Treasurer who, passing over, was caught in
a shower, and stepping into a goldsmith's shop for
shelter, found there a picture by Holbein, who had
lived in the house. The Lord Treasurer gave
100l. for the picture; but it was unfortunately
destroyed in the fire of London, which happened
before it could be sent home. Another individual
who has escaped oblivion is Lord Mayor Osborne.
He was apprenticed to Sir W. Hewitt, the wealthy
clockmaker (in Elizabeth's time); a careless maid-
servant—a maid-servant this time—dropped Sir
William's child into the river. Osborne "took a
header" into the Thames and rescued the mediæval
Colleen Bawn. The father rewarded him with
his daughter's hand when she grew up, and also
with an ample dowry. Hewitt was Lord Mayor
in 1559, and Osborne in 1582. Before the end

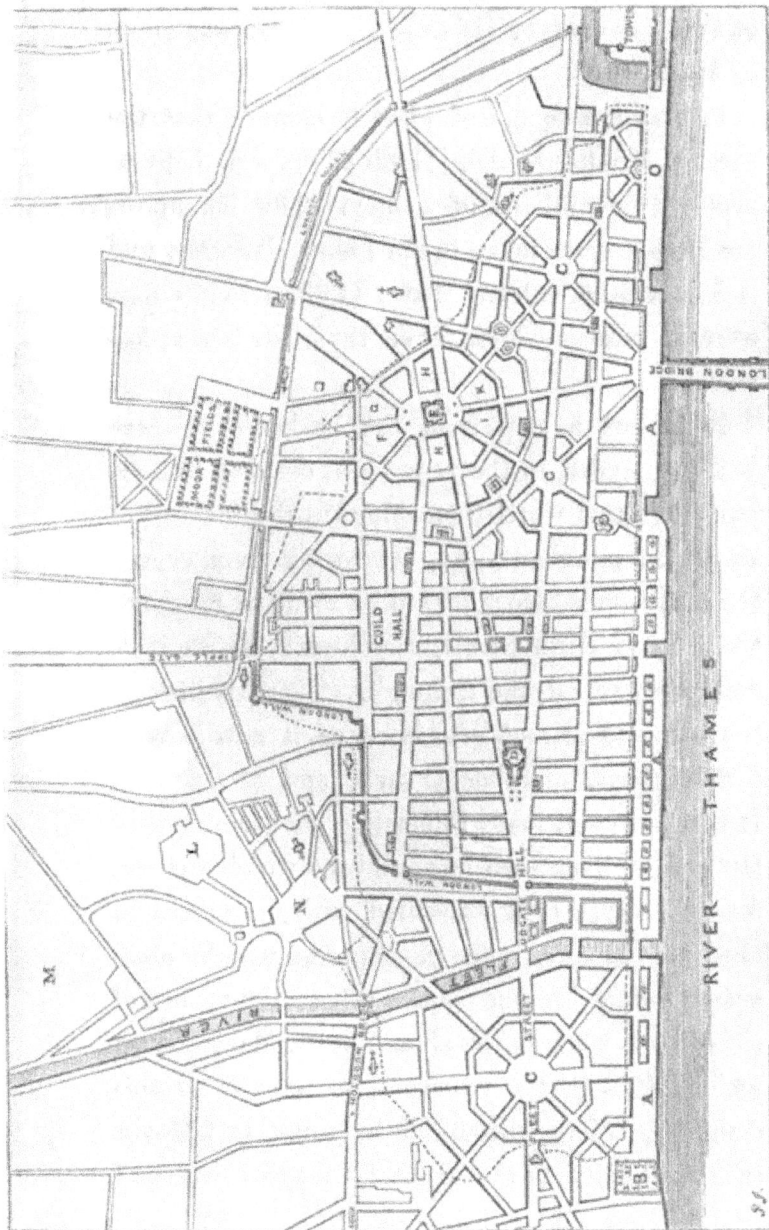

SIR CHRISTOPHER WREN'S PLAN FOR REBUILDING LONDON. (AFTER THE GREAT FIRE.)

A A Grand Terrace or Embankment.　a a a Halls of the City Companies.　B Temple Gardens.　C C C Piazzas.　D St. Paul's.
E Royal Exchange.　F. Post Office.　G Excise.　H H Goldsmiths and Money-changers.　I Bank.　K Mint.
L Charterhouse.　M Clerkenwell.　N Smithfield.　O Custom House.

of the next century Osborne's grandson was Duke
of Leeds.

It may not be out of place to mention that the
present London Bridge is built of granite, and cost
nearly two millions of money. The lamp-posts
are from cannon taken in the Peninsular war; and
it has been calculated that 20,000 carriages pass
over in one day—not fewer than 107,000 pedestrians.

It is but a step from the bridge-foot where
William Ryder, in the year 1564, chanced to see a
pair of knitted worsted stockings in the lodging of
an Italian merchant, and, borrowing them, caused
the first worsted stockings to be made in England.
Close by is High Street, Southwark, or, as it is
commonly called, the Borough. There is little in
the name to attract, associated as it now is with
hop-waggons, omnibuses, carts, and street cabs.
It has, however, many interesting connections with
the past, the outward memorials of which are fast
fading away. It is associated with the names of
Gower, Chaucer, and Shakspere, which must
excuse me for leading you for a few minutes out of
the old city walls to the church of St. Mary Overy,
which derives its name from the ferryman's
daughter, before introduced to you. It was the
custom to enter in the canon books the names of

those who benefited the church, and so Mary is here canonised, whilst *Over the Rhy*—the Saxon for over the river—is easily converted into Overy, and hence the name of the beautiful church which stands on the right-hand side of the bridge as you enter Southwark. Gower—"moral Gower," as Chaucer calls the oldest English poet—did much to beautify it, and his tomb has been carefully preserved in grateful remembrance of his benefactions. He was married here to one Alice Gwundolf, by William of Wykeham, but no trace is left of her tomb, although she was buried here. Gower, in the later years of his life, was blind, and he pathetically laments that he is compelled " to suffer life " deprived of sight, probably regretting most his inability to see any longer the beautiful edifice he had helped to adorn. It is a pleasant reflection to think that his memory still adds a glory to the little church, and contributed largely at a recent date to its preservation.

The tender Fletcher and the vigorous Massinger lie here. Shaksperian dust also mingles with that of its graveyard, for here rests Edmund, the youngest of the great poet's brothers. The interior of the church is very beautiful and interesting from its monuments. Clink Street, where Shakspere lived (1609), is near at hand; as was

also the Falcon Tavern, where Ben Jonson,
Burbage, and the players at the Globe may have
made merry with " Sweet Will." **The** only letter
to Shakspere now known to exist was addressed to
him while living here in **Southwark.** Its date is
October 25, 1598, and is from Richard **Quinney** to
his loving and good friend and countrie **man,**
Mr. W. Shakspere, and of course—what are good
friends made for ?—it requests the loan of 20*l.*
The money, no doubt, was repaid, as Richard
Quinney's son Thomas married Judith, the youngest
of Shakspere's daughters.

Time was when Southwark was the great
rendezvous for pilgrims on their way to À Becket's
shrine at Canterbury, and who met here to form
parties for mutual security and company. The
road to Canterbury, lined with hedgerows passed
over an arched bridge, called Locksbridge (discovered in 1847); and this road may be still
traced in some of the narrow lanes of Kent.

" In Southwark," says Stow, " be many fair inns
for receipt of travellers," the remains of which are
fast disappearing, together with the *long waggons*
for passengers and commodities. The " Tumble-
down Dick," a caricature of Richard Cromwell's
downfall, was once a sign in High Street; and
there are here and there portions of those old inns,

THE CANTERBURY PILGRIMS, AND THE TABARD INN, SOUTHWARK

with their external galleries and sloping roofs.
But we must not linger too long in old Southwark,
but pass at once to the Tabard. Chaucer's Tabard
is now called the Talbot; why the sign of the inn
was changed is uncertain, but it was since 1597.
Within the last thirty years there was the following
inscription over the gateway: "This is the Inn

THE TABARD INN, HIGH STREET, SOUTHWARK, 1826.

where Sir Jeffery Chaucer and the 29 Pilgrams lay
in their journey to Canterbury, 1383." (There are
thirty-one pilgrims by-the-by, including Chaucer
and the *three* priests.) The immortal verse of the
old poet will only preserve this inn, we fear, to the
next generation, for it is so little regarded that the
pilgrims' room (traced out by Mr. Saunders in

1841) is now a railway booking-office, and it is difficult for the most determined dreamer to people the Talbot yard with the pilgrim troop that Chaucer sent to Canterbury. There is the old sign of the Tabard, or " Herald's coat," over the booking-office, but so defaced and uncared for, that it might be a fancy sketch of Chaos.

Chaucer, when he retired from active life, wrote his " Canterbury Tales," and some of his early poems at Woodstock—Rosamond's Woodstock,—

> " Within a lodge out of the way,
> Beside a well in a forest."—*Chaucer's Dreams.*

When Caxton, a mercer of London, set up his printing-press, to the west of the Sanctuary of Westminster, nearly his first work was Chaucer's " Canterbury Pilgrimage." The first edition was very imperfect, and Caxton subsequently reprinted it with great care, and made a handsome apology to the author, like a printer with some manners in him. They are not all so polite. Tom Moore tells of an author who could never get any redress for having a lovely poem about " Freshly blown Roses" sent out to the world misprinted into " Freshly blown Noses."

Let us now take boat at London Bridge, with the honest ghost of William Fitzstephen, who died in 1191, and hear it tell of the " large river of the

Thames, well stored with fish, and covered with boats and barges and graceful swans. Think of that—fish and swans at London Bridge! Yet time was when our ancestors, tired of bowls, could step

CAXTON'S HOUSE IN THE ALMONRY, WESTMINSTER.

down to Queenhithe or the Temple, and have an afternoon's angling. Henry III. first carried the refuse of his royal kitchen into the Thames; and if he and those who drove the fish from the Thames are aground with Charon on the Styx, I for one will not lend them a tow. Our **ancient** spirit will also tell how **bold** Londoners at Eastertide "did run at the water quintain, regardless **of** a ducking or the laughter of the crowd." Or **we** will take barge with **moral** Gower when he went to meet Richard **II. on** the " Silent Highway " (as the river was called), **to** receive the royal command that "**some** new thinge he should book," and which resulted in *The Confessio Amantis.* The old poet's **fitting** monument is, as we have seen, by the **river side,** in his own church of St. Mary Overy. Or shall we go aboard the Duke **of** Norfolk's barge, in 1428, when it fell upon the piles and overwhelmed, which was (says the old chronicler) " the cause of spilling many a gentleman and others, the more the ruth was ? **But** they were saved through help of them above the brigg with casting down of ropes." This was at a time when, if ropes were arranged for noblemen or gentlemen, it was generally little to their advantage.

Such was once the danger of the Thames ; and we **can remember w**hen it required a cool head and bold heart **to shoot old** London Bridge with safety. The vile uses to **which our** noble river has been so needlessly and **recklessly** condemned have **de**prived London of **one** of its greatest beauties, and destroyed what was once the source of pleasure and **employment** to thousands. Let us hope that the embankments which were **begun** by the Romans, and are now in progress, may be completed before the advent of that New Zealander, who has become in our **time** almost **a** resident in this country.

The " Silent Highway " **will** never again, we **fear,** be thronged with royal pageants, **as** when **Henry** II. and afterwards **when** Queen Elizabeth **came** from Greenwich, " with her barges freshly furnished with banners and streamers of silk," and attended as, no doubt, Anna Boleyn was subsequently, " with trumpets, and shawns, and other divers instruments, all the way playing and **making** great melody."

> " Whilst from the barge
> A strange invisible perfume hits the sense
> On the adjacent wharfs."

You may almost see the perfume that hits the sense from the Thames now-a-days. Or when great Elizabeth showed her state upon the Thames, **and** Raleigh saw her from his prison window, " and brake into a great distemper, and sware that his **enemies** had brought her thither to brake his gall with Tantalus' torment."

We wonder **if** the vain, good old queen believed him, as he survived the sight many years?

"The Devil's Own," as the gentlemen of the Inns of Court delight to designate themselves, were gay water-dogs in the old time, and presented a sumptuous masque at court, on the marriage of James the First's daughter, Elizabeth (1613), to

QUEEN ANNE BOLEYN. (From a rare Print by Hollar after Holbein.)

the Palatine, going thither by water. The old river once used the lawyers very rudely, and rose so high at Westminster, that the learned in the law had to be taken out of the Hall in boats. That was in 1235. Such a visitation would have had small terror for such a lawyer as the late Sir

Lancelot Shadwell, who once heard a Chancery injunction case while swimming in the Thames— made a wet order, and dived out of court.

It must have been a pleasant voyage from London Bridge to Whitehall, when the banks of the beautiful " silver streaming Thames" (as Spenser calls it) were studded with noble dwellings of some of our proudest and richest nobility, their broad and tasteful gardens reaching to the river. Alas! those of the Temple alone remain to us. From the garden water-gates, and other landing-places (York Gate is alone left), went to and fro throughout the day private barges and 2000 public wherries bearing freights of beautiful women and gallant men, scarcely scaring in their course the flocks of swans sailing upon the river. No doubt Shakspere from his house in Clink Street, or from the windows of the Globe Theatre saw the Thames thus beautified ; and so the Swan of Avon remembers the Swan of Thames, when York describes the struggle of his followers at the battle of Wakefield :

> " As I have seen a swan
> With bootless labour swim against a tide
> And spend its strength with the o'ermatching waves."

When Charles I. was created Prince of Wales, he came from Barnes Elms to Whitehall in great

state; and when Henrietta Maria arrived in
London nine years later, it is recorded that the
king and queen in the royal barge, with many
other barges of honour and thousands of boats,
passed through London Bridge to Whitehall.

YORK GATE.

" The Whitehall to which the daughter of Henri
Quatre was conveyed," says Charles Knight, " had
another tale to tell in some twenty-three years, and
the long tragedy of the fated race of Stuart almost
reaches its catastrophe when, in a cold winter
night of 1688, the wife of James II. takes a

common boat at Whitehall to fly with her child to
a place of safety. A few weeks later, and the
doomed king steps into a barge surrounded with
Dutch guards, amidst the .triumph of his enemies,
the pity of the good men who blamed his obstinacy
and his rashness." " I saw him take barge," says
Evelyn—" a sad sight." Yes, and not the only sad
sight seen on the bosom of that bright river; for
how many a victim of tyranny and slave of ambition
has passed over it on his way to dusky death !

The old **river** has also had its solemn shows of
funeral pomp, as when the remains of Anne of
Austria and Queen Elizabeth were brought by
water to Whitehall, and in our day the body of
the heroic Nelson from Greenwich for **interment**
in St. Paul's.

The watermen of London were, **in** the olden
time, as musical **as** most other Englishmen, and
the old city chronicler, Fabian, **tells** us that John
Norman, mayor of **London in 1454,** was the first
of all mayors who broke **the** old, ancient, and continued custom of riding to Westminster. John
Norman was rowed thither by water, for which
the watermen made of him a " roundel," **or** song to
his great praise, the which began—

" Row the boat, Norman, row to thy leman."

The feeling of the honest watermen was better

than their poetry, which, by-the-by, was at one time not very remarkable for its intelligibility. The waterman's ancient chorus was—

"Heave how! rumbelow!"

whatever that may have signified. We have seen the last of the city water pageants, we fear; and we feel with our most valued friend Charles Knight, "that the water show of the Lord Mayor's day had a fine antique grandeur about it that told us that London and what belongs to London were not of yesterday."

It is somewhat curious that so little change should have been made in the names of the various landing-places by the river 400 and more years ago. Old Swan Stairs was called Old Swan Stairs and we had, as now, Temple Stairs, Queenhithe, Essex Stairs, York Stairs, Broken Wharf, Paul's Wharf, and others.* There was no other bridge than London Bridge over the Thames until 1750,

---

* It has been otherwise with streets; as Mr. Cunningham, in his admirable "Handbook of London," gives a long list of changes. We transcribe a few of the strangest transformations. Candlewick Street has been transmogrified into Cannon Street; St. Olaves, into Tooley Street; Sheremoniers Lane, into Sermon Lane; Snore Hill, into Snow Hill; Dermond's Place, into Deadman's; Strype Court, into Tripe Court; Knightenguild Lane, into Nightingale Lane; Hammes and Guynes, into Hangman's Gains; Blanch Apleton, into Blind Chapel Court. And many others too numerous to mention here.

when Westminster Bridge was finished. Black-friars was opened in 1770. Dr. Johnson wrote in favour of the unsuccessful competitor, and was not far wrong in attacking the other, whose bridge has but lasted a hundred years, and has passed away. And beautiful Waterloo was begun in 1811 and finished in 1817. The conservancy of the Thames is vested in the Lord Mayors of London, Richard II. having sold it to the City for 1500 marks, thereby constituting the Lord Mayor admiral of the Above-bridge Navy, as the penny boats are called.

Before we land, let us take a peep at Queen-hithe, so named because it belonged to Queen Eleanor, the mother of King John. This royal lady was particularly objectionable to the citizens of London, and they once pelted her with mud and stones as her barge passed under London Bridge, calling out, " Drown the witch !" a reputation the lady deserved if Peele's chronicle play of Edward I. be trustworthy, and wherein it is said that Queen Eleanor sank at Charing Cross and rose again at Queenhithe. When Eleanor was accused by Edward of her crimes, " she wished the ground might open wide, and therein she might sink," if she were guilty.

   " With that at Charing Cross she sunk into the ground alive,
     And after rose with life again in London at Queenhive."

So no doubt there was an underground railway or something like it in Edward's time.

Until 1464 Greenhithe continued to be the favoured landing-place, and all fish sold elsewhere was ordered to be seized. Old Fish Street and Old Fish Street Hill proclaim the site of the ancient fish-markets. Billingsgate, however, by advantage of situation, and possibly by power of tongue, in 1669 ultimately prevailed, and obtained the preference. When the use of fish was an obligation of the church, as well as part of the domestic economy of the times, many enactments were necessary, and so we find the sale of fish carefully regulated. Economy in its use is frequently insisted upon. Tusser, in his "Husbandry," advises—" Spend herring first and salt fish last, for salt fish is good when Lent is past." The Fishmongers' Company soon rose into great wealth and importance, and was, as it is now, we believe, second to none.

CHAPTER II.

WE will shoot the bridge with better fortune, let us hope, than attended our friend the Duke of Norfolk, and land at Tower Stairs, pausing for a few moments on Tower Hill. Yonder is the old Tower of London, a long history in itself, standing just *without* the old city wall, and therefore not within the scope of our present purpose.

On Tower Hill Lady Raleigh lodged during part of the time her husband was a prisoner in the grim old fortress. Here their son Carew was born. William Penn—over whose Quaker body there has been fierce battle since Lord Macaulay sought to demolish him—first saw the light in a court adjoining London Wall, on the east side of Tower Hill.* Otway the poet died at the Bull Inn, not

* William Pen, Esq., the famous Quaker Proprietor and Governor of Pensilvania, dy'd lately at Liege, after a long illness.—*Daily Post,* July 8, 1720.

exactly of want, but in scarcely a less painful manner—from eagerness to allay his want, when suddenly supplied. Felton, who stabbed the Duke of Buckingham, bought his knife (now in possession of Lord Denbigh) for one shilling on Tower Hill. Henry III. was the first king who caged wild beasts there—they were three leopards—and were succeeded by the lions, which, everybody knows, were washed in the moat. The lions were named after the reigning kings, and it was long a vulgar belief, that when the king died the lion named after the king died also.

Before the Tower lost its palatial character, numerous were the royal processions from it to the Abbey Church of Westminster. Here is a brief narrative of Richard II. "The young king rode forth clothed in white, with a multitude of nobles, knights, and esquires, the Lord Mayor and Corporation, and all the city glory. The streets were hung with floating draperies, garlands depended from shop signs, barriers were placed at the side of the streets" (we question if they were not always there as a protection to pedestrians), "and rows of citizens sat or stood within them." In Cheapside was stationed a castle with four towers, "from which," says Holinshed, "on two sides the wine ran forth abundantly; and at the

top stood a golden angel holding a crown, so that
when the king came near he bowed down and
presented it to him.   In each of the towers was a
beautiful virgin, of stature and age like the king,
and apparelled in white vesture.   The angel blew
into the king's face leaves of gold and flowers of
gold counterfeit.   On Richard's near approach, the
damsel took cups of gold, filled them with wine
from flowing spouts, and presented them to the
king and chief nobles, and so they went amid the
shouts of the people and the noise of music."

The part of the king in these displays must
have been what is theatrically called a "heavy
one," for Richard was so fatigued by his performance that he had to be put to bed as soon as it
was over.

Henry VII.'s queen, Elizabeth, we are told, on
her way to be crowned, wore a white curtal robe
of golden damask (evidently a polka jacket), and
her fair, yellow hair hanging down her back, with
a caul or network of pipes over it (we lately returned to that fashion).   As she passed by were
children arrayed in angelic costume, and singing
sweet songs.   In our royal progresses now-a-days
we substitute charity children, arrayed in anything
but angelic costume, with a selection from Stern-
hold and Hopkins for sweet songs.

All other pageants were the same in character, only differing in detail.

There were one or two circumstances attending Mary's coronation procession that are worth recalling.

She rode in a chariot covered with cloth of gold, followed by another, in which was no less a personage than her father's divorced wife, Anne of Cleves! —a touching tribute to the departed Blue Beard. The circlet of gold she wore was so heavy that she was obliged to rest her head upon her hand; and the Princess Elizabeth, who bore this crown from the waterside to Westminster Abbey, complained to Noailles of its weight. "Be patient," said he, "it will seem lighter when on your own head." Five years only passed and Elizabeth was Queen Regnant, and all that wealth and ingenuity could devise to show how welcome was her accession, met her everywhere on her way from the Tower to Westminster. Stately pageants, sumptuous shows, effigies of the queen's ancestors, not excepting Henry VIII. and the beheaded Anna Boleyn (funny fellows our ancestors), were seen on stages at the ends of the streets, and Gog and Magog (out for the day), stationed at Temple Bar, presented an ode in Latin, fortunately not preserved. Flowers were cast upon her, and a sprig

of rosemary, presented by a poor woman in Fleet
Street, was, it is recorded, noticed in her coach
when Elizabeth arrived at Westminster. (How
such small graces touch the public heart!) Elizabeth was moved by all this loyalty. " And be
assured," she said, " I shall stand your good queen,"
and she kept her word. The church bells were
rung on the anniversary of Elizabeth's birthday as
late as Charles II.'s time—a compliment paid to no
other sovereign as we remember.

In 1571 Elizabeth again visited the City in
great state, coming from Somerset House, and by
the sound of trumpet proclaimed the opening of
the first Great Burse, henceforward to be called
the Royal Exchange, which Gresham had built on
the site of the Old Tun Prison, and two little
alleys called Swan and New St. Christopher. It
was subsequently destroyed at the Great Fire of
London, when the only statue left standing of the
many it contained was that of the founder, Sir
Thomas Gresham.

The last of these processions took place April 22,
1666, when Charles, having come from Whitehall
to the Tower by water, created no less than eleven
peers and sixty-eight knights of the garter. The
citizens erected triumphal arches, and showed
such demonstrations of joy, that he must have

thought again, as he said on Restoration day, "that it was all his own fault that he had stayed so long in exile."

These gratuitous spectacles had their uses in making the workers among the people more tolerant of their burdens, becoming partakers, as it were, of the state and luxury of their masters.

Numbers of the old nobility had residences in the City, although the love of the country which still distinguishes the English aristocracy, prevailed possibly in a stronger degree in the olden time. Besides, a journey to London was no joke. Let us look at the domestic life of a jovial bishop.

In 1265 Swinfield, bishop of Hereford, had, it appears from his household roll, a palace at Hereford, a house at Worcester, and a house in London. He had many manor-houses and farms and stables, kennels for hounds, and mews for hawks. He brewed, baked, and made his own candles. He kept a tailor to make garments for himself and family. When he moved about his domestic utensils, brass pots, and earthenware went with him, as also carts laden with meat and wine and Bosbury venison. The bishop rode a palfrey, and his chaplain, house-steward, cook, farrier, palfrey-man, and household officers, all well armed, attended on him. There were fifty-one horses in the troop.

The bishop had spoons and forks of silver, though the finger and thumb did duty generally, and every man carried his own knife. The bishop and his retinue left Prestbury on the 20th of December, and arrived at his house in Old Fish Street on January 7th.

Before parting with this church noble, we may as well peep into his kitchen, and pry into his domestic arrangements. "He who leads a good life is sure to live well," so his cellars are filled with wine—there are spiceries and foreign luxuries. Every variety of fish—sticks of eels, twenty-five on a stick—salmon, tench, minnows, lampreys, and salt fish; oysters, mackerel, and trout; gruel in abundance and soup; salted greens and other vegetables; salted beef, pork, and venison, all prepared in the country. Then sugar and saffron, fowls and brawn, bread and cheese. His Christmas dinner has cost above 100*l.* of our money. John, his farrier, has 6*s.* 8*d.* half yearly; John's man, 3*s.* 4*d.* The falconer, porter, and carters have 3*s.* 4*d.* also. The launder, the palfreyman, the butler have 2*s.* 6*d.* The messengers (distinguished in Countess Leicester's family as *Slingaway, Bullett, Truebody,* and *Go a bit hasty*) have 2*s.* 6*d.* also. The younger domestics and pages have from 6*d.* to 2*s.* each.

When at home at the manor-house, which was
usually for the most part a hall, with one great
chamber allotted to the lord of the house, the
guests dined and drank their wine, and, as night
ended, slept on the wooden floor of the hall,
strewed with dry rushes in winter, and green
fodder in summer, the servants sleeping in the
kitchen away from the hall, or with the horses in
the stable.

Feather beds were rarely used (1450) except by
the wealthy, and frequently form an item in a
will. In 1463 John Barel bequeaths to his niece
" the round table for her term of life ;" and " pottle
pots," quart pots, tongs, bellows, brass pans, pewter
dishes and platters, sheets and blankets, are
frequently bequests, showing how deficient our
ancestors were in household goods and chattels.
The domestic servants of the middle classes were
treated kindly, and no dignity was compromised
by considering dependents as humble friends.   In
Henry VI. and Edward VI.'s time the Paston
letters show us that the daughters of a household
were kept in strict discipline, and even in matters
of love and matrimony had the goodness to comply
with their parents' desires. Females were generally well instructed, as we may judge from the
many excellent letters left to us, and were also

conversant with sewing, spinning, and housewifery.
They read novels, but novels in large folios, which
there was no slipping under the sofa cushion when
mamma or the family confessor came in.

We have not space to be a Court-guide of the
old time, but we must mention a few interesting
old houses in the City.

Castle Baynard, from which the ward takes its
name, was built by Baynard, a follower of the
Conqueror, and subsequently became the property
of Robert Fitzwater, whose daughter Matilda
figures in history with King John and Magna
Charta. Fitzwater fled to France to save himself
and daughter from the machinations of John. He
was afterwards permitted to return to England,
and became the general of the revolted barons,
under the title of the Marshal of the army of God
and the Church. Fitzwater was the hereditary
City Chatelain and Banner Bearer, and in time of
war presented himself at the west door of St. Paul's,
saying to the Mayor, " Sir Mayor, I am come to
do my service which I owe the City ;" whereupon
the City gave him a horse worth twenty pounds,
properly accoutred, and Fitzwater had twenty
pounds for his day's expenses and the city banner,
which he bore to Aldgate ; and for every siege in
which he should engage he had twenty pounds of

the Commonalty of London. The only remains of
this warlike demonstration is the City Marshal,

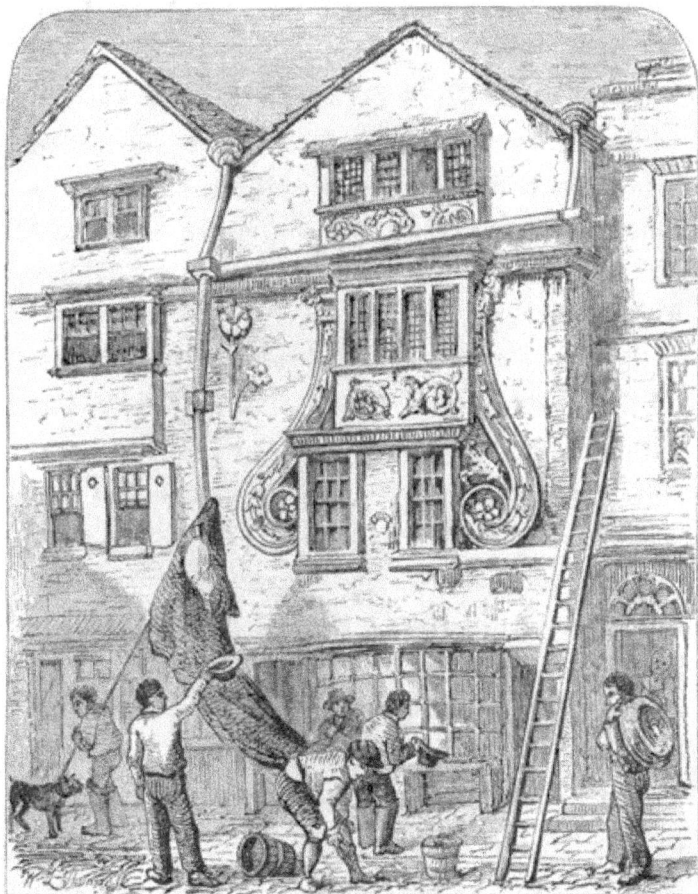

DOMESTIC ARCHITECTURE. Houses on the West Side of Little Moorfields.
(*Drawn in May, 1810.*)

with his cocked hat and truncheon. At Castle
Baynard Richard III. took on him the kingly
title, and Henry VII. and his queen resided there;

E 2

and, when it became the property of the Earl of
Pembroke, those who had proclaimed Lady Jane
Grey queen met there, and substituted the Lady
Mary.

The Ward of Castle Baynard was thickly studded
with the houses of the nobility; the attraction
being the King's Great Wardrobe, built in the
time of Edward III., and the secret letters and
writings concerning the estate of the kingdom
were kept there.

Baynard Castle was destroyed for the last time
in the great fire of 1666. So Eastcheap was
within easy distance of the West End of that day,
and Prince Hal and his equally riotous brothers,
Thomas and John, could make merry near their
own lodgings with Mistress Quickly and the
roisterers at the Boar's Head. This celebrated
hostel, preserved by Shakspere to all time, stood
on the site of William the Fourth's statue, and
was given by John Folstoffe, one of the bravest
generals under the fourth, fifth, and sixth Harrys,
to Magdalen College, Oxford. The Boar's Head
was destroyed in the Great Fire, and afterwards
rebuilt. When recently pulled down its stone sign
was deposited in Guildhall library, to be within
scent of the civic revelries.

A subterranean passage leading from Baynard's

Castle to a house formerly occupied by Fair Rosamond, was traced in Paul's Chain not very long
ago.

A great old house in Dowgate, called the Erber,
was inhabited by Warwick the King Maker until
he fell at the battle of Barnet. Clarence, before
his malmsey bath, resided here, and Richard III.
before his removal to Crosby Hall. Cicely, Duchess
of York, lived at St. Peter's Parva, Paul's Wharf.

Crosby Hall, with its fine open timber roof, still
remains to us in part. It was built about 1466 by
Sir John Crosby, grocer and woolman, knighted
by Edward IV., and buried in St. Helen's parish
church. Crooked-back Richard lodged here when
he entreated Lady Anne to leave him to perform
her husband's funeral whilst she should "presently
repair to Crosby Place." It subsequently became
the residence of (1542) Anthony Bouvier, a rich
Italian merchant, then of Alderman Bond, who
added a turret to the hall. It became a house for
the reception of ambassadors, and was bought by
Sir John Spencer, father-in-law of the first Earl of
Northampton, and who kept his mayoralty there.
In 1636 the East India Company held it. It
became a Presbyterian meeting-house in 1672,
then underwent partial demolition, and in 1831
what remained was carefully restored, and was

well worthy the trouble and expense bestowed on
its preservation.

A palace of stone stood near the east end of
Cannon Street, and is said to have been the
residence of the Black Prince. Winchester House
and Gardens were in Broad Street, formerly the
site of the Augustine Friars Church, and Token-
house Yard, near the Bank, occupies the site of
the Earl of Arundel's house and gardens.

About a century later than Henry II.'s time the
nobility began to migrate westward, as the marshes
of the Lea and the great fens of Finsbury were not
particularly attractive. London *elegant,* if not
London *proper,* has been moving westward ever
since, occasionally stimulated by a prod from some
silver-fork novelist.

Some few went northwards to Islington—
"those fond of ducking" we presume; some to
the vineyards, by the Old Bourne (now the sewer
of Holborn), but the banks of the " silver streaming
Thames " had the greater attractions, and the
palace of Westminster and the good things of the
court were also in that direction. The bishops
were among the earliest emigrants to Fleet Street
and the Strand, and were soon followed by other
nobility. We shall visit them in their new
residences when we pass through Temple Bar.

There was a **scrivener's** house in the **old city**
near to where the Compter formerly (1555) **stood,**
and once known **as** the Spread Eagle in **Bread**
Street. It was partly destroyed in the Great Fire.
John Milton was born there, and nearly opposite,
in Milk Street, Sir Thomas More first " muled and
peuked in his nurse's arms."

Milton was buried next his father in the chancel
of St. Giles' Cripplegate ; and his grave was said
to be under the spot where the clerk's desk stood
formerly. Certain parish ghouls, comprising the
churchwardens, vestry clerk, or others, opened the
supposed grave in August 1780, and discovered **a**
leaden coffin resting on a wooden one, supposed **to**
be that of Milton's father. The leaden **coffin,**
when opened, disclosed a body in a shroud. **The**
hair was six inches long, neatly combed and **tied**
together. A part of this was cut off, and some of
the **teeth** extracted, and then the remains were
left **to** be exhibited by the sexton, for money, to
the public. The remains, possibly, were those of
Milton, although some conjectured they were those
of a female, owing to the long hair.

Although Sir Christopher Wren did not believe
that the first Old St. Paul's had been a Temple of
Diana (as asserted), it appears that in Edward I.'s
reign **a** great number of oxheads were dug up,

and supposed to be the *débris* of the Tauropolia, celebrated in honour of *Casta Diva*. More bones

DOMESTIC ARCHITECTURE.   View of the Porch of an Old House in Hanover Court, Grub Street.
(*Drawn in July, 1809.*)

were found when digging the foundation of a new chapel on the south side of St. Paul's, and Selden has ingeniously suggested that London implied *Llan-dien*, or Temple of Diana, a more graceful derivation than Lud's town, from the old king buried on Ludgate Hill. We incline, however, to accept *Llyn-din*, the town on the lake—as the best derivation.

It appears that the first Old St. Paul's was begun in the sixth century, and destroyed by fire in the reign of William the Conqueror.

In the same fire that destroyed the cathedral the castle known as the Palatine Tower had suffered, and the materials were placed at the disposal of Bishop Maurice for the construction of a new church. For twenty years did the good bishop work, and then left the completion of his church to Richard de Beaumeis, who bestowed the entire revenues of his bishopric on the edifice. The wall which enclosed the church extended to Paternoster Row and Ave-Maria Lane on one side, and to Old Change, Carter Lane, and Creed Lane on the other. To the west it was open to Ludgate. The money to complete the building was raised (1240) by Bishop Roger granting indulgences. The people paid up liberally, and the subterranean church of St. Faith was begun in 1256.

Pictures, shrines, books, ecclesiastical habits, all more or less adorned with gold and jewels, were contributed in profusion, and in after years the accumulated riches of gold, silver, and jewels, golden basins, silver phials, silver candlesticks, crosses, cups, chalices, &c., occupied in their enumeration twenty-eight pages of the last folio edition of Dugdale.

There is a record of a festival on the feast of the conversion of St. Paul in the fifteenth century, too long to quote, which describes a scene of magnificence almost unparalleled in church history. Gold, silver, rubies, emeralds, and pearls seemed to lose their value from their profusion. Fragrance diffused from silver censers up the nave, through the aisles, and so to the back of the high altar, which was covered with jewels and precious stones of all kinds, small shrines, rings, and silver girdles, the gifts of the pious. Among the rings was the sapphire stone given by Richard de Preston, citizen and grocer of London, for the cure of bad eyes— and if Richard believed that he was not the man to see through a millstone.

In Edward III.'s time the Flagellants visited St. Paul's, scourging their naked shoulders and chanting hymns. One is not surprised to hear that they made no proselytes, and returned much sorer, if not wiser, than they came.

In St. Paul's King John acknowledged the

Pope's supremacy, and Richard II.'s body, after his murder at Pomfret, was there exposed, and visited by 20,000 persons in three days.

There were monuments to many names, great in our country's annals, in Old St. Paul's.

The most ancient were those of two kings, Sebba and Ethelred, the latter celebrated for Invasion Tariffs with the Danes, of whom he seems to have been a great encourager. He gradually increased the payment for a good Danish massacre and pillage, from 10,000 pounds of silver to 40,000 pounds. However, when Ethelred heard of Canute's arrival, he collapsed into bankruptcy, never sought for protection, but gave it up altogether, and died.

John of Gaunt was buried in Old St. Paul's, his tilting spear, ducal cap, and shield being over him. It was here, in 1337, that he stood in good stead Wickliffe, the Reformer, when cited before his superiors. Wickliffe died Dec. 31, 1384, in his sixtieth year, from a paralytic attack, which saved him from martyrdom; and it hurt him not that the Bishop of Lincoln, by order of the Council of Constance, nearly sixty years afterwards, dis-interred and burnt his bones, and cast the dust into the river Swift. From Wickliffe's rectory of Lutterworth seeds were to be borne upon the wind to bear fruit in other centuries.

Bishop Corbet, the founder of St. Paul's School, Sir Christopher Hatton (the dancing Chancellor), Sir Francis Walsingham, his son-in-law, Sir Philip Sidney, Donne the poet, and Vandyck had all monuments in Old St. Paul's.

A custom connected with the old cathedral was the election of the Boy Bishop on St. Nicholas Day (December 6th). This mock dignitary had the greatest authority until December 28th, and was attended and robed as a regular bishop, and if he died within the period named was buried as one. According to Hall " they were led from house to house blessing the people, who stood *girning* in the way, to expect that ridiculous business."

The nunneries had for their mock dignitary a little girl. The custom was put down by Henry VIII. and revived by Mary, but the Boy Bishop made his final bow in Elizabeth's reign.

The presentation of the banner of St. Paul's to Robert Fitzwater, the Castellan of the City, has been mentioned, and the tolling of the bell of St. Paul's warned the people to assemble together. That bell was never heard by the Jews of London without dismay, as its booming was too often the signal for the plunder of their race; and when De Mountford, in 1264, marshalled the Londoners

The Cathedral Church of St. Paul, as it was before the Fire of London.

to march against Henry III., his troops massacred
five hundred men and women and children of the
unhappy people, and filled their patriotic pockets
from the Jews' coffers.

Pardon Church Haugh, a chapel founded in the
reign of Stephen, and the story of its founder,
Gilbert à Becket, father to Thomas à Becket, is
known perhaps to many. Doubtless you remember
how he, following the fortunes of his lord, was taken
prisoner in Palestine and thrown into a dungeon ;
how the Emir's daughter beheld the captive, pitied
first and then loved him ; and how, when he had
returned by her means to England, her love would
not let her rest, but with two words—" Gilbert,"
" London "—to guide her, she travelled east and she
travelled west, until she found the one she sought
in Old London City. How the loving infidel was
baptized at St. Paul's and became the mother of a
sainted archbishop! Thomas, it seems, was also a
martyr during life to a very bad temper and a hair
shirt. He once excommunicated a man for dock-
ing his reverence's horse's tail—being very particular to a hair it seems. Before printing enabled
the truth of most matters to be disseminated, one
Lord Bateman appropriated the pretty legend we
have just narrated, and pretended that he was
the beloved of the Emir's daughter : he was an

impostor, and his proud young porter was a myth, let
our friend George Cruikshank draw what he will.

In 1535, Coverdale had completed his trans-
lation of the Bible, and Henry ordered divers
bishops to peruse it. They said there were many
errors in it, but no heresies. " Then in God's
name," said the king, " let it go forth among my
people ;" and the minister Cromwell ordered a
copy of the Bible to be chained to a pillar or desk
in every parish church. From that day to this,
the Book has never been closed in England.

Bonner, then Bishop of London, caused six
Bibles to be set up in St. Paul's, and they soon
found readers and commentators, to Bonner's great
annoyance. He was angry in vain! Edward VI.
struck off fifty-four officiating priests of St. Paul's,
and six years later—oh heavy day!—he stripped
the church of all its valuables—recollect, twenty-
eight pages folio contained their enumeration—
and left only two or three chalices and basins, and
a silver pot!

The centre aisle, adorned only by the tomb of
Sir John Beauchamp (usually called Duke Humphrey's, until the discovery of the true place of
sepulture of the duke at St. Albans), was named
Paul's Walk—the resort of the idle, the profligate,
and dissolute. The penniless loungers there were

said to dine with Duke Humphrey, "his grace
without meat." In Paul's Walk, Falstaff bought
Bardolph, and there, according to Decker, "you
might find in one and the same rank, yea foot by
foot and elbow by elbow, the knight, the gull, the
gallant, the upstart, the gentleman, the clown, the
captain, the appel-squire, the lawyer, the usurer,
the citizen, the bankrupt, the scholar, the beggar,
the doctor, the idiot, the ruffian, the cheater, the
puritan, the cut-throat, the high men, the low men,
the true men, and the thief. Thus whilst devotion
knelt at her prayers profanation walked under her
nose in contempt of religion."

One of the Law Hostels or Inns was in Dowgate,
and another in Paternoster Row, and hence originated, it is supposed, the custom of the serjeants-
at-law and their "apprentices" (the word is Dugdale's not ours) sitting in Paul's Walk each at his
own pillar, hearing his client's cause and taking
note thereof on his knee. A vestige of this custom
continued till Charles II.'s time, when a lawyer
called to the degree of the coif went to St. Paul's
to choose his peculiar pillar, and from the collection of rogues just enumerated they must have
been capital criminal lawyers, if practice make
perfect.

The boys of St. Paul's were accounted good

actors, and Pennant says were famous in mysteries, holiday plays, and even regular dramas, and often performed before our monarchs. We should consider most of the mysteries blasphemous now-a-days, though the whole Scripture history was performed some six years ago at Boulogne. We should feel the introduction of comic demons, bandying coarse jests, repartee, and practical jokes, provoking roars of laughter, as a sensation drama rather out of place. We have, it is true, distant approximation to funny men in the pulpit amongst us still, but then they are counterbalanced by preachers in theatres.

Outside the church various public proceedings took place. The first lottery in 1659 was drawn before the western door; it included 10,000 lots at ten shillings each; the prizes were to have been plate, but we are sorry to record were never forthcoming. The drawing continued day and night from the 11th of January to May 6th, and the profits were applied to the repair of the havens of England.

In St. Paul's Churchyard—at the west end of the cathedral—nearly on the spot were Queen Anne's statue stands, Digby, White, and Bates were executed for the Gunpowder Plot.

Old St. Paul's was 690 feet long, 130 feet broad,

F

and the spire was 520 feet high, having a ball
large enough to hold 10 bushels **of** corn.   It had a
cross on the top, making the entire height 534
feet; the space of ground occupied was somewhat
over 3 acres.

In 1600, Bankes' horse Morocco, a middle-sized
bay English gelding, went to the top of St. Paul's,
" to please," says Decker, " a number of asses below."   This was the horse shod with silver, which
Bankes **took** subsequently **to Rome,** and which
was unlucky enough to be burned there, with his
master, for supposed witchcraft.   Who were the
asses then ?

The tall steeple was destroyed **in Elizabeth's**
time, 1561, and the whole building was consumed
in the Great Fire of 1666.   The first stone of the
present edifice was laid June 21, **1675,** and was
completed in 1710, at a total cost of 1,511,220*l*.

Queen Anne, if we believe the scandal of the
time, did **not** originate **the** Teetotal Society, for
Damper, an under tutor at Eton has sung—

> " When Brandy Nan became our queen,
>   Twas all a drunken story ;"

but I have no doubt that statement was a libel, as
the Duchess of Marlborough, no friend to the
queen, has denied the allegation.

In the corner of the Churchyard was a public-

house, called "Tobit's Dog," and the statue of
Queen Anne stands, as you may have seen, offering
a stone pumpkin to the gentlemen on the knife-
boards of the passing omnibuses. It is necessary
that you should remember this fact and the libel,
and that her Majesty built a number of churches
in London, to understand the point of the lines
we are about to quote :—

> " Here mighty Anna's statue placed we find
> Between the darling passions of her mind,
> A brandy shop before—a church behind.
> Why here, like Tantalus, in torment placed
> Near those strong waters which she cannot taste ?
> Though by her proffered globe you may perceive
> That for a dram she would the whole world give."

We are now at Cornhill. It is the memory of
a May morning in the olden time. Bells are ring-
ing merrily, and the citizens of all classes are
returning from the neighbouring woods and
groves of Highgate and Hampstead (now miniature Londons), all bearing garlands of wild flowers
or green boughs wherewith to decorate the May-
pole, which hath rested over the booths of the
traders since last year, and is now drawn forth by
a yoke of forty oxen to be set up at St. Andrews
Undershaft. The lord and lady of the May, not
the grimy, shovel-beating mummers of our time,
but two of the likeliest youngsters in the ward of

OLD CHEAPSIDE, WITH THE CROSS.

Cheap, are installed in the bowers of greenery, decorated also with scarfs, ribbons, and other braveries. Dances, feasting, and merriment will succeed, and lusty London 'Prentices play at swòrd and buckler, and fair and modest maidens dance the *hay* for garlands until the closing day warns in doors the Lady May and her maiden court, all of whose pretty faces had been washed in May-dew to make them beautiful. Old Pepys, it may be remembered, went to Woolwich with Jane and W. Hewer, to gather May-dew, which Mrs. Turner had taught was the only thing in the world to wash the face with. " I am contented with it," says the old diarist; and indeed it is a pretty fancy—much more efficacious, we will warrant, than any enamelling plaster of Paris in vogue now-a-days.

Or perhaps we may witness what Hall chronicles he saw in his day : " A king and queen keeping May-day holiday in the wood under Shooter's Hill, with a Robin Hood and a Maid Marian, and feasting with them in an arbour and a hall made of boughs," eating an outlaw's breakfast of king's venison. Then to an open glade to see two hundred archers (all volunteers, of course) led by the Duke of Shoreditch, " loose at once their arrows, which whistle by craft of head, making a noise both **strange and** great," **and** then, no doubt, joining **their fellows** at Cornhill—for **such** were May-days in London until **the coming** of Evil May-day, as it is emphatically called.

"**A** great heart-burning," says Stow, "and a malicious grudge grew amongst the Englishmen **of** the City of London against strangers, because such numbers were permitted to resort hither with their wares, and to exercise handicraft to the great hindrance and impoverishing **of** the king's liege **people."** (We have heard some such reasoning in our **own day.)** Well, **their feelings** inflamed by John **Lincoln** a broker, and **Dr. Bell a canon,** "there rose," says Stow, " a secret **murmur,** and no man could tell how it began, that **on May-day** next following, the City would **slay all** aliens, insomuch that divers strangers **fled** out of the City." The king and council, **the** Lord Mayor **and his brethren, took instant** steps to prevent this **threat being carried** into execution ; but an alderman **imprudently interfered to** " put down " two apprentices playing at sword and buckler—the **cry** arose 'Prentices! 'Prentices! Clubs! **Clubs!** (the City war-cry), and the mischief **was** set on foot. Excited people rushed **from all** quarters. The prisoners were released, the doors and windows of the foreigners' houses were forced, the inmates beaten, and the goods destroyed. These excesses continued until three in the morning, when the Mayor, possibly assisted by the king's soldiers, captured three hundred men, and confined them in the Tower and elsewhere.

On the 4th of May they were tried at Guildhall, and on the 7th, John Lincoln and twelve of his associates were brought forth for execution. John Lincoln alone was hanged. "Four hundred men and eleven women, poor younglings and old false knaves, bound in ropes one after another in their shirts, with halters round their necks, were pardoned by the king at Westminster. But the punishment for Evil May-day did not end here, for the Londoners were deprived of their annual sport, and the May-pole, after resting over the booths for thirty-two years, was taken down and sawn into pieces by some fanatics who had been excited thereto by the preaching of some one at Paul's Cross." The May-pole, however, held up its head again in London, as we shall see by-and-by.

Cheapside, so named from Chepe, a market, was originally called Crown Fields, from the Crown Inn which stood there. The host was hung in Edward IV.'s time for saying his son was "heir to the Crown." The joke was not a very good one,

and there would be work for the gallows in **Fleet
Street**, we fancy, if **Edward** were king now-a-
days.

Many a show of joy and sorrow has old **Chepe**
witnessed. **Magnificent** tournaments, the streets
strewn with sand to give the horses foothold;
kings and queens witnessing the nightly sport
from the gallery of old Bow Church, whose tower
lanterns were once illuminated nightly, as beacons
to those who journeyed from the forest grounds of
Hampstead and **Highgate** to old London city.
Bow Bells were once rung every night at nine
o'clock, and at that hour, no doubt, Dick Whittington heard their pleasant voices calling him to
return and be thrice Lord Mayor of **London**.

Lord Say was beheaded in Chepe by order of
Jack Cade, and Perkin Warbeck sat there in the
stocks, and was then beheaded at Tyburn. At the
Standard William Longbeard was beheaded by
order of the first **Lord** Mayor of London, who
played king at home when Richard I. was in the
Holy Land. The people stole the gibbet, and
preserved pieces of it as holy relics. **Many** others
also suffered there, and Duke Humphrey's wife
Eleanor, charged with sorcery, walked through
Chepe in a sheet, with a taper in her hand, to
Paul's Cross. Pageants and bonfires frequently

amused the dwellers in the old street of markets; amongst them the mother of Herrick, the poet, who tells us, in

" Golden Cheapside, the earth
Of Julia Herrick gave me birth."

Isaak Walton there followed his trade of sempster and Sir Christopher Wren lived in Cheapside ; as did also John Beyer, the original of Johnny Gilpin —that celebrated train-band captain who " witch'd the world with civic horsemanship."*

We hinted that possibly the king's soldiers assisted the authorities in capturing the " poor younglings and old false knaves " on Evil May-day, as unless the Marching Watch—Henry had not yet put down that costly institution—stood true to the civic throne, the City police were not likely to have been victorious. If the old limners have been faithful transmitters of the ancient " Charley," he appears to have been a most feeble old party, quite a temptation to Corinthian rois-terers of the time. " Before the time of Henry III. it was a common practice in this city that a hundred or more in company, young and old, would make nightly invasions upon houses of the wealthy, to

* The gentleman who was so severely ridiculed for bad horseman-ship, under the title of Johnny Gilpin, died a few days ago at Bath, and has left an unmarried daughter, with a fortune of 20,000*l.*— *The Postman*, Nov. 1790.

the intent to rob them, and if they found any man
stirring within the City within the night, that
were not of their crew, they would presently murder
him, insomuch that when night was come no man
durst adventure to walk in the streets." So there
were *Mohawks* and *Tityre tus* in those days, as
there was in later times—

> " Who has not heard the Scourers' midnight fame?
> Who has not trembled at the Mohocks' name?"—

says Gay. One hundred pounds were offered by
royal proclamation in 1712 for apprehending any
one of them.

The state of the police in London may be judged
of by the following extract :—" The 11th of
February, 1592," says Gilbert Talbot, " Lord
Rytche, riding in the streets, a dagger was shot at
him ; " and it appears by the statutes of Henry IV.
and Henry VIII., that beating, wounding, maim-
ing, were common in the streets. During the civil
wars bloodshed in the public thoroughfares was
very common. The Coventry Act, passed temp.
Charles II., consequent upon the slitting of the
Earl of Coventry's nose in revenge for some
offensive words spoken in Parliament, did little at
the time to put a stop to open violence ; and Lords
Rochester, Mahon, Warwick, and many others
distinguished themselves by attacking the watch

and scouring the streets—running amuck like savages. The *Tryers*, the *Scowerers*, the *Sweaters*, the *Mohawks*, the *Tityre tus*, were formidable bodies of ruffians. Dryden, Shadwell, and Vanbrugh gave them too much encouragement on the stage, and Addison hardly condemns them. **For** further details, see Moser's *Vestiges*.

LONDON BY NIGHT (1604).

CHAPTER III.

THERE is scant record of the early City Watch.
The murder of Lord Ferrie's brother at his lodging
at the George Inn in Lombard Street, his body being
thrown into the street, is said to have originated the
night watchers in 1175.   In 1416, Henry Barlow,
then Mayor of London, is found to have ordered
lanterns and lights to be hanged out on the winter
evenings betwixt All-hallowmas and Candlemas.
In our Eighth Harry's night time the ordinary
lighting and watching of the streets were by one or

two cressets, which only served to make darkness visible, and a few watchmen armed with halberds and dim lanterns. But once a year, on Midsummer Eve, the City made a great show of the Marching Watch, and which King Harry witnessed in 1510, having come privily into Westcheap of London, clothed in one of the coats of his guard. On the occasion of these night marches an enormous bonfire blazed under the Cathedral of St. Paul's, lighting up every pinnacle and its many windows, as though a thousand tapers burned within. The streets were full of light ; over the doorways of the houses were lamps of glass with oil burning in them all night (mind, all night), and some hung out branches of iron curiously wrought, containing hundreds of lamps lighted at once. Tables were set out with ponderous cakes and flagons of ale and wine, and over the doors hung branches of birch, with wreaths of lilies and John's wort, " and pots of the green orpine, in the bending of whose leaves the maiden could read her fate in love." (Our authority for this is Stow.) The windows and galleries, then common to the houses of London, were filled with ladies, the men standing below within a barrier ; and between the gable roofs were servants and venturous apprentices. Music within, and the cadence of sweet voices singing in

harmony. Then with trumpet and drum onward
came the Marching Watch. The pitch ropes
which burned in the cressets sent up their tongues
of flame and wreaths of smoke. Seven hundred
cresset-bearers, besides two hundred and fifty
constables, minstrels, and henchmen, to the amount
of nearly 2000. There were demi-lances, gunners
with their wheel-locks and arquebuses, archers in
white coats, with bows bent and sheafs of arrows
by their side, pikemen in bright corslets, and bill-
men with aprons of mail. And so came and passed
the Marching Watch. And then for the rest of
the year was the old gloom upon the City—the
solitary cresset and the rare watchman.

In 1540 Henry put down the Marching Watch,
considering the great charge to the City; but it
was not until 1569 that the lovers of old pageants
consented to abandon it altogether. A substantial
watch was then projected for the safety of the
City, and consisted of an aged man armed, as we
have said, with halberd and lantern, whose business
it was to parade the streets, and see that the
proper lights were hung out by the housekeepers.
The cry was—

> " Lanthorn and whole candle light,
>   Hang out your lights. Hear! Hear!"

no doubt to give thieves notice of his coming, and

almost as effectively as the clump, clump of our policeman's highlows.

But, in Queen Mary's time, they "made night hideous" by one of each ward who went all night with a bell, and at every lane's end gave warning of fire and candle, and to help the poor and pray for the dead :—

> " From noise or scarefire rest ye free,
> From murders, Benedicite."

And the breed did not improve until the introduction of the new police ; for the *guardian of the night* was, within our recollection, merely a great Witney coat stuffed with a superannuated bricklayer's labourer, having sufficient intelligence to bawl the hour, and to "wink hard" (*i. e.* not see) when well paid for doing so. They had boxes to sleep in, absurdly called watch-boxes; and it was said by Lord Erskine that a friend of his, who could not obtain sleep by any of the usual means, put on a watchman's coat, got into a watch-box, and was asleep in five minutes.

In 1694 a company was formed to light the streets with glass convex lights ; but the company's lease expired in twenty-one years, and with it convex lights. Then every person whose rent was 10*l.* was compelled to hang out one or more lanterns to burn from six to eleven. So the cut-

throats and housebreakers were kept out of bed till
past eleven, unless there chanced to be clouds over
the moon, or the house they had selected to work
in was under 10*l.* a year, and without a lantern.
Wise forefathers of the City! It was not until
1744 that this state of things was materially
altered.

It will be seen, by a glance at the map of London
in Elizabeth's time, that Finsbury and Spitalfields
were as yet open spaces; and a proclamation was
issued by Elizabeth, dated from Nonsuch, forbid-
ding "the erections of new buildings where none
had existed in the memory of man." (We are
afraid the ghost of the gentle Elizabeth must have
an uneasy time of it in this brick and mortar age.)
This proclamation was made because the extension
of the City was calculated "to encourage the increase of beggars and the plague, a dearth of
victuals, an increase of artisans more than could
live together, and the impoverishing of other cities
for lack of inhabitants." (The population of
London, within and without the walls, was in
James I.'s time about 150,000, and is at present
nearly three millions.)

It was also stated "that lack of air and room to
shoot" arose out of the too crowded city. Even
in Henry VIII.'s time this "lack of room to shoot"

was complained of, and Henry was a great patron
of archery. " Before this time," says Hall, " the
towns about London, as Islington, Hoxton, Shoreditch, and others, had so enclosed the common
fields with hedges and ditches, that no Londoner
should go out of the City but in the highways."
Of course, such treatment could not be borne by
the gallant cockneys, " and a great number of the
City assembled themselves in the morning, and a
turner in a fool's coat came crying through the
City, ' Shovels and spades !' and so many followed
that it was a wonder."   Within a short space all
the hedges were cut down and ditches filled—the
workmen were so diligent, and this act the king's
council approved.

The great archery grounds were Finsbury Fields ;
and these extended from the open country to the
City wall—to Moorgate—and the only buildings
beyond were the dwellings of the bowyers, fletchers,
and stringers, the place since known as Grub
Street, now Milton Street. Dr. Johnson, in his
Dictionary, describes Grub Street as the name of a
street in London much inhabited by writers of
histories, dictionaries, and temporary poems, whence
any mean production is called Grub Street. The
first use of the term Grub Street in its present
offensive sense was made by Andrew Marvel (Cun-

ningham), and it has supplied abundant illustration for other writers. A certain Henry Welby lived in Grub Street forty-four years, and in that time was never seen of any one (1636). He was eighty-four when he died, possessed of very large estates in Lincolnshire. This seclusion arose from an attempt made on his life by a younger brother.

Beyond Grub Street, northward, the fields were studded with archery marks and pillars of stone, or wood, for targets, surmounted with some device, as a bird, a serpent, or a swan. In 1594 there were one hundred and sixty-four of those marks, each distinguished by a name, as " Dunstan's Darling," " Daye's Deed," " Parkes his pillar," " Partridge his primrose." Why Partridge should have had his mark called a primrose we can't imagine, unless for the alliteration, or perhaps his friends wanted to make game of Partridge. The shortest distance was nine score yards, and the longest nineteen, or three hundred and eighty yards. In Henry VIII.'s time no man was allowed to shoot at less than eleven score, and our old ballads tell of hazel-rods being split at twenty score, or four hundred yards, and sometimes with the " long bow," we fancy.

In 1737, however, the butts at Finsbury had

become reduced to twenty-one, and the longest
distance to thirteen score! the shortest to three
score, or sixty yards. Davenant has a hit at the
archers of his day, and laughs at the attorneys and
proctors who met in Finsbury Fields :—

> " Like ghosts of Adam Bell and Clynne—
> Sol sets for fear they'll shoot at him."

Shooting the sun was a new idea—shooting the
moon has long been a vulgar pastime on rent
days.

What the wits could not do the builders did;
they killed the archers, and 1768 saw the last
effort made to preserve the shooting-grounds at
Finsbury.   The most ancient Fraternity of
St. George, established by Henry VIII., has continued in name until the present time, although we
question whether nineteen score and a hazel wand
would not overtask the skill of their best marks-
man.

When we had the honour of associating with the
fraternity, the once celebrated Master Betty, the
young Roscius, was in figure and skill no mean
representative of Friar Tuck of Sherwood.   When
Master Betty was not quite thirteen he got fifty
pounds a night!

The worthy clerk of Copmanhurst naturally
suggests quarter-staff, a favourite pastime with the

youth of **London, and** many a bloody coxcomb has
been won in Chepe **and** Cornhill.

The formidable quarter-staff, which we believe **is**
peculiar to England, was about six feet in length.
It was grasped in the middle, and thus allowed free
play to the hands from end to end, and a turn of
the wrist could describe a circle difficult **to** enter.
It was a favourite game at all our country fairs,
particularly in the west of England. We never
saw it played; but **the degenerate** single-stick was
common **in our boyhood, and was** a pastime which
generally made a lasting impression upon one **of**
the **players at least.**

"The youths **of London** used on holidays, **after**
evening prayer, **at their** masters' doors, to exercise
their swords and bucklers, and the maidens, one of
them playing a timbrel, danced for garlands hung
athwart the streets." A pleasant picture this of
the old city, and somewhat difficult of realization
now-a-days, as the timbrel would have a sorry
chance against the " Paddington !" " Chelsea !"
" Hammersmith !" of our noisy omnibus conductors.
Card-playing was in fashion in Henry VII.'s time,
but apprentices were only allowed to indulge in **it**
on holidays, and **then** in their masters' houses, for
counters, nails, and points; though sometimes,
perhaps, they stole a visit like Jin Vin to the play-

table of " the Chevalier Beaujeau, flower of Gascony," and got fleeced for their folly. Chess was also in vogue.

Bowls were played in John's time, and the bowling-alleys appear to have been the admiration of all foreigners, and were " pleasant greeneries" in the midst of the City. In Henry VII.'s time Northumberland House in Fenchurch Street had been deserted by the Percys, and its gardens converted into bowling alleys, and its chambers into " dicing-houses." We remember seeing some thirty years ago a bowling alley somewhere in Clerkenwell, and which gave evidence of having been once adorned with bowers and alcoves. A memorial stone to some departed player displayed a poetical epitaph, in which the terms of the game were applied to describe the virtues of the deceased.

Bull- and bear-baiting were favourite sports with the Court of the gentle Eliza, and, with cockfighting,* continued long after to be popular pastimes of the Londoners. Boys brought fighting cocks to school on Shrove Tuesday, and fought them before their master,—an odd way of teaching a lad "his humanities, look ye !"—and some may

* Cockfighting was introduced into England by the Romans, though frequently suppressed.

perhaps remember to have heard the gross but graphic " Wednesbury " ballad, wherein the order of a main is described. Wrestling was perhaps, next to archery, the favourite sport of the Londoners, and there were doubtless many who could have withstood a Cornish hug, or Devonshire kick, and given a backfall or cross buttock to any man of our day. The prizes contended for were either a ram, a bull, a red gold ring, or a pipe of wine.

On the eve of St. Bartholomew the civic court were wont to take their way to Finsbury Fields, and there have men two by two set to wrestle before them. After all was over live rabbits were set loose among the crowd to make sport for them, and very probably to allow the Lord Mayor and Corporation to depart in peace without the tagrag and bobtail which accompany a Lord Mayor when on show now-a-days. " At times," says old Fitz, "all the youth of the City went in the fields to play at ball," and for which the 'Prentice club no doubt was used. The scholars had their ball—the tradesmen their ball, and "the anciente sort, the fathers and the wealthy citizens, came on horseback" to see the fun ; and these pleasant gatherings continued for more than four hundred years, and only passed away with the close of the seventeenth century.

Tennis **was also a** ball-game in vogue, we believe, **as early** as Henry V., and Shakspere is not guilty of an anachronism when he makes Henry say to the dauphin, who has brought the present of tennis balls,

> " When we have matched our rackets to these balls,
> We will in God's name play a set shall strike
> His father's crown into the hazard."

Tennis continued and continues a favourite game with those who have leisure for its exercise, and fine exercise it is.

The river of Wells flowed outside Cripplegate, and passing **through** the partially fenny ground of Moorfields, made near West Smithfield a large sheet of water, called the Horse Pool, where **the** beasts were watered on the Friday **cattle market.** Fitzstephen calls it that vast lake, and here, when it was hard frozen, the youths of London came to sport, riding on blocks of ice drawn over it as sledges; and skating " with the velocity of a bird," upon skates made of legbones of some animal, an **iron** shod staff being used as a propeller. Sometimes the skaters met in friendly battle, and wounds frequently ensued.

The citizens of London had the **right** of hunting in Middlesex, Hertfordshire, the Chilterns, and in Kent as far as the river Cray, and through

Cripplegate they went to hawking in the surrounding country.

These were some of the out-door pastimes of our gallant cockney ancestors; but even old Tom Rounding and the Epping Hunt are now things of the past!

It would be interesting, no doubt, to inquire closely into the government and commercial progress of a city which exercises so great an influence upon the rest of the civilized and uncivilized world, but such considerations are from our purpose. We must not pass by, however, the City Companies altogether, though the briefest notice shall suffice. There are ninety-one companies, of which the Weavers is the oldest, having been established in 1184. Mr. Madox, in his *Firmia Burge*, gives precedence to the bakers and saddlers. The Woolmen must have been incorporated very early, as wool was an article of considerable export. Dr. Hughson, writing in 1805, quotes "a late ingenious publication," to give some idea of the immense enhanced value of many manufactures from the raw or unimproved materials to their produce at market: "One hundred pounds laid out in wool, and that wool manufactured into goods for the Turkey market, and raw silks brought home and manufactured here, will increase that one hundred pounds to five **thousand pounds, which** quantity of silk sent **to New Spain would return** ten **thousand pounds.** . . . Steel may be made **near** three hundred times dearer than gold weight **for** weight, for six of the finest steel wire springs **for** watch pendulums shall **weigh** but one grain, and be worth two hundred and seventy-two pence **for the six, whereas one grain** of gold is worth but **twopence."** The history of the wool traffic is very **curious, but would occupy too much space for us to enter upon.** The Steel Yard Company also **existed from Henry** III.'s time to 1551, when **it lost its privilege.** It was composed of Flemings and Germans, and for many years they were the principal exporters of the staple commodities of England. **Twelve** companies are **styled the** Honourable, **namely,** Mercers, Grocers, Drapers, Fishmongers, **Goldsmiths, Skinners, Merchant** Taylors, Haberdashers, Salters, Ironmongers, Vint-**ners, and** Clothworkers, all celebrated for the **excellence** of their dinners and the largeness of **their charity.** Formerly the election of **officers** was attended with great state and **ceremony and** general feasting. Huge sideboards of **plate were** displayed; pyres of sandal-wood burned **in chafing-**dishes; tables laden with barons of beef and boars' heads, interspersed with dishes of brawn, fat swans, and conger, and sea hogs; great birds with little birds together; *lèche Lombard*, made (or rather *compounded*) of pork braized in a mortar with eggs, raisins, dates, sugar, salt, pepper, spices, milk of almonds, and red wine, the whole boiled in a bladder (what is a haggis to this?); and to these a multitude of other savoury dishes too numerous to mention. After dinner, whilst spiced bread, hippocras, and comfits went round, the election took place. And then came the master and wardens, with garlands on their heads (some we have known would have looked very comical in such headgear), preceded by minstrels, and that great English institution, the beadle. The garlands were removed, and, like Cinderella's slipper, tried on by many of the assistants, but, strange to say, fitted only their original wearers unless there was a vacancy to be filled up. Thus fate-selected, the wardens were chosen and duly sworn, the loving cup of spiced hippocras or claret wine passed from the old warden to the new, and then (they having drunk each other's jolly good healths) the new warden received his garland, and the congratulations of the fraternity. Some mystery or play followed, Noah's Flood was one of them (no doubt at Fishmongers' Hall), then another loving cup, and all departed. On the following Sunday a

mass was said for all brethren and sisters, the
quick and the dead, and a minor feast held,
and the liveries (in which it was a citizen's
pride to appear) paid for. Part of these cere-
monies, much shorn of their splendour, we have
seen; we believe each Company has its peculiar
formula.

The real duties of the Company were to bind
apprentices and keep the same in good order, to
preserve the respectability of the craft by fining
and imprisoning the unfair trader. One Simon
Potkin, of Aldgate, had been fined for putting
starch into his comfits (we moderns supplement
arsenic and verditer); Simon was fined again for
saying, "He had given money to his company to
sell at his own free will;" there was not much wit
in the remark, but Simon Potkin had to pay
3s. 4d. for a swan, "to be eaten by the Master and
—himself," and to incur the immortality now
given to his name and transgression. Freemen
were bound to keep the secrets of the trade, or be
heavily fined.

The apprentices were troublesome fellows, and
would not at all times confine themselves to "the
throwts, shirts, doublets, and coats which were
only honest and clean," but would now and then
appear "in a cloak of pepadore, with hose lined

with taffety, and **shirts edged with silver,"** and so get clapped up in prison.

In 1582 the 'prentices required an act of Common Council to keep them in order. They were ordered to wear no apparel but what they received from their masters, no hat, but a woollen cap without any silk in or about the same. **To wear** neither ruffles, cuffs, loose collars, nor other thing than a ruff a yard and a half long at the collar. To wear no doublets but of canvas, fustian, sackcloth, English leather or woollen, without any **gold,** silver, or silk trimming, and **no other colours** than **white, blue,** or russet, **and all of** the plainest cut. **To** wear **no** pumps, slippers, or shoes but **of** English leather, without being pinched, edged, **or** stitched, nor girdles nor garters **other than of** crewel, woollen thread **or** leather, **without being** garnished. To wear no sword, dagger, nor other weapon but a knife ; nor a ring, **jewel of** gold or silver, nor silk in any part of his apparel, on pain of being punished by his master for the first offence; **to** be publicly whipped **in hall** for the second, and for a third, to serve six months longer than specified in his indenture. Neither was **he to** frequent any dancing, fencing, or music schools— no Argyll Rooms, music halls, nor Cremornes, under the penalties aforesaid "How jolly awful," eh! young fellahs? Besides, you were ordered by your indentures "to make speedy return when you shall be sent on your master's or mistress's business. You shall be of gentle and lowly speech and behaviour towards all men, especially to all your governors."

Nor were the apprentices alone subject to restrictions in dress, as in 1597 (three years earlier) a proclamation was issued by Elizabeth against excess of apparel, gold chains, and cloaks—the latter made so long that they reached to the heels. Daggers were to be limited to twelve inches beside the hilts, and three feet only were allowed for swords.

Cloth Fair, Ironmonger Lane, Fish Street, were occupied by the trades they indicate; Foster Lane sheltered the Goldsmiths, and Cheapside, between Bow Church and Friday Street, was called the Mercery. Blackwell Hall claimed the Woollendrapers, and Soper Lane the Grocers or Pepperers, as they were named. Newgate Street and Stocks Market, the site of the present Mansion House, divided the Butchers, and the Tanners were found "without Newgate and without Cripplegate."

The companies rendered great service to the community by securing supplies of corn and coal, and selling them in time of scarcity to the poorer citizens at a moderate price. Sir Simon Eyre, at his own expense, erected public granaries at Leadenhall, and Sir Stephen Brown sent out ships to Dantzic for rye corn, whereby he brought down the price of wheat from three shillings a bushel to half that price: so Sir Stephen Brown seems to have been the first Free Trader. This was about the beginning of the fourteenth century, and the money for corn was so scarce, says the chronicler, " that the poor people were enforced to make their bread of fearne roots." Roger Achilly, Mayor in 1511, also deserves honourable mention, as in a time of prospective dearth he stored the Leadenhall granary with every species of grain. He likewise drained Moorfields, and made roads and bridges to the adjoining villages. As there was frequently great loss sustained by the Company and the Corporation on these sales of corn, it was arranged in 1578 that five thousand quarters were to be kept between the twelve Great Companies. At the Great Fire of London the public granaries were destroyed and never replaced.

The Companies were frequently called upon to assist the sovereign with loans, and so to supply the place of the Jews, who, after massacres and spoliations, were expelled from England by Edward I., and were not permitted to re-establish themselves

until Rabbi Manasseh Ben Israel of Amsterdam
obtained Cromwell's permission for their return.
(Jewin Street is on the site of the old Jewish
burying-ground, and the only place in England
where they were permitted to bury their dead.)
To the time of the exodus in 1290, the Jews had
been the principal money-lenders, their rate of
usury being in 1158 from twopence to threepence

EAST INDIA HOUSE, LONDON.   (Pulled down in 1862.)

in the pound per week, or at the rate of fifty or
sixty per cent. ; and that tradition amongst others
seems to have come down to the present generation
of money-lenders. The Jews became enormously
rich by their traffic, and consequently were hated
by the less prosperous and persecuted by the more
powerful.

When they were banished altogether from
England, and their departure soon made gold and

silver coin difficult to come by, the sovereigns
constituted the Companies their bankers. Queen
Elizabeth seems to have been a constant and irresistible borrower, paying no interest. Very like
"Stand and deliver!" with her. But the gentle
Eliza once found herself with a balance in hand,
and she made the citizens borrow their own money
of her in sums of fifty pounds to five hundred
pounds, on security of gold or silver plate at seven
per cent. In 1567 her Grace established the first
lottery, and compelled the Companies to take
shares. But it seems, as we have said, the prizes
were not forthcoming. Her Majesty also devised
patentees for almost everything but "bread."
Nevertheless, despite these bleedings, the Companies furnished no less than ten thousand men and
thirty-eight ships for the defence of the country
when the Spanish Armada threatened to invade us
—and would do so again in defence of "our tight
little island."

There is a Company, not one of the City Companies, which deserves a word or two—the East
India Company, established in Elizabeth's reign
(1601), to establish a commerce with Arabia,
Persia, India, China, and several of the Indian Islands, the first subscription being only
739,782l. 10s. It was subsequently increased to a

H

million and a half. The company underwent
vicissitudes of good and bad fortune ; but ultimately
attained to the government of 100,000,000 of
people, and maintained armies.

HET   HUIS   VAN ·DEN

OOST   INDISCHE   COMPACNIE   IN

LON   DEN

THE ORIGINAL EAST INDIA HOUSE, LONDON, 1648.

The first India House was a tenement called the
Green Gate, and was at one time occupied by the

benevolent alderman Philip Malpas, **whose** house
was sacked by Jack **Cade** and **his rabble.**
Henry VIII. gave it **to** the Frenchman, John
Mutas, who harboured many of his countrymen **to**
calendar " wolsteds." This, and other acts detri-
mental to the citizens, caused the riot on Evil May
Day, 1517, to which allusion has been made. The
Green Gate and the adjoining residences of Sir
William Craven (1610), father of the great Lord
Craven, remained the India House until 1726,
when a new one was erected, and which gave
place to the present building **in 1799,** being **subse-**
quently enlarged and ornamented.

We have spoken of the **conduits running with**
wine—white and claret **wine—the Great Conduit**
in Cheap, all one June afternoon (t. 1533) **on the**
marriage of Anne Boleyn ; but the most precious
liquor—water—first flowed from the conduit in
West Cheap in 1285, brought hither from Tyburn
through leaden pipes, which took fifty years to lay
down. Tyburn and Baynard's Water, **or** Bayswater, furnished ten more conduits, **and** were
periodically visited by my Lord Mayor and the
City Hunt when, before and after dinner, the hare
and the fox were hunted and killed even in
St. Giles's Fields. **The Mayor and** Corporation
then went to dinner at the Banqueting House, at

the head of the conduit in Oxford Road (where Stratford Place now stands), and when, no doubt, as the old song runs—

> " They dipped the fore-pad in a bumper,
>   And drunk my lord's health in good wine."

In James I.'s time the conduit water was carried

CONDUIT AT BAYSWATER.

about by a man **called a** Tankard Bearer. He
bore **a** large can **on his shoulders**, towels over his
breast and back, and disposed of the conduit waters
by the quart or gallon, and was, in fact, a walking
pump. In 1620, the New River Company was
incorporated to supply water through wooden
pipes. James I. took great interest in the under-
taking, and fell into the river. **Hugh** Myddelton,
the projector, was made a baronet, and we **are** glad
to know, from Mr. Smiles's recent research, **did**
not get into hot **water** as reported, but was **well**
rewarded **for his** enterprise. **The** shares of the
Company (seventy-five in number**)**, sold for many
years **at only five** pounds each, but within a few
years a share has realised ten thousand pounds.

In 1582, Peter Morris, a Dutchman, and denizen
of the City, erected engines for raising a water
supply from the Thames by converting the water-
courses into cataracts or rapids, to the great inconvenience of the navigation : these works were
partially destroyed by fire in 1774, and in 1822
were removed by Act of Parliament. When a boy
we **saw** them in operation. Two or three large
slimy wheels plashing and dashing, and working
cranks and rods. Terribly frightened we were!

The water supply somewhat incongruously re-
minds one of the great fires which have devastated

SIR H. MYDDELTON. Opening of the New River. (From an old Print.)

London. One in 1086, when St. Paul's and all the churches from the east to the west gate were burnt. Another in the reign of Stephen nearly consumed the City. The fire on London Bridge in 1212 has been already mentioned. Then there was the Great Fire in 1666. Mr. Pepys was called about three in the morning of September 2nd to see the beginning of this great fire, which was not to cease until the 7th. * Both he and John Evelyn were eye-witnesses, and saw " the sky like the top of a burning oven visible for forty miles round, and to which distance the smoke extended, the crackling of the flames, the shrieking of the women and children, the fall of towers, houses, and churches, was like a hideous storm, and the air about so hot and inflamed, that at last no one could approach it. The stones flew like grenadoes, and the melting lead ran down the street in a stream, and the very pavement glowed with fiery redness. The fire began at a baker's in Pudding Lane,* and destroyed in four days eighty-nine churches,

* The monument on Fish Street Hill, set up to commemorate this event, stands about 202 feet from the spot where the fire began. The shaft and base of the pillar are exactly of the same height, viz., 202 feet. It is said to be the loftiest isolated column in the world, there being 345 stairs of black marble, and the whole cost was about 14,500*l*. There were originally three inscriptions in Latin, and one in English, which were obliterated by James II.; re-cut in the reign of William III., and finally erased by order of the Common Council,

including St. Paul's, the city gates, Royal Exchange, Custom House, Guildhall, Sion College,
and many other public buildings, 13,200 houses,
and laid waste in all 400 streets. The ruins
covered 436 acres, and extended from the Tower
to the Temple Church on one side, Fleet Street
and to Fetter Lane on the other. On the north-
east they reached to Holborn Bridge. The streets
were very narrow, and the houses built of wood
and plaster—usually with a large well-staircase,
which acted like a chimney. Before the fire the
houses nearly touched each other at top, and light
and air were almost excluded. Possibly Elizabeth's "Non-such" proclamation led to this economy
of space, though the old houses destroyed by the
fire occupied more ground than those built upon

Jan. 26, 1831. The English version, which produced Pope's well-
known lines—

> " Where London's column pointing to the skies,
> Like a tall bully lifts its head and lies,"

as as follows:—

" THIS PILLAR WAS SET VP IN PERPETUALL REMEMBRANCE
OF THAT DREADFUL BURNING OF THIS PROTESTANT CITY,
BEGUN AND CARRYED OUT BY Y^E TREACHERY AND MALICE OF
Y^E POPISH FACTION, IN Y^E BURNING OF SEPTEM. IN Y^E YEAR
OF OUR LORD, 1666, IN ORDER TO Y^E CARRYING ON THEIR
HORRID PLOTT FOR EXTIRPATING Y^E PROTESTANT RELIGION
AND OLD ENGLISH LIBERTY, AND Y^E INTRODUCTION OF POPERY
AND SLAVERY."

This has been very properly erased.

GREAT FIRE OF LONDON, 1666

their sites, when their gardens and open spaces were covered with buildings.

The few streets which were paved sloped downward to the centre, and formed a channel filled mostly with no very agreeable or sightly matter. So the fire—dreadful calamity that it was—hurried forward the material improvement of our street thoroughfares.

Swithin's Alley, by the Royal Exchange, was a merchant's house of that name, and some twenty odd houses were erected on its site. Copthall Court was a Dutch merchant's house, and Princes Street, going into Lothbury, was occupied by one great house before the fire. King's Arms Yard in Coleman Street was an inn with stabling for horses ; so that more houses were erected, although the streets were widened and improved. The most authentic accounts of the fire are from the *London Gazette,* and the testimony of Lord Clarendon, who was an eye-witness of its progress.

Immediately after the Great Fire every alderman had to provide buckets and hand-squirts at his dwelling : hence, no doubt, the frequent appearance of the former in the old halls and warehouses in the City. There were many precautions to be enforced on the cry of fire : an armed man was to be placed at every doorway with a bucket of

water; lanterns were to **be** lighted and hung **out.**
All persons **except those** summoned by the Lord
Mayor **were** enjoined to keep within the houses,
and a **bell was** to be rung and the streets patrolled.
Brokers on 'Change were required to attend and
guard the goods committed to their charge ; and
these regulations continued in force, although neg-
lected in the observance, until the establishment of
the insurance companies, **and** a fire-watch, November, 1791.

One word on the old curfew bell, generally
regarded **as a** tyrannous institution of the Conqueror, and nothing else. It really seems to have
been **a necessary** act **of police to insure** the ex-
tinguishment **of fires in houses so very combustibly**
constructed **as were those of** our forefathers. **In**
the *Antiquarian Repertory* there is a drawing and
description of an ancient curfew, or cover-fire,
an instrument by which the embers on the hearth
could **be** effectually extinguished. It was shaped
somewhat like a Dutch oven, and formed **of** pieces
of copper **riveted** together, being about ten inches
long, sixteen **wide, and nine** deep. The curfew
bell was rung, **therefore, to compel** the use of **this**
instrument, and **not** merely **to** send naughty Londoners **to** bed whether they liked **it or** not.

CROSS IN CHEAPSIDE.   (From an Old Print.)

CHAPTER IV.

AT Paul's Cross, which formerly stood at the end
of Cheapside and St. Paul's Churchyard, were held
folkmotes, or assemblies of the people, until the
reign of Henry III.   In Stow's time it was a
pulpit cross of timber, mounted upon steps of stone
and covered with lead.   The first ecclesiastical use
to which it was put was "to curse all those who
had searched for gold in St. Martin's-in-the-Fields."
Sermons were regularly preached there, and in
1361 a bishop of London bequeathed one thousand
marks to be lent at the Cross to poor traders, on

pawns without interest. The earliest Paul's Cross sermon is preserved in **Fox's** *Book of Martyrs.*

Jane Shore did penance here, it is said, with sheet and candle, 1483; but others assert she only walked through Cheapside following a man with a cross. She was afterwards confined in Ludgate; but upon the petition of Thomas Hymore, who agreed to marry her, King Richard III. set her at liberty. According to the Harleian MS., Sir Thomas More saw her, and contradicts the story of her having perished by hunger. Hither was brought Elizabeth Barton, the Holy Maid of Kent, with Parson Masters, of Aldrington, Dr. Bocking, her confessor, Richard Deering, and others, **to do** penance. **They were all hanged** at Tyburn.

The wonderful **Rood or** crucifix of Boxley, in Kent, which was **wont** to move its eyes, shake **its** beard, nod its head, and bow to those who brought offerings, and had become famous all over England, was here exposed and broken into a thousand pieces by the enraged populace. **Elizabeth** Croft, principal performer in the imposture known **as** the Spirit in the Wall, did penance here. That must have been **a Protestant** spirit, as it denounced Queen **Mary, Philip of** Spain, and auricular con-fession. **Many other** penitents also appeared there, and **among them a** priest for "singing mass with good ale." He was probably the composer of *Pro Omnibus Bibo*.

On the 12th of May, 1521, the Pope's sentence against **Luther was** published at Paul's Cross, with **great state and** pageantry. Throughout Henry VIII.'s time, Paul's Cross was used by the defenders of the king's policy; and during Edward's short reign the most eminent Reformers preached here—Ridley, Latimer, and John Rogers. During a sermon before the Lord Mayor and aldermen, an order came from the Queen **to** levy a thousand able-bodied men to raise the siege of Calais, upon which they instantly quitted their devotion, and had the thousand men **ready** to march **in the** morning. (First-rate recruiting that!)

The Cross continued until 1643, when, by order of the Long Parliament, it was pulled down, as were all the other crosses in London and West-**minster.**

We have continual glimpses, most interesting, **in** the old chroniclers, of the manners and customs of their times; and from the great dramatists of Elizabeth's reign we get a knowledge of the daily life of Old London.

Shakspere does little for us beyond **those im-**mortal nights in Eastcheap, and the **smack of the** time which pervades his writings. **But Ben**

Jonson, the bricklayer's **son** of Hartshorn Lane,
and so Cockney-born, **has** left us photographs of
the form and body of the time in which he lived
and moved. We see by " Rare Ben " that there
were " Paul's men, who strutted through the
middle aisle with gallants who wore **silver** spurs
and jewels in ear, and the hand that hath the ruby
and a mirror in the hat," and some with ruffles
and worked shirt-fronts. The Puritan had texts
of Scripture upon theirs. **We learn** how a country
gentleman was made into a **town one.** **Thus he**
was to **" give** over housekeeping in the country,
having turned four or five acres of his best land
into two or three trunks of apparel, and to live
altogether in the City amongst gallants ; play at
primero and passage, feed cleanly at his ordinary,
sit melancholy and pick his teeth when he could
not speak." When he came to plays he **was** " to
be humorous, ruffle his face like a new **boot,** and
laugh at nothing but his own jest, **or else** as the
noblemen laugh "—that's a special grace he must
observe :—" pretend alliance with courtiers and
great persons." (How many a fine gentleman
now-a-days **is made** after the same fashion!) " Rare
old Ben " shows us how the rich trader, Gilthead,
trapped young spendthrifts, by getting them so
deeply in his books that escape **was** impossible,

unless, as Gilthead's son remarks—"**When** they
have **had** your **money** they **laugh at you, or** kick
you down stairs."

They had then the bold undertaker, or *procurer
of patents*, and the court lady who helped him to
them. Hear one of them:—

> " I'll drive his patent for him.
>   We'll take in citizens, commoners, and aldermen,
>   To bear the charge, and blow them off again,
>   Like so many dead flies, when it is carried."

They had the believer in alchemy, who sought
to make gold from lead (now we have the dabbler
in shares), the *gourmand*, **rival to** any member of
the *Bon Bouche Club*, **who had** " the beards of
barbels served instead **of salmon,** oiled mush-
rooms," for which he said unto his cook, " there's
gold; go forth and be a knight."

Then they had the sporting tobacconist. We've
no doubt Abel Drugger kept **a** betting-office, for
he backed Alchemist for half a crown to win a
fortune! Rather than so have wasted his sub-
stance, Abel had better given his roguish tobacco
to Captain Bobadil, who, according to his own
account, had, " with a dozen other gentlemen, not
received the taste of any other nutriment in the
world for the space of one-and-twenty weeks but
the fume of this simple only, therefore 'tis most
divine."

Londoners were then divided into tobacco lovers, like Bobadil, and **tobacco** haters, like Cob the water-bearer, who **declared** " it was only good **to** choke a man and **fill** him full of smoke and embers."

When Raleigh first introduced the smoking of tobacco, " silver pipes were the only wear." The weed was powdered, and the smoke passed through the nostrils. Some accomplished smokers **now-a-**days perform the same silly feat, and **call** it smoking by *inspiration!**

Mr. Walter Thornbury, in **a** communication to *Notes and Queries*, No. 210, writes :—" The tobacco merchant was an important person in the London of James the **First's time, with** his Winchester pipes, his maple cutting-blocks, his juniper-wood charcoal fires, and **his** silver tongs with which **to** hand the hot charcoal to his customers, although he was shrewdly suspected of adulterating the precious weed with sack-lees and oil. It was his custom **to** wash the tobacco in muscadel and grains, and to keep **it** moist by wrapping **it** in greased

---

* Tobacco was brought first to England by Sir John Hawkins, 1565 ; but Sir Walter Raleigh and Sir Francis Drake are thought to have been the first *smokers* of it in this country (1586), it having been previously manufactured only for exportation by one Ralph Lane. In 1791 the importation was 9,000,000 lbs.; but in 1861 it had increased to 52,854,392 lbs.

leather and oiled rags, or by burying it in gravel.
The Elizabethan pipes were so small, that now
when they are dug up in Ireland the poor call
them 'fairy pipes,' from their tiniess. These
pipes became known by the nickname of 'the
woodcocks' heads.' The apothecaries, who sold
the best tobacco, became masters of the art, and
received pupils, whom they taught to exhale the
smoke in little globes, rings, or the 'Euripus.'
'The slights' these tricks were called.

"Ben Jonson facetiously makes these professors
boast of being able to take three whiffs, then to
take horse, and evolve the smoke—one whiff on
Hounslow, a second at Staines, and a third at
Bagshot. The ordinary gallant, like Mercutio,
would smoke while the dinner was serving up.
Those who were rich and foolish carried with them
smoking apparatus of gold or silver—tobacco-box,
snuff-ladle, tongs to take up charcoal, and priming-
irons. There seems, from Decker's *Gull's Horn-
book*, to have been smoking clubs, or tobacco
ordinaries as they were called, where the entire
talk was of the best shops for buying the Trinidado,
the Nicotine, the Cane, and the Pudding; whose
pipe had the best bore, which would turn blackest,
and which would break in the browning.

"At the theatres, the rakes and spendthrifts

who crowded the stage of Shakspere's time **sat on**
low stools smoking; **they sat** with their three sorts
of tobacco beside them, and handed each other
lights on the points of their swords, sending out
their pages for more Trinidado if **they** required
it."

When the common sort adopted the habit of
smoking they used a walnut-shell and straw; then
came the clay pipe, which was sometimes handed
round the table from man to man. Tobacco was
sold for its weight in silver, and it was thought
scandalous for **a divine to** smoke, but tobacco was
used at all places of amusement—as it is now at
some, to the **great discomfort** of " young fellahs"
who fancy **it manly to** smoke, and pretend **they**
like it.

With their sporting tobacconist they had the
prototype of our Blackleg. Hear one at his calling
(Poor Pigeon if he heeds him!):

" There's a young gentleman is born to nothing—
forty marks **a** year, which I call nothing. He is
to be initiated **and** have a fly of ' the doctor.' He
will win you **by** irresistible luck, within this fort-
night, enough to **buy** a barony." (Tempting that!)
He is to be " the lion **of the season** and have the
best attendance, the **best drink, two** glasses of
canary, and pay **nothing; the** purest linen and

the sharpest knife ; **the partridge next his trencher "**
at the **ordinary.**

So our ancient fathers " made their game,
gentlemen," much as they did in St. James' Street,
when George IV. **was king.**

There was only one tavern in London when
Fitzstephen wrote (1191), three in Edward III.'s
time, one in **Chepe,** one **in** Walbrook, and the
other in Lombard Street; and in Edward VI.'s
reign there were forty taverns in the City, and
three in Westminster—there are now more than
seven thousand! The **Vintners'** Company of
London was founded in **1437, and** in James I.'s
time it was enacted that " none shall sell less than
one quart of the best beer or ale for **one** penny, or
two quarts of the smaller sort for the same sum."*
The power of licensing public-houses was granted
in 1621 to **Sir Francis Mitchel** and Sir Giles
Mompesson. Taverns had wonderfully increased
in Elizabeth and James II.'s time, for the ordinaries
are continually referred to both in play and narrative, and the cook's craft was as much esteemed
as now. Ben Jonson declares " a master cook to
be the man of men," **and he** is well worthy of consideration as the Minister of the Interior.

The varieties of American drinks, with their

* See " Tales of Taverns,"

extravagant names, had their prototypes in 1698, when M. Sorbiere, writing of the wonders of London, says : "They name several sorts of liquors in London as *Humptie Dumptie, Three Threads, Four Threads, Old Pharaoh, Knockdown, Hugmatee, Shouldree, Clamber-crown, Hot pots at Newgate Market, Foxcomb, Stiffle Blind* **Purneaux, Cock my** *Cap, Twopenny, &c."*

Our good old City, though circumscribed, **as we** see it was, by walls and Acts of Parliament, **was** large enough for knaves to find fools to prey upon. Coney-catchers, **like Bardolph's Nym and** Pistol, who carried **Master Slender "to a tavern and** made him drunk, **and then picked his pockets,"** were plentiful as blackberries. There were **three** parties to Coney-catching. The Setter, who found the Coney or Dupe; the Verser, who joined the hunt; and the Barnacle, who came **in** at the finish. "Then ere they part, they make him (the dupe) a coney, and so ferret and claw him at cards, that they leave him as bare of money as an ape of a tail." Robert Green, the dramatist—poor fellow! he **died of his** excesses, driven thereto by **his friends, who taunted him for** his sobriety, and called him Puritan—describes the scene from which **we quote.** The *modus operandi* **then in** vogue is **followed** by the **card** and skittle sharpers of our own time, and as one of them said, when lectured by a magistrate of our acquaintance—"they oughtn't to be punished—it was the fools who ought to suffer for tempting the ingenious."

The cheaters spoke a slang called Pedlar's French; and though they principally haunted country fairs, their head-quarters were in London. There was the Ruffler, the Upright Man, the Prigger of Prancers, the Abram Man, the Whip Jack, the Dummerer, the Counterfeit Crank, and others.

Southwark, Kent Street, and Bermondsey were the strongholds of the London tinkers, mumpers, and broom-men, and the places where the rogues disposed of their stolen gains. There was also the thief trainer, one Wotton, who had been a merchant and man of good credit, but set up a schoolhouse, like Old Fagan, to teach young boys to cut purses. There were hung up two devices—a pocket and a purse. The pocket "contained counters, and was hung about with hawks' bells, and over the top did hang a little scaring bell, and he that could take a counter without any noise was judged a nipper or cut-purse."

If Mr. Wotton's spirit is doomed for a certain time to walk the night with Hamlet's father, it must be very disturbed to see how little advance science has made in his direction.

Fleetwood, Recorder of London (in Elizabeth's time), was a terror to the fraternity, for he hanged nine out of ten one morning. "And I abroad myself," he says—"and I took that day seventy-four rogues." But Fleetwood's sport was sometimes interrupted by reprieves; the granting of them annoyed him sadly, and he writes, "It is grown for a trade now in the court." Poor recorder, poaching his gaol-birds!

Such of the London merchants who did not care to soil their shining shoes (once a distinctive sign of a London merchant), and those of the nobility who cared not to come in immediate contact with the commonalty, or to soil their delicate and embroidered pantofles or corked shoes, rode on horseback, the ladies sometimes on "one side," and sometimes on a pillion—a capital contrivance for sweethearting—bashful suitor in front, coy maiden behind. We remember so riding more than once, when, at the ripe age of eleven, we were "*cavalier seul*," to one "sweet Kate," who is now a grandmother! Sometimes ladies rode well — like Chaucer's "Wif of Bathe," whose

"Coverchiefs weren ful fine of ground;
I dorste swere, they weyeden a pound,
That on the Sonday were upon hire hede,
Hire hosen weren of fine scarlet rede.
Full streite yteyed and shoon ful moist and newe
Bold was hire face and fayre and rede of hew.

She was a worthy woman all hire life,
Husbonds at the chirche dore had she had five.

> *   *   *   *   *

Upon an ambler esily she sat,
Ywimpled wel, and on hire hede a hat.
As brode as is a bokeler, or a targe,
A fote-mantel about hire hippes large ;
And on hire fete a pair of sporres sharpe."

From this passage some have considered that the marriage was solemnized anciently at the church door, or that the ceremony commenced there ; and this would seem probable from Littleton's words (" Dower," sec. 39) :—

" When he commeth to the church door to be married there, after affiance and troth plighted, he endoweth the woman of his whole land, or of the halfe, or other lesser part thereof, and there openly doth declare the quantity and the certainty of the land she shall have for her dower."

It appears, however (sec. 41), that the woman, if she thought proper, might refuse such dower, and declare that she would rather abide by her future rights at Common Law. Lord Coke, commenting on these passages, says expressly, this dower must be made " ad ostium ecclesiæ sive monasterii," and that it is not good if made " ad ostium castri sive messuagii." He **also** expressly states :—

" This dower is ever *after* marriage solemnized ;

and, therefore, this dower is good **without deed**, because he cannot make a deed to his **wife**."

And Jacob ("**Law** Dictionary," *sub voce* "Dower,") **says it was made** " immediately after marriage."

Does not Chaucer, by mention of the church door, seem to infer that all her husbands were men of property ; and had each of them endowed the jolly lady " ad ostium ecclesiæ " with some of their lands and tenements ?

The English, until the beginning of **the** sixteenth century, were an equestrian people, and all the great processions were made on horseback. Henry IV. rode to Westminster attended by six thousand horse, and long after the introduction of coaches, in 1563, **it was** considered effeminate **to** ride in them, and was thought (says Aubrey**) " as** disgraceful for a young gentleman to be seen **in** one as in a petticoat and waistcoat," and a bill was brought into Parliament to prevent men riding in them **in** Elizabeth's time (1601). The postmasters, long before the post was established by law, kept **relays** of horses; but the carriers, with their train of packhorses, were the usual means of communication **between** distant places, and letters could be exchanged **between** London and Oxford in about a month **(1635). The** General Post Office was established **in 1660, and** regular postmasters appointed; they were usually innkeepers, and "made profit of their place," by many extortions.

"These are to give Notice that a Post will go and come every day between London and Reading, till further order.—Nov. 1688."—*Lond. Gazette.*

"There is lately set up a new Coach from Clapham, which sets out from Mr. Rawlinson's, near the Plough, every morning between 6 and 7, and returns from the Star by the Monument between 10 and 12, and from Clapham again between 4 and 5, and about 6 or 7 home again."—*The Postman,* June, 1710.

"That there is a Stage Coach sets out from the White Lyon in Chertsey, in Surrey, to the White Hart in Shug-Lane; and goes to the Bell in Bell-Savage on Ludgate-Hill, and carries Passengers at 3s. 6d. each to the said Inn, and for 3s. each to the White Hart in Shug-Lane; goes from Chertsey Mondays, Wednesdays and Fridays, and returns Tuesdays, Thursdays and Saturdays. Performed by John Hone, at the White Hart aforesaid. September 27th, 1729."—*Lond. Gazette.*

"To be Sold,

"At the Flying-Horse, in Lambeth-Street, Goodman's-fields,

"A Hearse, a Three End Coach, a Glass Coach, a

Chariot and Chaise, **and** five Hackney Coaches, with or without Horses, the Owner designing **to** leave off.—September **20,** 1729."—*Lond. Gazette.*

One **Hobson** was carrier and postmaster **at** Cambridge, and, from his custom of obliging his customers to take the horse next the stable-door, arose the saying of " Hobson's choice."

Hobson used to put up in London at the " Four Swans," in Bishopsgate Street; and Mr. Spectator tells us that he was there drawn in fresco with a 100*l.* bag under his arm, **with** this inscription—

" The fruitful mother of a hundred more."

Honest John Taylor, the water poet **(1623),** denounces **coaches in** prose and verse most heartily, for—

" When Elizabeth came to the crown
A coach in England was not known."

A doubtful statement, John, as **the** first coaches, called Whirlicotes, are said to have been introduced from France about Elizabeth's accession, by the Earl **of** Arundel, Steward of the Household to Queens Mary and Elizabeth; but Andrews, **in his** " History of **Great Britain,"** says they were known earlier. Three **only were** in use in Paris in **1550,** when Henry **IV. had** one without straps **or** springs; and some of **the** old hackney coaches we

remember must have been lineally descended
from it. They were called by the fast men of our
day "rattlers" and "bone-setters" — dislocaters
would have been the better term.

John objects :—

> "That fulsome madams and new scurvy squires,
> Should fill the street in pomp at their desires,
> Like great triumphant Tamburlaines each day,
> Drawn by the pampered jades of Belgia,
> That almost all the streets are choked outright,
> Where men can hardly pass from morn till night,
> Whilst watermen want work."

Ah! that was where the shoe pinched, honest
John! Yet John, one would think, had no need
to complain of business, as he plied at Bankside,
the landing-place where the inhabitants of the
Strand and Westminster came to visit the Globe
Theatre, the Paris Gardens, the Rose, and the
Hope playhouses, and there was no bridge but
London Bridge. In that locality were also the
bear-houses, to one of which Elizabeth took the
French ambassador, to witness the courage of
English bulldogs!* John took the new state of
things to heart, however, for he left London and
became a victualler at Oxford, and there died.†

* Lola Montes, the notorious Countess of Landsfelt, was the possessor of a bull-dog; and the man who sold it to her told us "that the countess was the loveliest thing he had ever seen—*on two legs!*" making pardonable reservations in favour of the bull-dog.

† The vehicle called a coach was a French invention, as was also the post-chaise, which was brought into England by Mr. John Tull,

It is somewhat strange that from the very
earliest time the City authorities were always

THE FORTUNE PLAYHOUSE, GOLDEN LANE, LONDON, 1820.

opposed to the players and playhouses, and in
1575 expelled them from the limits of the City;

son of Jethro Tull, the well-known writer on husbandry. John
Tull travelled in France and Italy, and having a turn for mechanics,
and being an extensive schemer, he introduced post-chaises and post
travelling, and obtained a patent in 1734. He started other projects,
and died a ruined man in the King's Bench.—See Hughson, vol. iii.

but the theatre in Blackfriars—its site now known as Playhouse Yard—was erected under the protection of certain monastic privileges. This house was called private : it was roofed over entirely. Two companies had the right of playing here—the Children of the Chapel, afterwards called the Children of the Revels, and the Chamberlain's Company, to which William Shakspere belonged, and for whose signature the Corporation of London paid 300*l*., to their great credit.

The performance of the play took place by candlelight, being frequented greatly by the higher classes. The first playhouse seems to have been called The Theatre. The Fortune was built by Alleyn and Henslowe on the site of a building formerly the nursery of the children of Henry VIII. It was finished in 1599, at a cost of 880*l*. It was a building eighty feet square, and partly raised upon piles. It was divided into three storeys, the first twelve feet high, the second eleven, and the third nine, which were formed in divisions of the gentlemen's and twopenny rooms. The interior was a square of fifty-five feet, open at top to the weather. The stage was forty-three feet in length, and with the tiring-room was covered.* Alleyn was the founder of Dulwich College, for whose

* See Hughson for further details.

restoration **to the** "**poor players**" **Mr. Webster**
of the Adelphi Theatre recently fought so earnestly
but unsuccessfully. So great was the wrong done
to the histrionic community, that funds were soon
found to establish the present admirable institution,
the Dramatic College, where many old public
favourites find

"Some pause between the theatre and the grave."

There **was also** The Curtain in Shoreditch, the
Belle **Sauvage** (probably on Ludgate Hill), Whitefriars, the Globe, the Swan and Hope at Bankside,
the Red Bull in St. John's Street, the Cross Keys,
Gracechurch Street, the Tuns, and the Nursery in
Barbican; but the City authorities closed all **they**
could. The first theatre that had a royal licence
was the Globe (1574). It was granted to Master
Burbage and four others, servants of the Earl of
Leicester. Almost the first act of James I. (1603)
was to grant a patent for the Globe and Blackfriars Theatres to Shakspere and his partners,
Fletcher, Burbage, Phillips, Hemming, Condell,
Sly, Armyn, **and** Cowley, and the drama assumed
a position it **had never before** attained, and which
it has never exceeded. **The** prices of admission
were, gallery, 2d.; **lord's room**, 1s.; and 6d. for **a**
seat **on** the stage. **And Paul Hetzner, who** visited

England, speaks of "the excellent music, variety
of dances, excessive applause," and the coming
round of oranges, nuts, apples, ale, and beer—and
perhaps a bill of **the** play, as there seems to be
little new under the sun or the moon either.

Greene, Peele, Decker, Webster, Beaumont,
Fletcher, Massinger, Ben Jonson, and William
Shakspere! To what meetings must the Mermaid
Tavern in Bread Street have been witness when
Raleigh, Selden, Cotton, and Carew were added to
the party! Many, we are told, were the wit com-
bats between Rare Ben and Sweet Willy. Jonson,
a Spanish galleon, solid, "but slow;" Shakspere,
the English man-of-war, **lesser in bulk** but lighter
in sailing, turning with all tides, tacking about, and
taking advantage of all winds by the quickness of
his wit and invention, heightened, as Jonson sings—

> " By a pure cup of rich canary wine,
>   Which is the Mermaid's now but shall be mine."

As we have endeavoured to confine this division
of our subject within the old Walls and so much of
Southwark as we have already visited, we defer to
another occasion further reference to the theatres
and taverns of London.

Old Guildhall was built about 1411, by subscription, **when Sir** Thomas Knowles was Lord Mayor.
The chapel was added by Dick Whittington, about

1411, and the east end of the hall was extended by
his means.   Sir John Shaw (1503) still further
enlarged it for city festivals, which had hitherto
been held at Grocers' Hall.   Guildhall was partially
destroyed in the Great Fire, looking like "a bright

GUILDHALL CHAPEL, LONDON.   (Pulled down 1822.)

shining coal, or like a palace of gold or burnished
brass :" the old walls and crypt alone remain.   It
was patched up by Wren, and in 1789 by Dance,
who added the present unsightly front.

There, in Guildhall, Buckingham sounded the

K

citizens as to Gloucester's elevation to the throne,
and there Anne Askew, one of the earliest Protestant martyrs, stood trial, and died at the stake
in Smithfield, after the rack had been used and
pardon offered in vain. There, six days after his
friend Wyatt's execution, stood the brave and
accomplished Sir Nicholas Throckmorton, opposed
to one of the most corrupt tribunals that ever
disgraced an English court of justice. Gallantly
he pleaded his cause, and nobly the jury who pronounced his acquittal did their duty. Their verdict
made Queen Mary ill for three days. They paid
for it, however, afterwards, by fine and imprison-
ment. The trial is to be found in Holinshed, and
will repay perusal. In Henry VIII.'s day the
poet Surrey was tried at Guildhall, as was Lady
Jane Grey in Elizabeth's time.

And there also, to compliment the citizens of
London for their loyalty—so said Lord Salisbury
and Sir Edward Coke—Garnet, the Jesuit, was
tried for the Gunpowder treason (March 26, 1606);
and there, during the Commonwealth, the poet
Waller was arraigned.

The Guildhall feasts have been famous for centuries, and the guests, kings, queens, emperors,
princes, and aldermen, the reeking of the viands
almost hiding the graver memories of the past.

Mr. Pepys, Mr. Cunningham says, gives the
earliest account of a Lord Mayor's dinner, when he
"sat at the merchant stranger's table; where ten
good dishes to a messe, with plenty of wine of all
sorts, but it was very unpleasing that we had no
napkins, nor change of trenchers, and drank out of
earthen pitchers and wooden dishes."

When Charles II. dined there, Lord Mayor
Viner seized the King's hand at parting, and
hiccupped—"Sire, you shall stay and take t'other
bottle." Charles smiled and hummed, "He that's
drunk is as great as a king," turned back, complied
with his host's request, and left another "dead
man" in Guildhall. Now Mayor Viner should
have been privileged, as is the Mayor of Norton
Basset. Whenever he is *plenus Bacchi*, and sees
two pigs in a gutter, he is permitted to join them.

The last dinner of the last century was very
characteristically illustrated. The outgoing and
incoming mayors were jovial fellows, and especial
lovers of good tobacco. As far as we can hear, this
was the only dinner at which smoking was permitted, or rather invited; and when the two mayors
alluded to lit their pipes at the same candle, the literary gentlemen present unanimously declared that
it reminded them of that famous passage, of the two
kings of Brentford smelling at the same nosegay.

K 2

From a clever review in the "Athenæum,"* of
*A Full and Particular Account of the Lord Mayor's
Procession by Land and Water*, we extract what
follows.

"The Roman Prefect and the Saxon Port-reeve
bequeathed a portion of their power as well as
duties to the Norman Mayor of London. We have
an instance of this in the circumstances attending
a City riot in the very olden time. The Mayor
was engaged in doing what would be tantamount,
in these days, to reading the Riot Act, in which
occupation he was pertinaciously opposed by a
roystering fellow whom his worship was unable to
reduce to silence, till he resorted to a very summary process, that of ordering the noisy rogue to
be dragged into a neighbouring street, where he
had his head chopped off! The affair was duly
represented to the king, but his Grace only laughed
his quiet laugh, and declared, by the Rood! the
Mayor was a lusty fellow and had done right
well.

"The Mayor's authority, too, was illustrated by
all sorts of honours, particularly when he was
willing to lend money to the king. In 1354,
Edward III. granted him the privilege of being
marshalled by gold and silver maces, copper

* Nov. 3, 1860.

(plated) being recommended for the chiefs of all other corporations. All writers on this subject have fixed the title of Lord as commencing with the grant of this regal bit of ceremony; but that distinction dates, we believe, from another year, and the right honourable gentleman had to pay for it. A subsidy was needed for a war in 1378. There was a general assessment according to the rank of the individuals. A question arose as to the proper position of the Mayor of London in the table of precedency. 'Have him among the earls!' was a suggestion readily adopted; and, in consequence of the honour, my Lord was assessed at four pounds, which, in present value, caused him to contribute little less than 100*l.* to the exigencies of the war.

" The above incident points to the reality of the Lord Mayor's grandeur; but there was also a recognised sacredness in his person, as may be seen in the fact that, in 1479, Sheriff Byfield, presuming to kneel too closely to the chief magistrate, at prayer, before one of the shrines in St. Paul's, was fined 50*l.* for his presumption. Twenty times that sum would now hardly represent an equivalent for the amount in which the audacious sheriff was mulcted; but the plague was about, and the Mayor might have caught it, and the City lacked conduits; and so the fine was levied, and therewith new conduits **were** built, or old ones repaired.

" Even with all possible care, and fines on too-familiar sheriffs, the sacredness of his Worship was not always inviolate. In 1484 London saw no less than three Mayors in succession, the first two having died of the fatal sweating-sickness. Now and then, highwaymen had as little respect for Mayors of London as Death himself. The latest example was in the person of the truculent Saw-bridge, who, in 1776, was crossing Turnham Green on his return from a state visit to Kew. The whole of his illustrious party were stopped by a single highwayman—even the swordbearer made no motion, but sat still while his lordship was stripped. When the fellow had thus outraged the City court, he rode off to Kew and insulted the church. He met the vicar on the high road, and after making him deliver all his valuables, even carried off his sermon, to the temporary relief of the small flock occasionally penned in that locality.

" With the power of the early Mayors there was connected, as we have said, much abjectness of condition. Of this there are innumerable examples. Money was generally at the bottom of it. Where

this was not forthcoming, the greedy monarch
would make seizure not only of the houses of
mayor and aldermen, but of their sons, as hostages.
Sometimes the first lady in the land could be as
savage as her lord. Queen Eleanor clapped the
Mayor, Hardell, into a dungeon in the Marshalsea,
and kept him there till he consented to pay the
arrears of an illegally-ordered subsidy for the war
in Gascony. It was a fashion with other sovereigns
in want of money to imprison the poor Mayor, to
degrade him from his office, and then compel him
to purchase liberty and his old position at the
price at which they were estimated by the father
of his people. In later days this quality of oppres-
sion was not possible ; and if these Mayors could
not cut off heads without having to answer for it,
their authority became more real and legally
recognised. The officials who thus irresponsibly
acted were but phantoms compared with Sawbridge
sweeping the king's pressgangs out of the City—
with Wilkes bearding the entire Government—or
with Beckford, to-day lecturing his bewildered
sovereign, and the next haughtily receiving Lord
Barrington's humble apologies for having ordered
a body of soldiers to march through London, from
Spitalfields to the Strand, without permission from
the mayor and aldermen.

"This spirit in the mayoralty had grown up since the days of the Commonwealth. Refractory Mayors could only be subdued by tenderness. The pressure of knighthood bought as well as rewarded services; and to these other honours were occasionally added, as when the Duke of Newcastle, in 1749, was installed Chancellor of Cambridge. On that occasion he obliged two valuable friends, and made London's Mayor, Sir William Calvert, an LL.D. ; while the Duke of Richmond received the more burlesque honour of Doctor of Physick !

"Charles II., perhaps, took the most pains to obtain City rulers prepared to gratify him, and whom he was not unwilling to gratify in return. For this purpose it was necessary he should know his men; and, accordingly, there was at one difficult period of his reign, drawn up for him a clear sketch of the characters of the Court of Aldermen and Common Council. This document, which has been printed, enters not only into the tempers, failings, virtues, or vices of the City potentates in whom the king took an interest, but it spoke of how their domestic life was illustrated, in what sort they lived with their wives, and the degree of estimation accorded by their wives to *them!*

" We are all familiar with the almost comic helplessness of Bludworth in the year of the Great

Fire, with his 'Lord! what can I do?' and his whinings about lack of rest, and his ejaculations of weariness, and his yearnings for refreshment for the inner man. To render him true justice, however, Bludworth was rather wanting in head than in heart. The Mayors, in the days of pest and sweating-sickness, exhibited no inconsiderable alacrity in avoiding all suspected localities. Tradition tells of Craven, who founded the line of earls of that name, that, terrified at an outbreak of plague, he took horse, rode away westward, and never stopped till he reached those wild Berkshire Downs, where he found refuge in a farm-house, and subsequently built Ashdown House, on the spot now occupied by a more recently erected mansion. The old local story-tellers inform us that four avenues led to the house from the four cardinal points of the compass, and that in each wall of every room there was a window, in order that if the plague entered on one side, it might find issue by the other!

"Of all the Mayors who have stood in the presence of a king, no one is so conspicuous for his boldness or audacity as Beckford. If, for a time, he was something of the mere demagogue, he was not altogether void of the qualities which distinguish the patriot. The two characters are, perhaps, combined in the speech delivered by him on his first retirement from the civic throne in 1763. On that occasion he said, among other strong things, that 'under the House of Hanover alone, Englishmen *could*, but under the House of Hanover Englishmen were determined they *would* be free.' The memory of the man who uttered that compliment and comment may continue to be honoured, despite the expressed contempt of Gifford.

"But it was through the famous incident of Beckford's second mayoralty, in 1770, that his name chiefly lives. The unconstitutional return at the Middlesex election, where the candidate in a minority was declared to be the sitting member, brought the Lord Mayor to the foot of the throne with the famous Remonstrance. The king, it will be remembered, censured the citizens in his reply; and thereupon the Mayor gave tongue to a rejoinder, in defence of the censured, which astounded the unprepared monarch, who, according to the *Public Advertiser*, had no sooner terminated the reading of his own reply, than he 'instantly turned round to his courtiers and burst out laughing.' How he looked and acted when Beckford delivered his *impromptu* rejoinder—a better one, probably, than that afterwards written and received as the true one by Horne Tooke—let Walpole show : 'It is always usual to furnish a copy of what is to be said to the king, that he may be prepared with his answer. In this case he was reduced to tuck up his train, jump from the throne, and take sanctuary in his closet, or sit silent and have nothing to reply. This last was the event, and a position awkward enough in conscience.'

"In old times, people who had a respect for fashion—

> 'Commended the French hood and scarlet gown
> The Lady Mayoress passed in through the town
> Unto the Spittle sermon.'

"That occasion was one of her gala days; but *the* day which was to be marked with the whitest stone of all, was that on which a king met this vice-queen of the City within the limits of her husband's authority, and that king her husband's guest for the time being. Her privilege then was to be saluted with a kiss from the lips of royalty ; and the privilege did not expire without a vehement outcry on the part of the claimants to that pleasant distinction.

"Towards the middle of the seventeenth century, there was a rough country boy, a pupil of St. Paul's School, who stood watching a procession of the Judges on their way to dine with my Lord Mayor. The father of the boy wished to bind him

apprentice to a mercer, but the aspiring lad, as he
looked on the train of judges, registered a vow
that he too would one day ride through the City,
the guest of the Mayor, and die a Lord Chancellor.
His sire pronounced him mad, and resigned
himself to the idea that his obstinate son would
one day die with his shoes o n.

"The boy's views, however, were completely
realized, and the father's prophecy was also in part
fulfilled. The connection of the notorious Jeffreys
with the City was, from an early period, a very
close one. He drank hard with, and worked hard
for, the City authorities, and was as well known in
the taverns of Aldermanbury as Shaftesbury was
in the same district, when he was inspired by the
transitory ambition of himself becoming vice-king
in the City. From the time that Jeffreys became
Common Serjeant, but more especially from the
period he became Recorder, he kinged it over the
vice-king. He was Lord Mayor, Common Council,
Court of Aldermen, and Supreme Judge, all in
one ; and the first-named officer had really a
melancholy time of it during the period Jeffreys
had sway in the City. At the feasts he was a
tippling, truculent fellow, browbeating the men,
and staring the most dauntless of the women out of
countenance. In the latter pastime he was well

matched, perhaps **excelled,** by his **learned brother**
Trevor; and my Lord Mayor Bludworth had good
reason to remember both of them. The Mayor had
a fair daughter, the young and wild widow **of a**
Welsh squire, and one who made City entertain-
ments brilliant by her presence, and hilarious by
her conduct and her tongue. There was a wonderful amount of homage rendered to this Helen, to
whom it mattered little in what form or speech
the homage was rendered. The rudest could not
bring a blush upon her cheek; her ear was never
turned **away from any suitor** of the hour, and
every lover was received with a laugh and **a**
welcome by **this most** buxom of Lord Mayor's
daughters.

"There is not one man in a thousand, probably,
who is aware that the blood of Jeffreys and **the**
Mayor of London's daughter afterwards flowed in
noble veins. They had an only son, a dissolute,
drunken fellow, with whom even aldermen were
too nice to have a carouse, and whose appearance
at a feast scared Mayors who could take their claret
liberally. **This** likely youth, whose intoxication
broke down **the solemnity** of Dryden's funeral,
married, in spite **of** his vices, a daughter and sole
heiress of the House of Pembroke. The only child
of this marriage was Henrietta, who married **the**

Earl of Pomfret, and enabled Queen Caroline to
have a granddaughter of the infamous judge for
her lady of the bedchamber.   One of Lady
Pomfret's many children, Charlotte Finch, was
well known to many of our sires.   She was
governess to George III.'s children, whom she
often accompanied to the City to witness the
annual show.

" From City men who have borne high, and
some the highest offices in the corporation, are
descended not a few of the noblest of our peers.
Nearly four hundred years ago the ancestor of the
valiant and pious Cornwallises was keeping the
peace of London.   The noble Capels spring from a
Mayor, as do the sober Dartmouths and the gallant
Cravens.   From metropolitan eminence among
fellow-citizens have also arisen, or descended, the
Thynnes and the Pulteneys, both destined to wear
the title of the Bath ; the dignified Cowpers, the
learned Coventrys, Hill of the flashing sword, the
Denzel Holleses, the Romneys, one of whom gave
an earl's coronet to the daughter of Sir Cloudesley
Shovel, the admiral who had made shoes in his
'prentice days, and Osborne, whose love for his
master's (the goldsmith's) daughter, and courage
in saving her when in peril, were the first steps by
which he ascended to the City throne, and sowed the

seed which came up in strawberry-leaves for the
ducal coronets of the Dukes and Duchesses of Leeds.

"If, during the Commonwealth, the head lay uneasy which wore a civic crown, neither was there
a bed of roses for the London dignitary under
Charles II. This condition of little-ease was at its
worst in the three years, 1680-1-2. The Lord
Mayor's pageants, on his own day, were nothing
to those which passed through the city on the 17th
of November, in honour of the birthday of Queen
Elizabeth and the Protestant religion. At that
period the Court was in fear, the Mayor in alternate
fume and fright, and the orthodox, hard-drinking,
rollicking 'Green-Ribbon Club' in a frenzy of
drunkenness from claret and zeal for the Church.

"The name denoted the token by which they
recognised each other in the streets, but their
peculiar place was in the balconies of the King's
Arms Inn at the corner of Chancery Lane. Thence
they saw defile before them the pageants of Pope
and Devil, and of great personages supposed to
favour popery, all of which were committed to
the flames in front of the house, while the Club,
above, drank, shouted, and waved their hats on
their pipes; while the tipsy but 'right-thinking'
crowd below yelled like fiends exulting in the light
of their native home.

"The Green-Ribbon Club, invented for the
defence of all honest men who dreaded being
massacred by the Duke of York and the Papists,
a pocket-weapon, harmless to look at, but effective
enough when employed, as it sometimes was, not
against 'Papists,' but in knocking down adverse
pollers going up to vote at elections. The handle
is described, by gentlemen who grasped or felt it,
as resembling a farrier's bleeding-stick ; the fall
was joined to the end by a strong nervous ligature,
'that in its swing fell just short of the hand, and
was made of *lignum vitæ*, or rather, as the poet
termed it, *mortis*.' Contemporaries called this the
'Protestant Flail.' We know it now as the 'Life
Preserver.' Such was the invention. The new
word then coined let handsome Roger North
explain. 'I may note,' he says, 'that the Rabble
first changed their title, and were called " the
Mob " in the assemblies of this club. It was their
beast of burthen, and called first *Mobile vulgus*, but
fell naturally into the contraction of one syllable,
and ever since is become proper English.'

"From the earliest times there has always been
a certain unpleasant familiarity maintained between
the spectators in the street and those at the
windows of the houses on the line of the procession. In years gone by no cavalier would pass on

foot through **Cheapside, at** this festival time, **in a** new mantle of **silk** or velvet ; and in Queen Anne's days men **of condition** who ventured into the street left their superfine cloth at home, and only went abroad in ancient ' drab-daberries.' In that Queen's reign the Lord Mayor's mob was a mere mass of howling, filthy savages. **Behind the old** tapestry and Turkey worked **table-cloths which** covered the balconies the ladies **sat unmolested till** the actors in the show had defiled. **But, on the** very instant, they flew **within,** for **it was the** custom of the sovereign **people below** to assail them with ' kennel ammunition.' The show then consisted of a succession of pageants with intervals in their passing. It was chiefly at these intervals that the ladies had **to fly,** with scarfs and **new** commodes irremediably soiled, before volleys **of** every species of filth provided by **the** unclean savages for these especial **occasions. If it** were possible that anything could be **worse than** the missiles, **it** was the language with **which they** were accompanied. **In** this matter, however, the people were **not always** unprovoked. Looking back into the **streets of those days,** we see several gentlemen at the **lower windows** provided with huge bullocks' horns ; **these are full of** dirty water or some un-savoury **liquid; and** the funny object here is to pour the contents down the neck of some unlucky spectator below. The eagerness with which this fray is carried on is often expensive to the finer folks, and is doubtless the cause of certain advertisements which soon after appear in the papers, offering a 'guinney for a very large watch-case, studded with gold, dropt from a balcony in Cheapside.'

"Gradually the mob became rather satirical than aggressive. The beauty of the women seems to have softened them, though occasionally that beauty must have been put to hard trial by the cruelty of fashion. It is said that, in 1776, there were never seen so many beautiful English faces together as on the Lord Mayor's Day at the windows in Cheapside. But there was never such a hideous spectacle as the head-dresses above those very faces. A calculator who carefully went through the statistics of the day, and who was, perhaps, a speculator in the staple commodity of the nation, came to a conclusion that though wool was a light object, there could not have been less than twelve hundredweight of it carried on the heads of the ladies, maids and matrons, who on that day looked down on Mr. Mayor from the windows of Cheapside.

"Down to 1663, and continuing much later, the

guests were not treated on an equality. There
were various tables in the several courts as well as
in the hall, and at those assigned to the men of
lowest rank there were no napkins, one plate
served throughout the dinner, the meats were
served in wooden dishes, and the wine, such as
it was, and no stint, was circulated in earthen
pitchers.

"The Great Fire burned out the show and
dinner too, for a time, and the Mayor and Sheriffs
rather sneaked slowly up to Westminster Hall
than triumphantly progressed thither, as they had
been wont to do. Gradually the procession,
hardly less affected by the Plague than it was
subsequently by the Fire, resumed its old forms,
and the streets had their Saturnalia again, particularly if royalty had been to the City that day. In
such case the streets were illuminated, and, as the
said royalty, with all the guards that had been
drinking hard at various renowned inns in the
City, rolled back again westward, the balconies
were filled with roystering gentlemen, who tossed
off their mantling bumpers, and saluted the royal
diners-out with very tipsy huzzas."

"A love of sight-seeing," writes Mr. Fairholt,
" was a characteristic feature in our forefathers,"
and the remark made by Trinculo in the " Tem-

pest," "that when they will not give a doit to a
lame beggar, they will lay out ten to see an
Indian," was a most truthful saying. Yes! the
Londoners have always been great sight-seers, and
the Lord Mayor's show was a sight worth seeing.
It was formerly called a Riding, and originated
from the necessity of the Lord Mayor elect presenting himself before the king at Westminster.
That venerable institution, the Lord Mayor's
coach, would have found it difficult travelling as
the Strand and Charing were in times past, and
one need not wonder that Sir John Norman before
mentioned introduced water pageants. What these
displays were we gather from a description of the
pageant which attended Anna Boleyn from Greenwich (1533), and which "was to be likewise as
they used to do when the Mayor was presented at
Westminster:"—gay barges, streamers, sackbut,
shawm, and other noises of music, made up these
water pageants, the Mayor's barge being preceded
"by a wafter, or foist, full of ordnance, in which
was a great dragon, continually moving and
casting wildfire and making hideous noises to clear
the way;" and so from Greenwich to Westminster,
and afterwards from London to Richmond and
Greenwich, when whitebait was discovered, and
salmon was declared to be intoxicating.

The land pageants were all more or less like
those already described, save that there were

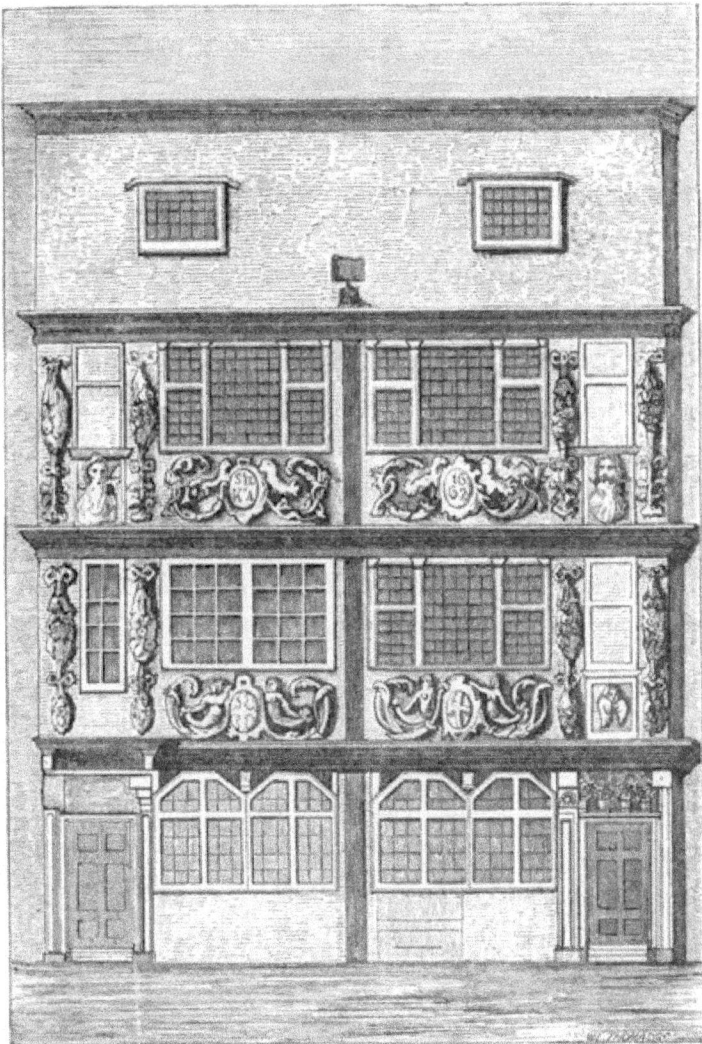

HOUSE IN GREAT ST. HELENS.   The Residence of Sir John Lawrance, Lord Mayor
of London, A.D. 1665.

occasional attempts at punning realizations of the names of the Lord Mayors. John Wells had three wells running with wine; that was a capital joke, and had no doubt a popular run. William Webb had a child representing Nature with a distaff spinning a web; rather a hazy metaphor, unless William came from the fens at Finsbury, and was web-footed. But the most strikingly original was when Sir John Leman was Mayor, 1616. He actually exhibited a lemon tree in full fruit, displaying an amount of mild invention very much to his credit as a father and a citizen. The devices for these pageants were numerous; but we fancy their general effect is pretty truthfully satirised by Clod in Shirley's "Contention for Honour and Riches" (1633), who declares that he cares not a bean-stalk for the best "What-lack-you" (or apprentice), and ridicules their galley foists and pot guns, their paper whales and ships that swim upon men's shoulders, and Hercules clubs that spit fire, and declares that the "children, which show like a painted cloth, catch cold, and are only kept alive with sugar-plums," and that they all "look upon the giants and feed like Saracens, till they have no stomach for Paul's in the afternoon." From 1639 to 1655 no pageants were exhibited, nor again from the

year after the Great Fire until 1671. In 1702
these great pageants ceased, their memory preserved by the Lord Mayor's coach—

" A thing of beauty and a joy for ever,"

the fly-borne aldermen, the men in armour, and
the noisy mob of the great non-ablutionists of
London.

And so we take leave of Old London City
within the Walls.

CHAPTER V.

IT has been said that great men lived, but they
lacked a poet, and have died. In revenge, how
many thousand flies have been uselessly embalmed
in poetic amber ! How many popular blunders,
prejudices, and fallacies have the bards preserved,
until the bards themselves get quoted as history !
The Tower of London, to whose outside we are
about to introduce you, has had its walls inscribed
with many a bardic legend, and millions believe
that the Tower was built by Julius Cæsar, because
Gray has told them so—

> " Ye towers of Julius, London's lasting shame,
>   With many a foul and midnight murder fed."

But, in spite of Mr. Gray, and according to " a
fayre register Book of the Bishops of Rochester,"
it was not the First Cæsar, but the First William
(1078), to whom London owes its lasting shame.
The Conqueror began the old White Tower,

William Rufus completed it : and the Red King was evidently the man to deal with refractory builders and stonemasons ; for it is recorded that he compelled the building of the Tower until many men perished thereby. It was the employers, it seems, that practised striking in those days.

The Tower is the history of England in stone. To study that history would occupy the whole space set apart for these jottings. We shall therefore detain you but a few minutes on what, in old times, was doubtless the safe side of the moat.

Charles, Duke of Orleans, who was taken prisoner at Agincourt and confined in the Tower, has left in a volume of his poems an illumination * representing the fortress at that period. It is a view of the Tower nearly five centuries ago. The Duke, you will see, has ingeniously shown the interior and the exterior at the same time ; and could, we have no doubt, have complied with the difficult requirement of the dramatist, who desired the representation of a moon behind a cloud, and been, like the Irish bird, " in two places at once ;" for you will observe that the Duke is writing his poem, looking out of the window, and receiving a friend at the same time. He also gives us a notion of the rush of waters through old London Bridge,

---

* This illumination has been frequently engraved.

and which accounts for the "spilling of," to quote
an old chronicler, the Duke of Norfolk's party,
long years ago.

CONVENT OF ST. CLARE. (From an Old Print, 1757.)
PARTS OF THE NORTH AND EAST WALLS OF THE CONVENT OF ST. CLARE, OR
MINORESSES, as they appeared after the Late Fire.
[This Convent, for the reception of Poor Ladies of the Order of St. Clare, was founded by
Blanche, Queen of Navarre, and her husband, Edmund, Earl of Lancaster, in 1293. The
fire happened on Thursday, the 23rd March, 1797. The walls were of Caen stone and
chalk, the timber was oak and chestnut.]

Rufus added a deep ditch, and Edward III. built the Church of St. Peter's ad Vincula, now sadly disfigured by alterations. We concur in opinion with Lord Macaulay, that it was barbarous stupidity which transformed this interesting little church in the Tower into the likeness of a meeting-house in a country town, as in truth there is no sadder spot of earth than this little cemetery, when we remember who sleep there, and how they were done to death. Beneath the altar lie Anna Boleyn and her brother Rochford (1536), without any memorial of their resting-place; Catherine Howard, the last of the Plantagenets (1542); the venerable Countess of Shrewsbury (1541); Cromwell, Henry's minister (1540); the brothers Seymour, both beheaded, one by order of the other (1549); John Dudley, Earl of Warwick; the Duke of Northumberland (1553); and so, as Stow says, there lie two dukes between two queens, and all four beheaded; Lady Jane Grey and her husband (1553-4); Elizabeth's Earl of Essex, and the murdered Overbury (1613); Sir John Eliot (1632), whose body Charles I. would not allow the younger Eliot to remove from the Tower; Okey the regicide; Monmouth (1685) beneath the communion table; Rotier the medallist; the Jacobite Lords Kilmarnock, Balmerino, Lovat. Talbot

Edwards, who so gallantly resisted Blood when he stole the crown, sleeps in the nave.

So leaving the Tower's story untold, let us walk to the Minories.

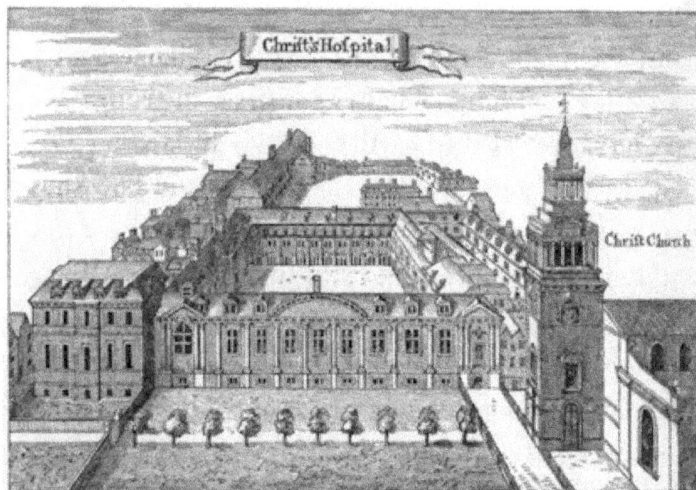

CHRIST'S HOSPITAL.   (From an Old Print.)

[This Hospital (formerly a House of Grey Friars) was first founded by that pious Prince Edward yᵉ 6th, & has since received many Donations from other Persons; by which Charities poor Children to the Number of about 820 Boys, and 80 Girls, are not only provided with Lodging, Diet, Clothing, & Learning, but when dischargᵈ yᵉ House are bound out Apprentices, & some of the Boys who have made large advances in Learning are sent to yᵉ University. The House is divided into handsome Wards, where the Children lodge, and a particular Ward to wᶜʰ yᵉ Sick are remov'd. For their Instruction here are a Grammar School, a Mathematick School, a Writing School, a School where yᵉ Girls learn to Read, Sew, & Mark, & of late Years yᵉ Boys have been taught to Draw. This Hospital is under yᵉ Care and Patronage of yᵉ City, and by yᵉ prudent Care taken thereof it has produc'd many famous for Wealth, Learning, & Serviceableness to yᵉ Publick.]

The Minories derived its name from the Sorores Minores, or Nuns of St. Clair (1293), whose convent stood in this street on the site of the Church of the Holy Trinity, and was founded by Blanche,

Queen of Navarre, the wife of Edmund, brother of Edward I., and the order continued until th e suppression, when the site was granted to the Bishop of Bath and Wells. The nuns of St. Clair sold milk to Stow, three ale pints for one halfpenny, always hot and the same as milked, and strained. That was before the discovery of the " chalk formation " in London lacteals. We wish some Sisters of Mercy and milk would open in London a dairy of St. Clair now-a-days. After the dissolution, armourers' workshops were erected. The Spa Field rioters, when on the way to the Tower, robbed the gunsmiths' shops in our time. The ladies, strange to say, have been great encouragers of the Minories' armourers, so says Congreve to Sir N. Temple.

> " The Mulcibers, who in the Minories sweat,
> And massive bars on stubborn anvils beat,
> Deformed themselves, yet forge those stays of steel,
> Which arm Aurelia with a shape to kill."

What should we say if any lady wore " steel " for this purpose now-a-days ?

The old convent fountain is in Haydon Square, where Newton lived when Master of the Mint. Regulations for the government of the Mint were first issued by Athelstane, A.D. 928. Stow says, that in Edward I.'s time, 1278, the Mint was kept by Italians, the English being ignorant of the art

of coining. Edward III. formed the operators
into a corporation, consisting of a warden, master,
comptroller, assay-master, workers, coiners, and
subordinates, and the first entry of gold brought to
the Mint was *tempo* Edward III., 1343. Charles II.
had tin coined into money, and James II. sent
gun-metal and pewter for the same purpose. Sir
Isaac Newton was warden, 1699-1727, during
which time debased coin was called in.

Let us pass into Spittal-Fields, or Lolesworth, as
it was called (the burial-place of our Roman con-
querors), where stood the Priory and Hospital of
St. Mary Spittle, " strongly built of timber, and
with a turret at one angle :" its ruins were revealed as late as the last century. At the north-
east corner of Spital Square stood the pulpit-cross,
in the open air, and where the celebrated Spittal
sermons (still continued at Christ Church, Newgate
Street) were first preached, and at which the blue-
coat boys were condemned to be regular attendants.
The pulpit-cross was destroyed in the civil wars.
The old map of Elizabeth's time shows Spital-fields
an open space, but before another century numerous buildings had been erected here and elsewhere
in the suburbs of the City. The celebrated Lord
Bolingbroke lived here, as did Culpepper the
herbalist, hard by the Priory in Paternoster Row.

Tarleton, the player at the Curtain Theatre, kept an ordinary in those pleasant fields! and in Cock Lane, now Pelham Street, Milton's granddaughter, Mrs. Clark, was allowed to keep a chandler's shop, and, certainly, a "New Defence of the People of England" was more needed than ever. Queen Caroline (wife of George II.) sent her fifty guineas, and on April 5, 1750, "Comus" was played for Mrs. Clark's benefit, and realised one hundred and thirty pounds.

Here the weavers most do congregate, the loom having been first introduced by the poor Protestant strangers, Walloons and French, and who soon produced fabrics as good as those of France, and worth 300,000*l.* annually. The Spitalfield weavers are great birdfanciers, and singers at their work. Falstaff had been among the weavers, and so had Ben Jonson. "I would I were a weaver," says Sir John, "I could sing all manner of songs." "He got his cold," says Ben, "sitting up late and singing catches with weavers." Spitalfield and Coventry weavers—we speak on the authority of Mr. John Timbs—have very small heads, varying from six and half inches to six and three-quarter inches, and the medium size of an Englishman's head is seven inches. There's a nut for the phrenologists to crack!

Moorfields and Finsbury bespeak their swampy origin. In Edward II.'s time Thomas Falconer, Lord Mayor, had broken a way through the wall, built Moorgate, and made "causeys" for the citizens to walk towards Islington and Hoxton. The fields were ditched and drained, and afforded walks for the peaceable citizens and their dames, or, as Shadwell says, " haberdashers walking with their whole fireside."

Here were the bleachers and laundresses, " whose acres of linen," says Davenant, "show like the fields of Carthagena when the five months' shifts of the whole fleet are washed and spread." The walks and grass-plat shaded by trees were called the City Mall.

In the old time, we are sorry to say, it was the fashion for fine ladies to swear. We find Hotspur actually scolding his affectionate Kate for using too gentle an oath, a tameness worthy, he says, only of city dowdies.

HOT. Come, Kate, I'll have your song too.
LADY P. Not mine, in good sooth.
HOT. Not yours, in good sooth! 'Heart, you swear like a comfit-maker's wife! Not you, in good sooth; and, As true as I live; and, As God shall mend me; and, As sure as day:

> And giv'st such sarcenet surety for thy oaths,
> As if thou never walk'dst further than Finsbury.
> Swear me, Kate, like a lady, as thou art,
> A good mouth-filling oath: and leave in sooth,
> And such protest of pepper-gingerbread,
> To velvet guards and Sunday citizens.

Here was the muster-ground for the train-bands
of London, formed at the threatened Spanish invasion, and their first place of meeting was in
Artillery Close; but when the alarm was over
they dissolved, and left the Artillery garden to the
Tower gunners. The train-bands were re-formed
in 1610, and, when the civil war broke out, they
sided against the king, and did good service at
Newbury, Brentford, and elsewhere. They mustered about twelve thousand, and Cromwell esteemed them highly. That distinguished equestrian, John Gilpin, you remember, was a train-
band captain of London town, and the famous
Honourable Artillery Company are their lineal
descendants.

Here the weavers, despite the smallness of their
heads, did by the boldness of their hearts, as
Pepys records, gallantly thrash the butchers in a
set battle, and drove them out of the field, and
then went forth offering 100*l.* for a butcher!
And here the old diarist (and so also Evelyn)
saw the tents and sheds raised by the houseless
Londoners, when the Great Fire had consumed
their city.

Second-hand bookstalls were formed under the
trees in Moorfields, to be represented in later
years by the Temple of the Muses, built by James

M

Lackington, who made 5000*l.* in one year by the sale of old books. A coach and four horses were once driven round his shop by a consummate master of the ribbons.

The Common Hunt was kept here at the Dogge House; and that city "meet" must have been a sight to have seen, with the Swordbearer perhaps as huntsman, and the Remembrancer as first whip, in his funny fur cap, which looks as though he had been so frightened "that each particular hair doth stand on end;" a lunatic apparition which may remind us that Old Bedlam Hospital stood on the south side. It was built after the model of the Tuileries, which gave the French king great offence accordingly.

A barbican, or watchtower, built on high ground, and whence a man might view the whole city towards the south, and also into Kent, Sussex, and Surrey, and also every other way, says Stow, gave the name to a spacious thoroughfare connecting Finsbury with Aldersgate Street. It was once the mart for old and new apparel. In Dryden's time Barbican had fallen into disrepute.

> "A watch-tower once, but now, so fate ordains,
>   Of all the pile an empty name remains."

The Clerk's Well (*fons clericorum*) gave the name to the locality where formerly stood the

magnificent monastery of the Knights of St. John
of Jerusalem, and where King John resided, and
more than one of our sovereigns held councils
within its walls. Wat Tyler's mob destroyed the
whole commandery, and beheaded the prior in the
courtyard, now the site of St. John's Square.
The last prior but one rebuilt the monastery late
in the fifteenth century, and his successor died of
grief when the priory was suppressed. Five years
later the church was a storehouse for the king's
nets and tents for hunting, the rest of the site
being given to Lord Lisle for his service as High
Admiral. The church was afterwards blown up
by gunpowder, and the materials used by the Protector Somerset in building old Somerset Place in
the Strand. The gate was, however, preserved,
and remains to this day as the Jerusalem Tavern.
Cave the printer occupied it beforetime, and the
names of Savage, "poor and friendless," Goldsmith, "glad of hack-work,"Johnson and Garrick,
make the spot classical. Johnson there ate his
plate of victuals behind a screen, his dress so
shabby that he durst not make his appearance ;
and Garrick, an actor worthy of his "Critics,"
played the "Mock Doctor," in the room over the
archway, the other parts in the farce sustained by
the journeymen printers. In St. John's Square

died the bold Bishop Burnet, and near there formerly stood the house of Oliver Cromwell, where some suppose the death-warrant of Charles was signed.

In Clerkenwell stood also the nunnery of St. Mary, when the River of Wells, or the Fleet, ran trickling to Holborn Bridge, and a Coppice and Wilderness, and Saffron Gardens, and Vineyard, all preserved by localities so named, stretched away to the village of Islington. The pass to that then distant region was so dangerous that people waited at Wood's Close—now Northampton Street—until they mustered in good force, and were then escorted on their way by an armed patrol. A friend informs us that an old gentleman of ninety-five (who claims to be a descendant of the first lord mayor) remembers being one of such a party. Here resided many noble folk, among them the eccentric Duchess of Albemarle (1669), who, when a widow, and immensely rich, became so elated by her wealth, that she vowed she would marry none but a sovereign. The first Duke of Montagu won the mad lady by declaring himself to be the Emperor of China. He married her—for her money—and kept her in such strict seclusion, that her friends demanded her production in open court. The Duchess survived the

Duke many years, and died at ninety-six—constantly, it is said, treated by her household as a sovereign, and served on the knee.

Near the northern end of St. John Street, Clerkenwell, stood the Red Bull Theatre in Red Bull Lane, and the place retained its name until the beginning of the last century, when it was called Woodbridge Street. When the "poor players" were suppressed by the Puritans they assembled at this place during Christmas and Bartlemy Fair time, under the direction of Alexander Goffe, the celebrated woman-actor of the Blackfriars Company. Drolls, put together by Robert Cox from the comic scenes of Shakespeare, Fletcher, and others, were very popular at the Red Bull, and the nearest approaches to the regular drama which the actors dared to attempt. A collection of these drolls—now extremely rare —has a curious frontispiece with a singularly incongruous variety of characters upon the stage. *Sir John Falstaff* and *Dame* **Quickly**; *Clause* in the "Beggar's Bush," *Changeling* and *Simpleton* from a piece written by Robert Cox, whilst *Tu Quoque Green* is advancing from behind the curtain with a label in his mouth. Before the suppression of the theatres the Red Bull appears to have held but an inferior position, for in a poem addressed to Sir W. Davenant (1633), it is described as

"That degenerate stage
Where none of th' untuned kennel can rehearse
A line of serious sense."

Some months before the Restoration the Red Bull was reopened, and on the king's arrival the company took the name of the King's Servants, and soon after removed to Vere Street, Clare Market, fixing themselves at last at the Cockpit, Drury Lane.

Hicks' Hall—everybody has heard of Hicks' Hall—whence the miles on the great north road were measured, and some have wondered where it "formerly stood!" It was in St. John's Street, opposite Ben Jonson's Windmill Inn, where Formal invited Brainworm, that he might "bestow a quart of sack upon him." It was named after Sir Baptist Hicks, who built it in 1612. In this hall the good Lord William Russell was condemned to death. Who forgets "that sweet saint who sat by Russell's side," and whose wifely devotion was the single ray of sunlight upon a scene of dark and cruel tyranny?

Thomas Britton, the musical small-coalman, lived at the corner of Jerusalem Passage, and had his musical meetings in a low narrow room over his coal-shop, and to which all the fashion of the

time sought admission, Britton himself playing the
viol de gamba. Perhaps from him comes the slang
word for chorus—" Coal-box "—if we might mention anything so ungenteel. Near the well in
Ray Street was the bear-garden of Hockley-in-the-
Hole, where noblemen, ambassadors, and bobtail
met to witness bull- and bear-baiting, and the
whole science of defence, until Figg, the prize-
fighter, opened his booth in Tottenham Court
Road. Broughton had a booth also behind
Oxford Road (1742), and schools for teaching
boxing as a science were opened in different parts
of England. Mendoza taught at the Lyceum in
the Strand (1791), and boxing was greatly
patronised up to 1830 ; since that time it has been
going out of favour, though the public enthusiasm
was aroused when Tom Sayers (5 ft. 8 in.) drubbed
Heenan, the Benecia Boy (6 ft. 1 in.), April 16th,
1860, Tom fighting with one arm broken. Sayers
died in 1865.

Numerous spas and medical wells were once in
fashion at and about Clerkenwell, but they have
given way to bricks and mortar, and left no wreck
behind—not even Bagnigge Wells garden, rendered
pictorially famous in later times by Seymour the
caricaturist, as the locality where " the two teas
and a brandy and water " ran away without paying.

The parish clerks of London were famous
actors of mysteries, and in 1390 they came to
Skinner's Well, near to Clerken Well, and did
enact interludes, which play continued three days
together, the king, queen, and nobles being

THE TILT YARD—COMBAT A L'OUTRANCE.

present (we are very glad we were not); and in
Henry V.'s time they played one which lasted
eight days, and was "matter from the Creation of
the world"—one would almost think to the end
of it. We once knew an unappreciated poet who

had written a tragedy in thirty acts, and which he proposed to play five acts every night during the week. The subject was the entire history of Poland, but the parish clerks beat him hollow.

It is Michaelmas Sunday, if you please, in Richard II.'s time (1377), and to celebrate the marriage of Charles VI. of France the king hath commanded a tournament, the English knights challenging all comers. There are, says Froissart, threescore knights apparelled for the jousts, each knight attended by a squire riding a soft pace; then threescore ladies of honour mounted on fair palfreys richly dressed, and each lady leads a knight with a chain of silver, and on they come with a vast number of trumpets and other minstrelsy. The twenty-four challengers have their armour garlanded with white hearts, and their necks with crowns of gold, and so on to where the queen awaits them in Smoothfield, or Smithfield, as it is better known. It was sometimes called Ruffian Hall, from its frays and common fighting with sword and buckler, and deserved the name for many a day later, and until the market was removed. Here was fought the combat of *Horner* and *Peter* in Shakespeare's Henry IV. The scene of the dramatist is founded on fact. " A certain armourer had been

appeached of treason by a false servant of his own.
For proof thereof a day was given to fight in
Smithfield; but the armourer's friends gave him
wine and strong drink in such excessive sort that
he reeled as he went, and so was slain without
guilt." Dramatic justice was done, however, on
the false servant. He was convicted of felony and
judged to be hanged, "and so he was at Tyburn."
Why they should have taken the culprit to
Connaught Terrace, Edgeware Road—the site of
the old Tyburn tree—we cannot say, the Elms
(now known as Cow Lane) being at hand, and
where the gallows stood. The trial by battle was
abolished only in 1819, shortly after a most
fearful crime had roused the indignation of the
nation, and the lawyers discovered that the
miscreant who was guilty had a right to his wager
of battle. There also, as Master Tommy knows,
Wat Tyler was stabbed in the throat by Lord
Mayor Walworth; hence it was thought the
dagger in the City arms—but, no; the dagger
was there before the valiant Mayor was even a
London 'prentice.

"How blest are we that have not vulgar minds!"

Here, also, were kindled the martyr fires of
London from the accession of Henry IV. One of

the first martyrs was John Bedby, a tailor, in
1410, and the last is said to have been Bartholomew Leggatt. But the punishment by fire for
other crimes than keeping a conscience was long
retained, as Evelyn speaks of seeing a miserable
creature burning who had murdered her husband.
We believe, however, that such agonies were
shortened by strangulation. Among the old
woodcuts in the first edition of 'Fox's Book of
Martyrs,' is the burning of the brave, good, and
witty Anne Askew, and from that it appears the
martyr fires were usually kindled just outside the
gates of St. Bartholomew's Priory. Bones marked
by fire have been found buried there. Should
not the place have a martyrs' monument ?

In Henry VIII.'s day three poisoners at different times were boiled to death ; one, a cook,
put poison in his caldron, and, all things considered, received poetical justice; and in Queen
Mary's reign 277 persons suffered by fire in
Smithfield. In 1575, Elizabeth being Queen, two
Dutchmen, Anabaptists, were burned with much
" roaring and crying," as the chronicle records
with a sort of strange wonder that Anabaptists
should not like to be burned. Matters, however,
changed greatly for the better, and roods and
church images were the victims of martyr fires;

and St. Bartholomew's day was kept as a day of triumph for the Protestants, the booksellers displaying only Bibles in their shop windows.

But enough of these sad memories; and let us seek for pleasanter recollections in the other uses of old Smithfield.

The first fairs were formed by the gathering of worshippers and pilgrims about sacred places, on the feast-days of the saints enshrined within them. Grant of tolls to a fair was then a concession from the Crown of no mean value; and Prior Rayere, jester at one time to Henry I., and founder of St. Bartholomew's, very knowingly secured those of Bartlemy Fair to the uses of his church and hospital; for shortly before the demolition of monasteries, St. Bartlemy received about 300*l.*, equivalent to not much less than 3,000*l.* now-a-days. When Sir Thomas Gresham, the Lord Mayor, with the aldermen and citizens of London, saw how matters were going with the religious houses, they petitioned Henry VIII. for the governance of the three hospitals, St. Mary, St. Thomas, and St. Bartholomew, for the "aid of poor and indigent people, and not to the maintenance of priests, canons, and monks, carnally living as they of late have done." The king granted the City's prayer, provided it would find

the requisite **funds for the** support of the hospitals; and five **hundred** marks a year were voted
forthwith : **a tax which** was, in fact, a poor's rate ;
and the **hospitals for** the sick have grown and
multiplied in **the** land—thanks, in no small
degree, to the enlightened liberality of the medical
profession.

All goods were sold *absolutely* at fairs, however
bad the title to them of the seller, saving only the
rights of the king. This, we suppose, was called
fair dealing. The resident traders were compelled
to close their shops during fair times, which **was**
pleasant. For many years fairs continued to **be the**
chief resorts of traders, and stewards of country
houses made purchases at fairs a hundred miles
away from home as late as the sixteenth century.

As every fair was called after the saint whose
feast-day it celebrated, the one we wish you to
visit was called St. Bartholomew, or, in the spirit
of abbreviation distinguishing the commonalty of
London, " Bartlemy," in the same way as an
omnibus is called a " bus," a cabriolet a " cab," and
the City the " stee." Our fair was granted, as we
have said, **to Rayere, the** king's jester, **by**
Henry I. A **clever,** cunning fellow was Father
Rayere ! as **Henry** I., according to Fabian's
" Chronicle," **had** divers monitions and visions,

and Rayere was just the monk to make the most of them. When kings dream it is bad for their pockets, or, rather, for those of their subjects.

St. Bartholomew was the principal cloth fair in England until the time of Elizabeth, and when our fine broadcloths were sent to Holland to be dyed, the art not being understood in England until introduced by one Brewer, from the Low Countries, 1667. The first cloth weavers, composed of seventy families, came over from the Netherlands on the invitation of Edward III. The clothiers had their stands in the churchyard, and Cloth Fair still marks the site. Fit persons were appointed by the Merchant Tailors' Company to attend and test by their silver yard the measures to be used. Mercers especially frequented fairs, and sold gay haberdashery, toys, and even drugs and spices ; whilst others dealt largely in silk and velvet, and eschewed the haberdashery traffic. Our old friend Dick Whittington was a mercer, and no doubt had a stall at Bartlemy Fair.

As the frequenters of fairs were here to-day and gone to-morrow, it was necessary that their disputes should find immediate settlement; so there was a court regularly called the Court of Pie-Poudre, which had to do with fair business only, and gave as summary judgments as our

County Courts, and probably, like those, generally found for the plaintiff. Pie-Poudre is corrupted from the French for "dusty-foot." The ancient Scotch law-writers called a wandering trader a "dustifute."

When the City obtained a share of the tolls, the fair was proclaimed by the Lord Mayor at the entrance to Cloth Fair. His lordship then called upon the keeper of Newgate, and had a cool tankard of wine, nutmeg, and sugar, and the custom only ceased on the second mayoralty of Sir Matthew Wood. One Sir John Shorter, maternal grandfather of Horace Walpole, and Lord Mayor in 1688, lost his life by letting the lid of the tankard flap down with too much force. His horse started, his lordship was thrown to the ground, and never recovered the tumble. He should have studied either good manners or good horsemanship. The mayor was evidently not master of the horse.

When the hospital of St. Bartlemy was disposed of to the City, Sir Richard Rich, Chancellor of the Court of Augmentation, was very early in Smithfield. At the time when he was Solicitor-General, he gave a turn with his own hand to the rack by which Anne Askew was tortured; so he was quite at home already in Ruffian's Hall. Rich had an

easy conscience, betrayed his friends, and served
his sovereign and himself. **As** Chancellor of the
Court **of** Augmentation, he augmented his own
income **by** purchasing Bartlemy Priory and all its
belongings for 1064*l.* 11*s.* 3*d.*—he was very
particular, like Mr. Mantalini, to "the dimnition
threepence," you see—and so continuing to buy
similar bargains, he became very Rich indeed, and
was made Lord Chancellor in the next reign ;
when, to quote Mr. Morley, the admirable historian
of Bartholomew Fair, " The way of society was not
the less surely forward and upward because it was
marching with soiled feet on a miry path."

Well, Rich—Lord Rich now—bought St. Bartholomew, **and there had his** town mansion, and
all the tolls of the **fair and** the market which had
pertained aforetime to the old Priory. Oh,
Father Rayere! where be your jibes now ? and all
that you thought of your house for ever ? There is
now remaining of the old Priory only fragments
of walls—one called Middlesex Passage—and part
of the great crypt overhung by the wreck of the
great hall, now divided into compartments, and
used as a tobacco factory. The old church of
St. Bartholomew the Great is externally as it stood
in Rayere's time, and within **is a** portrait statue of
the monk-jester.

The descendants of Lord Rich became Earls of Warwick and Holland ; one of whom, a temperate supporter of the Puritans, was Parliamentary Admiral, and Cromwell's fast friend, and helped to robe him as Protector. To Warwick's grandson Robert, Cromwell gave his youngest daughter Frances for a wife ; and when doing so, threw sack-posset over the ladies' clothes, daubed the stools with sweetmeats, and pulled off and sat upon the Admiral's wig—possibly after the wedding breakfast.

The Bartlemy property then passed to Elizabeth, heiress to Sir Walter Cope of Kensington She is supposed to have originated Lady Holland's Mob—a riotous assemblage of the showmen and traders at Bartlemy, some five thousand strong, which proclaimed in its own way that the fair was opened. Lady Holland's grandson married Charlotte Middleton, the daughter of a Welsh baronet. The earl died, and the lady afterwards remarried Mr. "Spectator" Addison, and for that reason we have told you the pedigree of the Lord of Bartlemy Fair.

So let us enter Bartlemy Fair, as it was in the days of Ben Jonson (who has founded one of the best and most valuable of his comedies upon the fair) and in subsequent years. We will take the

N

utmost care of you, ladies, and will warrant that
no one shall offer you the slightest impertinence.
Now, then!*

The first object we behold is a Miss Tom Thumb.
Listen to the showman :

" A Wonder of Nature : a girl above sixteen
years of age; only eighteen inches long, having
shed the teeth seven several times and not a
perfect bone in any part of her, except her head ;
yet she discourses, reads very well, sings, and
whistles—all very pleasant to hear."

"Here's the much-admired Gyant-like Young
Man of prodigious bigness.—If he lives three
years more and grows as he has done, he will be
bigger than any of those gyants we read of in
story.   He can already reach with his hand three
yards and a half."

> " In houses of boards, men walk upon cords
>   As easy as squirrels crack filberts.
>   For a penny you may see a fine puppet play ;
>   And for twopence a rare piece of art."
>
> " We've patient Grisel here, and Fair Rosamond there,
>   And the History of Susanna."

And a hundred other wonders.

Here are your " Bartholomew birds ;" your
"sword-and-buckler man ;" your " Kindheart if
anybody's teeth should chance to ache."   Here's

---

* See Professor Morley's " Memoirs of Bartholomew Fair."

your juggler "with a well-educated ape to come
over his chain for the King of England and back
again for the Prince, and to sit still for the Pope
and King of Spain." Here's "Leatherhead, the
hobby-horse man!" "the too proud pedlar, who is
puft up with the pride of his wares." Here's
"Trash the cake woman, whose gingerbread
progeny" is scandalized by her neighbour as
"made of stale bread, rotten eggs, musty ginger,
and dead honey."

"Buy any pears? buy any pears?" of the
costard-monger; or listen to Nightingale the
ballad singer—

> "Now the fair's a-filling,
>   O for a tune to startle
> The birds o' the booths here billing
> Yearly with old St. Bartle."

"Buy any ballads? new ballads?" Make way
there, for here comes Ursula, who wastes her
youth and prime in roasting pigs. Pluto's underground residence, heated by volcanoes, is a cold
cellar to her booth. Over it is writ in large
letters—

> "HERE BE THE BEST PIGS, AND SHE DOES ROAST THEM AS WELL
>   AS EVER SHE DID."

Quick! a bottle of ale to quench her who is all
fire and fat, and who fears to melt away to the

first woman—a rib again. More ale and a whiff of tobacco, if you wish her to hold life.

She charges threepence a pipe—the tip of your little finger would fill the bowl—though her tobacco is mixed with coltsfoot. She will have six-and-twenty shillings profit on her barrel of beer, and fifty shillings a hundred on her bottled ale! Five shillings apiece is the price of her pig, and sixpence extra to ladies, if she sees that a lady is in an interesting condition, and particularly urgent on her husband to treat her. "Have you any corns on your feet and toes?" If so, here's the corn-cutter; or, will you "buy a mouse-trap, or a tormentor for a flea?" Here they are to hand. Take care of your pockets, for there is Zekiel Edgeworth the civil cut-purse, "he of the horn thumb on which he nicks the pocket." Hear what he says to his "pal" the ballad-singer : " All the purses and purchases I give to-day, bring hither to Ursula presently. Here we will meet at night in her lodge, and share!" (Wicked old pig woman.) "Look you, choose good places for your standing in the fair when you sing, Nightingale." So our every-day thieves are no cleverer than their fore-fathers.

Here are the posturers, fire-eaters, mountebanks, and nostrum vendors. Here's one who declares

(like all his craft) he is not " an upstart pill-gilding
apothecary ; no, he's a physician that has travelled
most kingdoms in the world, and not a person to
fill your ears with hard words; not bothering you
with the nature of Turpet mineral, Mercuri Dulcis,
Balsamum Capiviet, Astringents, Circulations,
Vibrations, and Scaldations. *Tantum?* No; he
will present you with his cordial pills, being
tincture of the sun, having dominion from the
same light, to comfort mankind and to cause all
complexions to smile or laugh in the very taking
of them," and so on. When he has ended his
appeal, the Jack-pudding will dance on the tight-
rope, until his master recovers breath.

" Here's Dives and Lazarus, and the world's Creation,
  Here's the tall Dutch woman, the like's not in the nation ;
  Here's the booth where the high Dutch maid is ;
  Here are the bears that dance like any ladies.
  Tat, tat, tat, tat, says the little penny trumpet ;
  Here's Jacob Hall that does so jump it, jump it."

Jacob Hall, the Leotard of the seventeenth
century, was a celebrated rope-dancer, and reputed
rival of King Charles in the affections of Lady
Castlemaine, as is well known to the readers of
Dryden, Pepys, and other writers of that day. He
had, by reason of his lady patroness, a booth at
Charing Cross, and was considered a nuisance to
the parish. Hall was a great favourite with the

quality, and was followed by them and Lady Castlemaine to Bartlemy Fair, **where** they purchased fairings, as even did dear Lady Rachel Russell, as she writes to her husband, in 1680, three years before his judicial murder.

There are records of other rope-dancers whose feats are quite as astounding as anything presented by M. Blondin ; and Joseph Clarke was a famous posture master, who could imitate every sort of deformity, and so disguise his identity, that he paid successive visits **to** an eminent surgeon, who did not recognize his former patient, but examined him for all kinds of horrible dislocations and contortions : his portrait **testifies** to his wonderful twistibility.

Among the piemen none were more famous than Ford, or Tiddy Doll—Tiddy Doll, the gingerbread baker, immortalized by Hogarth, in **the** picture of the Idle Apprentice's execution at Tyburn. Tiddy's disappearance from his usual station in the Haymarket, in 1752 (when he had gone to the country fairs), occasioned a Grub Street account of his murder, which sold amazingly. Tiddy Doll was well made and handsome, **and** dressed like a nobleman, in a white **coat laced with** gold, ruffles, silk stockings, laced hat and feathers, and clean white apron. His usual address was,

" Mary, Mary, where are you now ? I live, when at home, in Little Ball Street, two steps under ground, with a wiscum, and a wiscum, and a why not ? Here's your nice gingerbread ! It will melt in your mouth like a red-hot brickbat, and fill you like Punch and his wheelbarrow !" Poor Tiddy Doll was drowned during a frost fair on the Thames by the breaking of the ice.

Charles II. made Killigrew Master of the Revels, and all ballad-singers, mountebanks, prize-players, and the like had to be licensed by him. " Bartholomew fairings " were oftentimes political pamphlets and drolls, sometimes against the Pope, and sometimes against the Puritans, who had closed the theatres, but could not put down Bartlemy. To Bartlemy Fair we are indebted for the pride and delight of every nursery, Bartlemy babies, as they were called, *dolls*, as they are now named. The modern origin of the word, we are inclined to believe, was from an old word of endearment, quoted by Richardson, of " pretty little poll—doll " —a pretty little Mary Dorothy. Some have supposed that these darling images were named idols, the i having dropped out on their way up the nursery stairs. Every mamma has seen them adored in a way to justify such a supposition.

Elkanah Settle, once the feeble rival and antago-

nist of Dryden, and who disgraced himself by his
animadversions on the last speech and confession
of Lord William Russell, here at Bartlemy Fair
was manager of the pageant of the burning of the
Pope, and afterwards turned actor in Mrs. Myon's
booth at the fair, and played the Dragon in a
green case of his own invention.

Dr. Young alludes to this circumstance in his
epistle to Pope :

> " Poor Elkanah, all other changes past,
> For bread in Smithfield, dragons hissed at last ;
> Spit streams of fire to make the butchers gape,
> And found his manners suited to his shape."

He ultimately obtained admission to the Charterhouse, and died there Feb. 12, 1723-4. According
to a writer in "The Briton," who thus speaks of
him, " He was a man of tall stature, red face, short
black hair, lived in the City, and had a numerous
poetical issue, but shared the misfortune of several
other gentlemen—to survive them all."

At Bartlemy Fair also, principally at the George
Inn Yard, Smithfield, Henry Fielding, one of the
greatest of the great English prose writers, kept a
theatrical booth for nine years. "The Booth,"
says his handbill, "is very commodious, and the
Inn Yard has all the convenience of coach-room,
lights, &c., for quality and **others,** and shall

perform this evening **at** four, and every day during the Fair, beginning exactly at two, and continuing every hour till **eleven** at night." Fielding's connection with Bartlemy Fair continued for nearly ten years, and was a great source of income to **him.** He ceased to be manager when he joined one of the Inns of Court. In the "Daily Post" of Aug. 30, 1732, we read : "Yesterday the Prince and Princess went to Bartholomew Fair, and saw Mr. Fielding's celebrated Droll called **the** ' Earl of Essex' and the 'Forced Physician,' and were **so well** pleased **as** to stay to see it twice **performed."**

Drury Lane and the other West-end theatres closed during the fair, and some of their best actors played at Bartlemy, tempted thereto by the increased pay of the booth. Amongst others, Doggett, the giver of the "Coat and Badge," Cibber, Fat Harper, who, like Stephen Kemble, **played** Falstaff without stuffing, Yates, and Edward **Shuter,**

> " Who never cared a single pin
> Whether he left out nonsense or put in,"

Mrs. Pritchard, and other names famous in dramatic annals, the last distinguished manager being Master Richardson. **We** were once introduced to the celebrated Muster Richardson, and were presented

with a free admission to his "Theater, as one of
the purfession." The drama was called the
" Wandering Outlaw, or the Hour of Retribution,
concluding with the death of Orsina and the
appearance of the Accusing Spirit." We did not
enjoy it very much, as the rain came through the
canvas, and the principal tragedian and the ghost
had the influenza. Richardson claimed to have
had under his management the elder Kean, Wallack,
Barnes the favourite pantaloon, and other cele-
brities. He had a fine appreciation of genius, that
Muster Richardson, and left a gentleman of the
Fair — the original "Mazeppa" at Astley's—a
handsome legacy because he was *a bould speaker*.
We will not detain you longer in Bartlemy Fair,
which died of inanition about 1849, after giving
the City authorities a great deal of trouble; but
we refer those who take an interest in such matters
to "The Memoirs of Bartholomew Fair," by Professor Henry Morley.

From gay to grave, from the players' booths to
the prison, to which, we dare say, the fair and its
temptations led many in their time. So passing
by Snow Hill—once called Snore Hill—remembering that at the Star, then Studwick the grocer's
sign, died that good man John Bunyan—let us
pause at the OLD Prison of Newgate, originally

Chamberlain Gate. It was a prison in the reign of King John, and rebuilt by Sir Richard Whittington's executors, and his statue (with the Cat, mind), placed in a niche on the wall. (*Timbs.*) It was merely a tower which stretched across the west end of Newgate, yet until Charles II.'s time it was sufficient prison-room for the City and county. After the Great Fire it was restored by Wren, and burnt by the rioters in 1780, the keys having been thrown into the basin of water in St. James's Square.

The prisoners were formerly crowded together in dark dungeons, and the foul air caused the gaol fever, of which they perished dozens by the day, and on one occasion sixty persons died from this pestilence in the Sessions House. Our prisons were very dreadful places in former times; women were packed in Newgate like slaves in the hold of a ship, having only eighteen inches of sleeping room, gaming, fighting, singing, dancing, drinking, and dressing up in men's clothes, whilst the males added card-playing and gambling of all kinds.* Garnish, or footing, or chummage, as it

---

* The 22 & 23 **Charles II.** c. 20, s. 13, recites:—" That whereas it has become the common practice of the gaolers and keepers of Newgate, the Gate-house at Westminster, and sundry other gaols and prisons to lodge together in one room or chamber and bed, prisoners for debt and felons, whereby many honest gentlemen,

was called, was demanded of all prisoners, " pay or
strip " the order of the day, and money or clothes
went towards the riotous entertainment of the
older prisoners, who added something to the
garnish. The untried were mixed with the convicted, and the young and repentant with the
hardened and profligate offenders. Some were
lavishly supplied with luxuries by their friends,
others were nearly starved, having to cook and
provide their own food, and the wardsmen derived
great profit from supplying the prisoners with
various articles. Some women that Mrs. Fry saw
were destitute of clothing and unfit to be seen,
and one girl spent ten shillings in beer in one day.
We have reformed all this indifferently well, and
in some cases have run into the other extreme.

A late humane governor, Mr. Wontner, lost his
life in saving that of May, convicted with Bishop
and Williams for burking an Italian boy. Bishop
and Williams having confessed that May was
innocent, Mr. Wontner travelled to Windsor and
back during the night, and arrived with the
reprieve just before the hour of execution. The

tradesmen, and others (prisoners for debt), are disturbed and hindered
in the night time from their natural rest by reason of their fetters
and irons, and otherwise much offended and troubled by their lewd
and prophane language and discourses, with most horrid cursing and
swearing, much accustomed to such persons," &c., &c.

exertion **brought on an** attack of which the excellent **governor died.**

The **gallows** used to stand on what is now
Connaught Terrace, and the Tyburn procession
was one of the grim things of the past. It was
John Howard who caused the gallows to be
removed from Tyburn to the Old Bailey, and need
enough for the change, when sixty persons have
been seen on one Sunday in the condemned pew.
The names of the more hardened among the
prisoners were often found cut on the wood-work
of the pew. The *Old Press Yard* was the place
where prisoners **were** PRESSED when they refused
to plead in **order** to preserve their property
forfeited to the Crown. A horrible cruelty, and it
was thought a humane thing to allow friends **of**
the prisoners to pile quickly additional weights on
the victim to hasten his death. Now, if a prisoner
will not plead, we record a plea of " Not Guilty "
for him, and try him just the same as if he had
spoken. The press-yard was the last memorial of
the **old** torture.

Stow could not **tell** the original of the Poultry
Compter, pertaining to one of the sheriffs of
London, it having been so kept and continued
time out of mind. It ceased to be a prison in
1804. The Marshalsea and King's Bench were

both very old prisons. Ludgate was a free prison,
and all freemen of the City were imprisoned there
for debt, trespasses, and contempt. The poor
prisoners begged at a grate (as they did within
our recollection at the Fleet), and handsome
Stephen Foster, who was Lord Mayor in 1454, is
said to have won a rich widow whilst so suppli-
cating charity. The happy pair built a chapel at
Ludgate, and made some provision for future
destitute inmates—

> " So that for lodging and water prisoners here naught pay,
>   As their keepers shall answer all at dreadful doomes day."

Among the City prisons of the past was the
" Fleet ;" it is a glad tiding to know their numbers grow less and less with the advance of time
and its teachings. The old prison originally
belonged to the See of Canterbury, and the
wardenship was held by several eminent persons,
together with the custody of the Palace at Westminster. The rents of the shops in Westminster
Hall belonged to the said warden, and pretty
fellows some of them were, guilty of all sorts of
crime and cruelty. Edward VI. and Mary sent
thither many victims of religious bigotry, and
Bishop Hooper laid there until sent to the stake at
Gloucester, his bed having been a little pad of
straw with a rotten covering. It was the prison

of the Star Chamber, **in** full activity from Elizabeth to Charles I., **and** many a man distinguished by piety, learning, and patriotism was shut within those gloomy walls; " Freeborn " John Lilburne, **and** Prynne, the Puritan denouncer **of plays,** among the number.*

After the abolition of the Star Chamber, the Fleet became a prison for debtors only, and those committed **for** contempt, **but** the **wardens** continued their extortionate fees and loading debtors with **irons.** This **state** of things continued until Bembridge and Huggins (wardens), and some of their servants, **were tried for** murder, and **acquitted. Hogarth has** immortalized the principal scoundrels in his " Trial of Bembridge."

* William Prynne's " Histriomastix; or, a Scourge for Stage-players," was a severe attack not only upon the stage, but also upon dancing, hunting, public festivals—especially the keeping of Christmas—decking houses with ivy, bonfires, maypoles, music—especially church music—new year's gifts, images, curled hair of men and women, and the wearing of perukes. It declared " that our English ladies shorn and frizzled madams have lost their modesty; that they that frequent plays are damned; and that princes dancing in their own persons was the cause of their untimely ends." Among the heads of the index of the work was " Women actors notorious ———" and this was unjustly made to apply to the queen, who had a short time before (but after the publication of the book) acted in a pastoral at Somerset House. The sentence passed upon Prynne by the Star Chamber was that his book should be burned by the common hangman, that he should be excluded from the bar of Lincoln's Inn, degraded from the university of Oxford, stand in the pillory at Westminster and Cheapside, lose an ear at each place, be fined five thousand pounds, and imprisoned for life!

The Fleet was twice burnt—once by Wat Tyler, and again in the riots of 1780. The mob politely sent notice to the prisoners of their intended coming, and on being informed that the lateness of the hour would be inconvenient, the rabble postponed their visit until the next day. No such instance of true politeness occurred during either of the French revolutions, that we remember.

The rules and day-rules of the Fleet may be traced to Richard II.'s time, and gave the prisoners the liberty of going abroad, with certain limits, on the payment of heavy fees, and on the obtaining of good securities. The Fleet and Queen's Bench were the only prisons in the kingdom having this privilege, and there is a story told of a prisoner having a day-rule (as these permissive orders were called) who from the force of habit determined to spend it in the Fleet. A man was also said to have so far gained the confidence of the gatekeeper of the Fleet as to be allowed to spend, occasionally, an evening at a public-house opposite the prison; but on one occasion, having overstayed his time by a quarter of an hour, he was threatened to be *locked out* altogether the next time he offended. The poor prisoner was so alarmed at the possibility of such a catastrophe that he never **went** out again. This story is true, and what a tale **it tells** of an utterly hopeless and friendless man.

There **is one** serio-comic association with the Fleet to which we must refer, the Fleet marriages, **and** which were held—although illegal—to be valid and indissoluble. These marriages were performed sometimes in the chapel of the prison, **and** at others at alehouses **and** brandy-shops. The parsons were generally inmates of **the** Fleet and the **rules** thereof, and, necessarily, profligate and vicious, **and in no way** deterred by the penalty of 100*l.* for **solemnizing** clandestine marriages. Any one could **be married for five or** six shillings— sailors were capital **customers.** A Captain **Saun-** ders, Member **of** Parliament, stated in the House that he had once given forty of his crew leave **to** go on shore, and they all returned married. **Others, of** high degree, were occasionally buckled **together by** these clerical blackguards; **in** some **cases, to procure** an antedated certificate, or to **conceal** the fact of their union; and, **occasionally,** even their **names, as shown by an entry :** " Wil- liam —— and **Sarah** ——; he dressed in a gold waistcoat, like an **officer; she, a beautiful young** lady, with two **fine diamond rings and a black** high crown hat, **and very well dressed."** Some

overseers had paupers married at the Fleet to get
rid of settlements—many an unwilling swain con-
senting rather than go to prison.

The first parson who dispensed with banns and
licences was Adam Elliott, and the register shows
entries of 40,000 marriages in twenty-seven years.
This gold-ring digging was put a stop to; but
after some delay, Elliott was allowed to resume his
vocation. **During his** suspension the Fleet marriages began. The books—some 300 large ledgers,
and about 1000 mere pocket-books, in which the
Fleet parsons made their entries—were bought by
the Government in 1821.

TEMPLE BAR, LONDON.

CHAPTER VI.

RECURRING to Fleet marriages, some of the extracts, made by Mr. Burns from the parsons pocket-books are worth narrating :—

"Geo. Grant and Ann Gordon, bachelor and spinster, stole my clothes brush; another couple had before stole a silver spoon."

There were fellows who acted as "common husbands," who for a fee married women in debt, so that they could plead a coverture; the fellows foregoing all claims upon their wives.

"John Ferren, Gent., sen., of St. Andrew's, Holborn, br., to Deborah Nolans, ditto, sp."

The supposed John Ferren was discovered, after the ceremony, to be in person a woman — no doubt to free Deborah from her debts, and to avoid the common husband. This trick was frequently played, sometimes for the reason named, and frequently as a joke.

The fees were sometimes compounded for by silver buttons, worth two shillings, and a ring of small value.

"Lydia Collet and Richard Turner, brought by Mrs. Crooks, behaved vilely, and attempted to run away with Mrs. Crooks' ring"—lent, it is conjectured, to perform the ceremony.

"John Newsam and Ann Laycock, widow—ran away with scertificate, and left a point of wine to pay for." No doubt a suggestion of the widow— if Mr. Weller's estimate of widows be a correct one.

One party was "married upon tick;" and a coachman came, and was half married, and would give but three shillings and sixpence, and went

off. On the trial of John Miller, for bigamy, it
was sworn that any one might have a certificate
for two shillings and sixpence, without any ceremony of marriage whatever. This was reducing
the business to such extreme simplicity, that a new
Marriage Act was passed, although Walpole wrote
against it, and many of the most distinguished
members of the House of Commons uttered wilder
opinions than he in opposition, one declaring that
" it would shock the modesty of a young girl to
have it proclaimed to the parish that she was
going to be married," and Charles Townsend declared " it was one of the most cruel enterprises
against the fair sex that ever entered the heart of
man, and that, did he promote it, he should expect
to have his eyes torn out by the young women of
the first country town he passed through "—and all
because it compelled the rich heiress and the peer's
son to wait until they were of age before they
could marry whom they pleased, and required
Dolly to be cried three times in the parish church
before she could become Mrs. Giles Jolter.

The Old Bourne, from which Holborn takes its
name, broke out, says Stow, about the place where
the bars do stand—now Brook Street—where
Chatterton died, at Mrs. Angel's, a sack-maker's;
in Fox Court, running out of it, the Countess of

Macclesfield gave birth to Richard Savage, naming
her boy after herself, for she certainly was a
savage. So leaving Farringdon Street on our
left for the present, ascend High *Old*bourne Hill,
formerly the road from the Tower and Newgate
to the gallows in St. Giles's, and its successor at
Tyburn. Some may remember poor Polly's—Mac-
heath's wife's—lament. " Methinks I see him
already in the cart, sweeter and more lovely than
the nosegay in his hand. What volleys of sighs
are sent from the windows of Holborn that so
comely a youth should be brought to disgrace."
No doubt, had social and not poetical justice been
done on the Captain, **he** would, like Swift's " Tom
Clink,"

> " Have stopped at the George for a bottle of sack,
> And promised to pay for it as he came back."

It is narrated of an old counsellor in Holborn,
that on every execution day he turned out his
clerks with this compliment—" Go, ye young
rogues, go to school and improve."

On our right are the remains of Field Lane,
where Mr. Fagan tutored the Artful Dodger and
Charley Bates (as Wolton did years ago) in the
art of picking pockets. Annexed is Saffron Hill,
so named from the saffron gardens there. Nearly
opposite is Shoe Lane, where formerly stood Old

Bourne Hall. Here Pepys came to a cock-pit and "found strange variety of people, from the Deputy-Lieutenant of the Tower to poorest 'prentices, bakers, brewers, butchers, draymen, and what not, and all these fellows, one with another, cursing and swearing," and he soon had enough of it. Here died Samuel Boyce, the poet, from want, unable, however, to eat the roast beef brought to him because there was no ketchup. In Gunpowder Alley lived Lilly, the astrologer, who pretended to discover stolen goods, and on the site of the present Farringdon Market was the burying-ground of Shoe Lane workhouse, and there was the grave of the highly-gifted and unhappy poet Thomas Chatterton.* On the site of Wren's church stood a former St. Andrew's, of which two or three old Gothic arches remain. Sir Edward Coke was married there (1598) to the Lady Elizabeth Hatton. She was young, very beautiful, and rather eccentric, and attracted the regards of Coke and Bacon. Essex supported the suit of Bacon with all his influence ; but whether the lady discovered that the great philosopher deserved the estimate given of him by the late Gilbert A'Beckett, who says—"The character

* The parish register records — " Aug. 28, 1770. — William (Thomas) Chatterton [with ' the poet' added afterwards], interred in the graveyard of Shoe Lane workhouse."

of this Bacon was rather streaky,"—and so declined him, we know not, but she married Coke and rejected a chancellor. Bacon had a lucky escape, for Lady Hatton turned out a tartar, and Coke found that, as Douglas Jerrold has since written, "she leaned her back against her marriage certificate and defied him." Those who marry widows should require to have "good characters from their previous situations," we fancy.

Over the way was the hostel of the Bishop of Ely, with its vineyards, garden, and orchard, as the Protector Gloucester knew full well, and remembered when meditating the death of Hastings and the arrest of the Bishop: "My Lord," said he, merrily, "you have very good strawberries at your garden in Holborn, I require you let me have a mess of them."—"Gladly," quoth the bishop, and sent for them immediately; but notwithstanding his civility Gloucester had him locked up that same morning. Many great personages occupied the Bishop's house. John of Gaunt, when driven from the Savoy by Wat Tyler's mob, lived and died there. The conspiracy which gave Protector Somerset's head to the block was hatched there. Many memorable feasts have been held in Ely Place, given by the newly erected serjeants-at-law, and in 1531, when eleven new serjeants were

made at once, **they** gave a feast worthy the
calamity. **It took five** days to get through the
bill **of fare.** Sir Christopher laid out about 6000*l.*
of our money upon Ely House when he came into
possession—and well he might, for Elizabeth made
the original bargain for him, and agreed **that he**
should pay only 10*l.* in money, ten loads of hay,
and a red rose (afterwards increased **to** twenty
bushels). It was to enforce this enforced bargain
with Bishop Cox that Elizabeth wrote the letter
remarkable for its brevity and emphasis, in which
she swore a good Tudor oath to unfrock Cox :—

" PROUD PRELATE,—I understand you are back-
ward in **complying** with your agreement; but **I**
would have **you** to know that I who made you
what you are can unmake you : and if you do not
forthwith fulfil your engagement, by G—d! I
will immediately unfrock you.

" Yours, as you demean yourself,

" ELIZABETH."

Elizabeth, who seldom gave loans, and never for-
gave due debts, subsequently pressed the payment
of a **sum of** 40,000*l.* arrears, which Chancellor
Hatton could **not meet,** so that it went to his
heart, and he **joined his** last dance—the Dance of
Death.

When Gondomar, the Spanish ambassador, lay there on Good Friday, 1633, a thousand persons were present to witness the stage play of Christ's Passion, being the last performance of the religious mystery in England. The chapel of St. Etheldreda, in Ely Place, and which still remains to us, was built about the thirteenth century, then standing in a field planted with trees, and surrounded by a wall.

For a long time Holborn had a single row of houses on the north side, and Field Lane was only a lane, and Saffron Hill a fair meadow, with a footpath across it, bounded by Turnmill Brook, and the walls of Ely Place. Leather Lane, or Lither Lane, as it is sometimes called, was a lane leading to a field (afterwards Furnival's Inn), in which stood the house of Sir William Furnivale.

At the George and Blue Boar was intercepted Charles I.'s letter to his queen, in which Cromwell and Ireton, disguised as troopers, discovered the king's intention to destroy them. This letter is said to have brought about Charles's execution. Opposite was the Red Lion, where the bodies of Cromwell, Ireton, and Bradshaw were carried from Westminster Abbey, and next day dragged on sledges to Tyburn. "So doth the whirligig of time bring about its revenges."

We are at **Gray's Inn** Lane, now the outlet for
dirty courts and dirtier inhabitants, though Pym
and Hampden resided in this lane when the ship-
money question was about to make England a
battle-field. Away northward **is the** old **hostel,**
the Pindar of Wakefield, and **Battle Bridge, so**
named because it once pertained to Battle **Abbey.**
There stood a marvellous statue of George IV.,
made of cement and brick by a journeyman bricklayer; but that ornament **of** the metropolis has
vanished, **and might advantageously** be followed
by a good many other of our statues at large and
in little. **Gray's Inn Lane was the** only place
known to Dr. **Willis** where grew the herbs bearing
a yellow flower, called the small Black Cresses **of**
Naples, **and** which sprung up in such **profusion**
among the ruins of Old St. Paul's after the **Great**
Fire.

Let us retrace our steps to Fetter Lane, or
Fewter's Lane, as it was called from the idle
people lying there when it was a road to the
gardens by the Thames side, and to those **in** Old
Bourne. Hobbes of Malmsbury lived here, and so
did Dryden, **at No.** 16, it is said. For more than
two centuries **both** ends of Fetter Lane were used
as places of execution. Fetter Lane seems to have
been **a** rival to Lombard Street, for Ben Jonson

makes Fungoso say that he " can borrow forty
shillings on his gown in Fetter Lane." Praise-
god Barebones, the leatherseller, and his brother,
Damned Barebones, lived at the corner of Fleet
Street and Fetter Lane, both in the same house.
A lady of rather unenviable notoriety resided
at the right-hand corner of Fleur-de-lis Court,
and may as well be introduced ; we refer to
that amiable flagellant Mrs. Brownrigg. " She
whipped two female 'prentices to death, and hid
them in a coal-hole," says Canning, parodying
Southey.

Staple Inn was the Inne or Hostel of the merchants of the (Wool) Staple. The Holborn front
is of the time of James I., and nearly one of the
oldest existing specimens of street architecture.
In Staple Inn Dr. Johnson wrote the " Idler,"
seated in a three-legged chair, his only one, so
scantily were his chambers furnished.

Barnard's Inn was the Dean of Lincoln's house
in Henry VI.'s time, and Thaive's Inn, originally the dwelling of Thaive, an armourer in
Edward III.'s day. Thieves' Inn, therefore, as a
derivation, is a piece of rudeness to the lawyers,
who, we dare say, are not worse there than elsewhere.

Just through Holborn Bars, you had, says Stow,

" in old time a Temple built by the Templars."
This was afterwards called the Old Temple. The
site was bought by the Earl of Southampton, now
Southampton Buildings.

Lincoln's Inn Fields produced **apples**, pears,
nuts, and cherries, flowers, and vegetables, and
there was a walk under elm-trees where Philip
and Mary walked. It was the cony garth, and
well stocked with rabbits **and** game.

Holborn was paved at the expense of Henry V.,
when the highway **was so** deep and miry that
many perils and hazards were occasioned to the
king's carriages, **and to those** of his faithful subjects. **Chancery** Lane, formerly New Lane, **was**
no better in Henry **III.**'s time, when he of a **Jew's**
house founded **a House of** Converts. (There **have**
been many converts to the folly of debt **in Jews'**
houses in our time in Chancery Lane.) Edward III.
annexed the House of Converts to the office of the
Master of the Rolls, and called **the** road thereto
Chancery Lane. The great Lord Strafford was
born there, and Lord William Russell inherited a
house **on the site of** Southampton Buildings.
When passing **this** house on the day of his execution, the fortitude of the martyr forsook him for a
moment, but, overmastering his emotion, he said,
" The bitterness of death is now passed." **From**

this house several of Lady Rachel's letters are
dated.

Honest old Izaak Walton, that benevolent
torturer of fish and live-bait, lived in Chancery
Lane, as did the Lord Keeper Guildford, who,
objecting to have the contents of the cesspools
pumped out into the street, procured the proper
drainage of the same, and made it the respectable
place it is considered to be by the profession.
Jacob Tonson, before he removed to Gray's Inn,
had his shop at the Judge's Head, near the Fleet
Street end of Chancery Lane. In Cursitor Street
was Lord Eldon's "first perch," as he says, "and
often thence ran down to Fleet Market with sixpence in his hand to buy sprats for supper." He
found better fare from the Courts in that neighbourhood in after years. Two or three *removes*,
and plenty of Cabinet pudding. Erskine, when he
was Chancellor, was asked by an old lady if " the
Esquimaux really lived upon seals?"—" Oh, yes,"
said Erskine, "and very good living they make, if
you only *keep them* long enough." Until the widen-
ing of the Fleet Street end, a fine example of an
old London house stood at the corner of Chancery
Lane.

Temple Bar divides London and Westminster,
and marks the boundary of the city and the shire.

In Shire **Lane was the** celebrated Kit-cat Club, so named from **certain** pies—

"**For kit-cat wits** first sprang from kit-cat pies."

Not a very pleasant association, I **must say.**

The Club consisted of thirty-nine noblemen and gentlemen attached to the House of Hanover; and the pies referred to really derived their name from no feline construction, but from Christopher Katt, the maker of them, and who lived near the tavern in King Street, Westminster. Pope or Arbuthnot has said that the Club was named—when it became the custom to toast ladies after dinner—from the old cats and the young kits, whose names were engraved on the members' glasses.

Jacob Tonson, the celebrated bookseller, was the secretary, and had the portraits of the members painted all of the same size, to suit the room. **Hence** the term "Kit-cat size" **for** certain can-**vas.** The portraits are, we believe, still preserved. **The Tatler's** Trumpet tavern was also in Shire **Lane.**

The bar consisted formerly of a post and rails, a chain and a barre, and were repainted and newly hung at the coronation of Queen Mary. The bar gave place to a house of timber across the street, with a narrow gateway beneath, and was destroyed

after the Great Fire. The present bar was built
by Wren, and the old oak gates still remain. These
gates were formerly closed at night, and on occasions of tumults or royal visits to the City. Elizabeth had to ask for admission when on her way to
St. Paul's after the defeat of the Spanish Armada.
So had Fairfax and Cromwell when on their way
to dine in the City; and Queen Anne had to send
in her card after Marlborough's victory. Our own
gracious Queen, on her accession, and when the
Royal Exchange was opened, recognized the civic
right of knocker. Above the centre of the pediment
the heads and limbs of persons executed for high
treason were placed on iron spikes, and " people
made a trade of letting spying glasses at a penny a
look" (Walpole), to those desirous of seeing them.
And there those grim mementoes remained until
blown down by the wind—some, like Counsellor
Layer's, having been there for thirty years. The
remains of the spikes were removed within our
recollection.

Let us return to the old Fleet River (navigable
in Henry VII.'s time to Holborn Bridge, but now
carried through a huge iron pipe), and then take
our way up Fleet Street, one of the most ancient
thoroughfares of London. Before the Great Fire
the street was badly paved (and so continued long

after), and the **houses, mostly** of timber, were **built** higgledy-piggledy—the shops dark sheds, with overhanging **pent-houses** beneath, where the traders **and their** 'prentices stood to solicit custom by calling out to every passer-by, " What do you lack, gentles ? What do you lack ?" The space for foot passengers was defended by rails and posts, and the latter served for the exhibition of the performances at the theatres, and other matters requiring publicity. Hence the word " posting-bill."

Bridewell, long the terror of refractory London 'prentices, the idle, and the abandoned, was a king's palace before the Conquest, and said to have been partly of Roman construction. Most of **our** Norman kings held their court there, and when **it** was rebuilt, Henry I. gave the stone for that purpose. The name is derived from St. Bridget, and her holy well, now represented by an iron pump **in** Bride Lane. The palace afterwards came into **the** possession of Cardinal Wolsey, and there Cardinal **Campegius** was brought, with numbers of King **Henry's** nobility, to hear the royal speech on his majesty's marriage with Katherine **of** Arragon. **And** there the heads of the religious houses in England were summoned when Henry determined upon their suppression. After Wolsey's disgrace the palace reverted to the Crown, but

Henry, from some unpleasant connubial recollec-
tion, we presume, allowed it to fall into decay.
After the suppression of the religious houses, and
Edward VI. had succeeded his many-wived father,
Bishop Ridley, in a sermon which he preached
before the king, begged the "wide large empty
house" as a poor-house and house of correction.
And Edward

> "Gave this Bridewell, a palace in old times,
> For a chastening-house of vagrant crimes."

So runs the legend beneath his portrait in the
chapel; and Fuller quaintly says; "The house of
correction is the fittest hospital for those cripples
who are lame through their own laziness," and
thinks the king was as truly charitable in granting
Bridewell for the punishment of sturdy rogues, as
in granting St. Thomas's Hospital for the relief
of the poor. The Great Fire entirely destroyed
Bridewell, and it was afterwards rebuilt, with its
principal front to the Fleet River. The old hall
still remains, and contains a picture by Holbein of
Edward presenting the charter of the hospital to
the Lord Mayor and citizens. Hogarth, in the
fourth plate of his "Harlot's Progress," has preserved to us its former condition. Women and
men are beating hemp, and an idle apprentice is
in the stocks. The floggings took place in the

presence of the court of governors, and were continued until the president struck his hammer on the table, and "knock, good sir, knock," was the common cry of those under flagellation. A certain Madam Cresswell, infamously celebrated in the plays of Charles II.'s time, died in Bridewell, and bequeathed 10*l.* to have a sermon preached, in which nothing but what was *well* of her should be said. The sermon is said to have been written by the Duke of Buckingham, and we shall preach it to you. " All I shall say of her is this, she was born *well*, she married *well*, she lived *well*, and she died *well*,—for she was born at Shad-*well*,—married to Cress-*well*, — she lived at Clerken-*well*,—and died in Bride-*well*."

The first church of St. Bridget, or St. Bride, was destroyed in the Great Fire, one relic only being preserved in the present building—the arch to a vault on your right as you enter. In Bride's churchyard Milton lodged when he married Mary Powell, and before his removal to his quiet garden-house in Aldersgate Street, " because there were few streets in London more free from noise than Aldersgate Street." In Bride Lane is Cogers' Hall, where the Cogers have met since 1757 ; and the corner of Bride Court is one of the town residences of our distinguished friend Mr. Punch.

Opposite Shoe Lane stood the famous Fleet Street
Conduit, which had angels with sweet-sounding
bells before them, and they, " divers hours of the
day and night, with hammers chimed such hymns
as were appointed."   St. Dunstan's clock, with its

OLD ST. DUNSTAN'S CHURCH, FLEET STREET.   London, 1829.

two savages who struck the quarters upon two
bells, was long a London wonder, and the pavement in front was a fine harvest-ground for pick-
pockets.   The clock is now at Lord Hertford's in
the Regent's Park.

Let us recross the street into Salisbury Court,
once the residence of the Bishop of Salisbury, then
of the Sackvilles (whence Sackville House, and

Dorset Street) where formerly stood a theatre, being the seventeenth stage or common playhouse made within threescore years in London and its suburbs, destroyed in the Great Fire. Sir C. Wren built for Davenant the Duke's Theatre, opened in 1671, where Betterton played. It was close to the silent highway, and the City gas works now occupy its site. Richardson wrote "Pamela" in Salisbury Square; and there, in Richardson's printing-office, Goldsmith acted as a reader about the time when Hogarth and Dr. Johnson visited the author-printer. John Dryden and Shadwell resided in Salisbury Court, and, in Dorset Court, John Locke.

Alsatia, as it was called (1608), extended from Water Lane to the Temple walls, and from the Thames to Fleet Street. It was the resort of fraudulent debtors, violators of the law, and abandoned women, who spoke a cant language, and boldly resisted the execution of every legal process. They were governed by laws of their own, presided over by some Duke Hildebrod, to whom they paid garnish and swore allegiance as Scott has it—

> " From the touch of the tip,
>   From the blight of the warrant,
> From the watchman who skip
>   On the Harman beak's warrant;

I charm thee from all.
  Thy freedom's complete
As a blade of the Huff,
  To be cheated and cheat,
To be cuff'd and to cuff,
  To stride, swear, and swagger,
  To drink till you stagger,
  And to brandish your dagger;
To eke out your living
  By wag of your elbow,
By fullum and gourd,
  And by baring of bilboe ;
To live by your shifts, and to swear
  By your honour,
Are some of the gifts
  Of which I am the donor."

The Ducal Exchequer might have been in Lombard Street, for it had its Lombard Street without its three balls. One of the houses there was old enough, when we first knew it, to have been Trapbois' dwelling-place, and within its crazy walls (until the next house fell down), many, many numbers of " Punch " were prepared for the press, and afterwards printed on the site of Shadwell's Alsatian Tavern, " The George," now the printing-offices of our excellent friends, Messrs. Bradbury and Evans. Mitre Court was also a sanctuary ; and here, at the Mitre Tavern, as everybody knows, Johnson drank his bottle of port and kept late hours, and here Boswell and he planned their tour to the Hebrides. The last of Dr. Johnson's Mitre friends—Mr. Chamberlain

Clarke—died in 1831, aged ninety-two. Opposite
Mitre Court was hanged Sarah Malcolm, a washer-
woman in the Temple, for no fewer than three mur-
ders, and the MS. of her confession sold for 20*l*.
Over the way is Bolt Court, where Dr. Johnson
lived and died, after leaving Gough Square,
where he lost his beloved wife Letty. Behind his
lodging was a garden, which he took delight in
watering, and the whole of the two pair of stairs
floor was made a repository for his books, one of
the rooms thereon being his study. Dr. Johnson
never suffered a lady to walk from his house to
her carriage unattended by himself, and his appearance in Fleet Street always attracted a crowd,
and afforded no small diversion. Johnson's fond-
ness for tea is well known, but we have never
seen a record of the number of cups he could
drink. The grandmother of a lady with whom
we are intimately connected once poured out for
him seventeen cups; the cups were small china
ones, and the Bohea was 38*s*. a pound.

Ferguson, the astronomer, died at No. 4 in Bolt
Court.

The Bolt in-Tun, an old inn in Fleet Street,
mentioned in 1443 as pertaining to the Whitefriars, was related in some way to Bolt Court, we
presume. In Wine-office Court, opposite, Gold-

smith lived, and there began the " Vicar of
Wakefield."

" THE HARROW," an old Inn in Fleet Street (corner of Chancery Lane), adjoining
the residence of Izaak Walton.

Ram Alley, opposite Fetter Lane, was long
famous for its taverns and cookshops; and was
also a sanctuary.   It is now called Hare Court.

In Fleet Street was the second or third coffee-
house opened in London, and was kept by Farr, a
barber.   It was presented by the parish inquest

for selling "a sort of liquor called coffee, which was a great nuisance and prejudice," we suppose, to the other drinking-houses. The first coffee-house in England was at Oxford, opened by Jacobs, a Jew; and the first in London was in George Yard, Lombard Street, kept by one Parquet, a Greek. Coffee-houses were suppressed by proclamation in 1675, but the order was revoked the next year.

The Rainbow, upon the site of Child's Place, was the Devil Tavern (the sign being the legend of St. Dunstan pulling his bad eminence's nose), where Ben Jonson and his boon companions held many a liberal meeting. Over the door of one of the chambers was inscribed :—

> " Welcome all who lead or follow
> To the oracle of Apollo."

And within this was the penetralia—in after years degradingly called the club-room. It was afterwards fitted with a music-gallery, although the 24th rule of the Apollo Club, translated, ran thus :—

> " Let no saucy fiddler dare to intrude
> Unless he is sent for to vary our bliss."

In Marmion's " Fine Companion " (1633), acted

before the king and queen at Whitehall, **and at
the theatre** in Salisbury Court, we have the
following description of a meeting at the Apollo.

> CARELESS. I am full
> Of oracles. I am come from Apollo.
> EMILIA. From Apollo!
> CARELESS.   From the heaven
> Of my delight, where the boon Delphic god
> Drinks sack, and keeps his bacchanalia;
> And has his incense and his altars smoking,
> And speaks in sparkling prophecies; thence I came.
> My brain's perfumed with the rich Indian vapour,
> And heightened with **conceits.** From tempting beauties,
> From dainty music **and poetic** strains;
> From bowls of nectar and ambrosiac **dishes;**
> From **witty** varlets, fine companions,
> **And** from a mighty continent of pleasure,
> **Sails thy brave** Careless.

Old Simon Wadloe, "the King of Skinkers,"
who kept the Devil Tavern, was the original of
Squire Western's favourite song, "Sir Simon the
King."

John Cottington, *alias* Mull Sack, the famous
highwayman, who had the honour of picking
Cromwell's pocket and robbing Charles **II.,** when
in exile at Cologne, of 1500*l.* worth of plate, was
a frequenter of the Devil Tavern, and passed for a
gentleman. He was hanged at Tyburn for murder. From the days of Ben Jonson to those of
Samuel, the Devil Tavern was the resort of
Pope, Swift, Addison, Garth, and other literary
giants.

The Fleet Street bankers are among the oldest in London. (Stone and Martin are said to be successors to Sir Thomas Gresham.) Richard Blanchard and Francis Child first made banking a business, and had running cashes in Charles II.'s time—according to Mr. Cunningham, to whose researches we have been frequently indebted. Mr. Blanchard's account for the sale of Dunkirk to the French is among the records of the house. Blanchard was ruined by the shutting up of the Exchequer, when the king owed the goldsmiths nearly a million and a half of money. The old sign of the house—the Marygold—is still preserved.

James Hoare, at the Golden Bottle—the old Leathern Bottle—was a goldsmith, with a running cash, 1667 ; and Goslings kept shop at the Three Squirrels, over against St. Dunstan's, 1673-4.

Before this, the London merchants had been accustomed to deposit their money in the Tower, in the care of the Mint Master ; but Charles I. borrowed 200,000l. of .these moneys without asking the owners to lend it. So no more money found its way to the Mint for security, you may be sure, and merchants confided their surplus cash to the care of their clerks and confidential ser-

vants—such was the terrible state of insecurity
before the civil war.   When that broke out, clerks
and apprentices joined the King or Parliament, in
many cases forgetting to leave their master's
deposits; therefore, the merchants began to place
their cash in the hands of the goldsmiths, who
gave receipts for the moneys, and these, passing
from hand to hand, became virtually bank notes.*

The goldsmiths had thus large funds at their
disposal, which they lent to Cromwell on the
security of the public credit.   So here we have the
beginning of a national debt, and all the main
features of modern banking.†

Before we leave Fleet Street for the Temple, let
us take a parting look down the old thoroughfares, and recal some of the familiar ghosts of men
and things which can never cease to haunt it.
Every November the 17th, in Charles II.'s reign,
in Fleet Street, was burned the effigy of the Pope
—the torchlight procession starting from Moor-

* The Bank of England was projected by a merchant named
William Paterson, and incorporated 1694, in consideration of the
capital, 1,200,000l. being lent to the government at 8 per cent.
When first established the Bank notes were at 20 per cent. discount,
and as late as 1754 they were under par.

† In one of the old Bartlemy fairings Goldsmiths' Hall is called
the Milch Cow of the State, as it was the Parliamentary exchequer,
and there the women of the Commonwealth sent their jewels and
trinkets to aid the funds for payment of the army.

fields to the Temple Gate. After the expulsion of
James, the anti-popish mummery was transferred
to November 5th. In Fleet Street were the
earliest printing-offices,* and the stationary mart
for books; and here the old printer Wynkyn de
Worde lived, at the sign of the Sunne. Edmund
Curll, the bookseller, and Lemuel Gulliver, were
there also. Jacob Robinson kept shop down
Inner Temple Lane, and there Pope and War-
burton first met. Puppets and nine days' wonders
found a home in Fleet Street, and Mrs. Salmon's
wax-work was a marvel in its days. No doubt it
had its Chambers of Horrors, its Moll Cutpurse,
who robbed General Fairfax on Hounslow Heath,
and other Tyburn and St. Giles' heroes. Mrs. Salmon first lived in Aldersgate, the sign of her fishy
namesake only in gold—it being impossible, said
Mr. Spectator, " for the ingenious Mrs. Salmon to
have lived at the sign of the Trout." There was
a song of the style which used to be called
humorous, and in which the lady's name is preserved, by an Irishman who was not to be
deceived.

> "Says I, Mrs. Salmon,
> Come, none of your gammon,
> Your statues are no more alive than yourself."

* See Charles Knight's " Old Booksellers."

Mrs. Salmon removed to Fleet Street, and when at the age of ninety her exhibition passed to Surgeon Clarke, the wax-work finally dissolving about 1820.

In the year 1128, Hugh de Payens, the head of the Knights Templars, came to England to extend the influence of his order. The Templars called themselves the poor fellow-soldiers of Jesus Christ, and were banded together to protect the Christian pilgrims to Jerusalem—then recently recovered from the Saracens. Hugh de Payens, the first master of the order, set out with four knights only, and returned to Palestine with three hundred, chosen from the best families of England and France, so that the days were at an end when —as shown in the seal of the Templars—two knights were compelled to ride one horse. Numerous Templar establishments arose in England, and the one erected in Holborn, on the site of Southampton House, was called the Old Temple; when the one in Fleet Street was built and named the New Temple. The Knights Templars became immensely rich, and their wealth proved their ruin. Edward I. and Edward II. had both been nibbling at their possessions, and Philip the Fair of France robbed and persecuted them. By one decree fifty-four were burnt in Paris in the most

barbarous manner. In 1208, the Templars in
England were arrested and their property seized;
and so persecuted were they, that one Peter
Auger, a favourite valet of the king, had to carry
his Majesty's warrant to wear a long beard, and so
declare he was not a Knight of the Temple.

We will not dwell upon the cruel story, nor on
the beautiful Temple Church, worth a day's talk,
but speak of the Temple as an Inn of Court, and
some of the memorable associations connected with
it. An inn—as no doubt you know—signified a
mansion, and not simply a tavern.

> "Now whereas Phœbus with his fiery wane
> Unto his inne began to draw apace,"

sings Spenser. The Knights of St. John of
Jerusalem—who, by the influence of the Pope had
become residuary legatees of the Knights Templars
—gave the Outer, Inner, and Middle Temple to
certain law students who had had a temporary
residence at Thavie's Inn, in Holborn. Henry III.
suppressed the other law schools in the old City:
and so in the Temple with its beautiful gardens,
and (says Fortescue) " out of the City and the
noise thereof, and in the suburbs of London,
between the City and Westminster, the practisers
of the law lived in peace and quiet—imparting
learning to the noblest of the land, and en-

couraging them also to dance, to sing, and to play
on instruments on *ferial* days, and to study
divinity on the festivals."

In the last year of Henry V.'s reign, only
threescore gentlemen of blood and perfect descent
were students there. In a few years the number
of law students greatly increased, and Gray's Inn
and Lincoln's Inn were added to the Inner and
Middle Temple. There were also ten Inns of
Chancery, of which Clifford's Inn only remains.
During the rebellion of Wat Tyler, the Temple
was invaded by the mob, and most of the books
and records destroyed. The division of the Inn
into the Inner and Middle Temple then took
place.

Whenever there was a riot in former times, the
mob always began with the lawyers. Jack Cade's
friend Dick, you remember, proposes, " The first
thing we do, let's kill all the lawyers." " Nay,
that I mean to do," says Cade. " Is it not a
lamentable thing that the skin of an innocent
lamb should be made parchment? that parchment
being scribbled o'er should undo a man? Now
go, some pull down the Savoy, others to the Inns
of Court; down with them all!" And well was
the demagogue obeyed. The Temple libraries
were burned, the students and practisers murdered

and ill-treated. The mob, no doubt, had good reason to hate the lawyers as vendors of the "commodity of justice," and of which they might have been the unwilling purchasers; or some might perhaps have translated the Horse and Lamb over the Temple gates as the epigrammatist did years after :

> "As by the Temple gates you go,
> The Horse and Lamb displayed
> In emblematic figures show
> The merits of their trade.

> "It's all a trick, these are all shams,
> By which they mean to cheat you;
> But have a care, you are the lambs,
> And they the wolves that eat you.

> " Nor let the thought of no delay
> To these their courts misguide you;
> 'Tis yours the showy horse, and they
> The jockeys that will ride you."

The beautiful Temple Gardens were long the favourite lounge of some of our most distinguished men, and here Shakspere has laid the origin of the factions of the Red and White Roses—

> "In signal of my love to thee,
> Against proud Somerset and William Pole
> Will I upon thy party wear this rose."
> 1 *Hen.* 6, *Act* 2, *Scene* **4**.

Here hung **the** leaden coffin of Mandeville, the excommunicated Constable of the Tower, until his burial beneath **the** porch of the Temple Church.

Q

And here, in later times, have walked and talked
the cruel Jefferies, Wycherley, Evelyn, the judi-
cious Hooker, Blackstone, Thurlow, Eldon, Cow-
per, Johnson, Goldsmith, Curran, Tenterden—
others whose names the world will not willingly
let die.

On the site of the present Inner Temple Hall
stood an older one, of Edward III.'s time ; and
good cheer was to be found there at Christmas
tide, Halloweve, Candlemas, and Ascension Day.
The Queen's privy council were the guests ; and
once upon a time King Charles came there in his
barge from Whitehall. There was once a great
scaffold in the hall, on which was enacted " Ferrex
and Porrex," probably the most ancient tragedy in
the English language, and certainly the most
stupid. After another play, one of the barristers
sang a song to the judges and benchers, who,
escorted by the Master of the Revels or the Lord
of Misrule, led the dance round the sea-coal fire in
the hall, until the younger ones tired them down as
it was said or sung of Lord Chancellor Hatton :—

> " Full oft within the spacious halls,
>   When he had fifty winters o'er him,
> My brave lord keeper led the brawls,
>   The seal and mace they danced before him."

The Christmasings lasted several days, and

carols were decently performed, and minstraylsie
after a breakfast of brawn, mustard, and malmsey.
In 1794, **nine** hundred pairs of small dice were
found which had dropped through the chinks of
the boards.—So perhaps the Devil's Own for the
Templars was not once a misnomer.

The Lord Mayor, so says Mr. Pepys, once met
with rough usage there, **and** because he would
carry his sword up, the students pulled it down,
shut up the Majesty of the City in **a** counsellor's
chamber, **from** which he escaped by stealth—for
the honour **of** the City—with his sword up.

The present hall of the Middle Temple took ten
years **in building. Its** carved screen and music-
gallery, the **old arms** and armour, the raised dais,
the massive **oaken tables,** are all of the past, **and**
carry the imagination back to that time **when**
John Manningham wrote thus in **his** little **Table**
Book :—"Feb. 2, 1601. At **our feast we had a**
play called 'Twelfth Night; or, What **you Will,'**
much like the 'Comedy of Errors ; or, **Menech-**
mis in Plautus ;' but most like **and** neere **to that**
in Italian called *Inganni*." Yes, **the** actual roof,
says Charles Knight, **under** which the happy
company **of** benchers, barristers, and students
listened to that joyous and exhilarating play, full
of the truest and most beautiful humanities, fitted

for a season of cordial mirthfulness—exists, and it is pleasant to know that there is one locality remaining where a play of Shakspere was listened to by his contemporaries—and that play "Twelfth Night."

Yes, Mr. Knight! it is very pleasant to walk in that stately hall and remember this;—and pleasant also to recal the masques and merry-makings, and the glad Christmas feastings, believing that such festivals often bring estranged friends together, and make many a weary heart lighter for the interchange of kindly greetings and honest hospitalities.

CHARING CROSS, LONDON, about 1720.

CHAPTER VII.

WE will now pass westward through Temple Bar,
and as we glance at that erection—a standing
proof that threatened buildings, like threatened
men, live long—we remember Dr. Johnson and
Boswell, and the sly glance at the Jacobite heads
then exposed on the Bar, and the neat application
of the classical quotation—" Perhaps our ashes
may mingle with theirs "—the old Doctor's Jacobite
theories surviving, though his sound good sense
made him an eminently practical Loyalist.   And
now we are, as the beggars well know, out of the

jurisdiction of the City Police, and in the Strand.
This, a friend of ours, who writes novels,
Mr. Shirley Brooks, declares to be " the pleasantest
and handsomest, and most English street in
London," and says that " to walk the Strand is to
obtain a liberal education." We dare say that
many of our young friends would like to be
educated upon those easy terms, in the school of
Peripatetic Philosophy.

But the Strand was not always handsome and
pleasant. It was, in the time of the unfortunate
Edward II., merely a road between the two cities,
the footway overrun with thickets and bushes, and
not paved until great Harry's day, when the
owners of the land between Charing Cross and
Strand Cross were compelled to make a sound road
and build three bridges—one at Strand Bridge
Lane, another at Ivy Bridge Lane, and a third
eastward of St. Clement's Church.

The first ascertained inhabitant was Henry III.'s
uncle, Peter of Savoy, and the bishops were the
earliest emigrants from the City as building closed
up its streets, their sacred calling making them less
anxious for the security afforded by the City walls.
At the period of the Reformation nine bishops
possessed inns, or hostels, by the river side, and all
these inns had gardens stretching to the silent

highway of the Thames, which was then preferred to the street as a means of transit.

Essex House — so named from Elizabeth's favourite (Essex Street and Devereux Court mark the site)—had been the town-house of the see of Exeter, and passed from Dudley Earl of Leicester to Essex, the liberal friend of Spenser—

> " He ofte gained giftes and goodly grace
> Of that great lord."

The story of the rebellious, headstrong, and ungrateful Essex is too well known to be repeated now, and we will only remind you that he came hither determined to die rather than be taken. A great force soon hemmed him in, and planted artillery against the house—one piece on the tower of St. Clement's Church. The result you know. Essex and his friend Southampton were sent to the Tower, to be tried and suffer death on the morning of Ash Wednesday, Raleigh looking on from a window of the Armoury. Essex's son, the Parliamentary general, was born here. A pair of fine large pillars, perhaps belonging to the water-gate, are all that now remain of Essex House.

In the next great house in the Strand, Arundel House, died the Countess of Nottingham, who received (by the mistake of the lad who conveyed it) the ring Essex sent to Elizabeth. The Admiral

forbade its delivery to the Queen, and when the
Countess on her death-bed made this discovery,
and begged the Queen's forgiveness, says Dr. Birch,
" her Majesty answered, 'God may forgive you, I
never can !' and left the room with great emotion."
The Queen was so struck with the story that she
never went into bed nor took sustenance from that
instant, but lay upon the carpet with cushions

ARUNDEL HOUSE, STRAND, LONDON. (From an Old Print.)

around her, in the profoundest melancholy. Elizabeth died on the 24th of March, three days after
the funeral of the Countess had been kept at
Chelsea."   So ends the story, which we were
bound to tell you; but are equally bound to add
that historians, who do not copy everything set
down by their predecessors, disbelieve the whole
of it.

Arundel House was sold by Edward VI. to
Henry Seymour, during whose possession strange
intrigues and dalliances are recorded, and in which

the Princess Elizabeth figures, it is said, somewhat
equivocally. Seymour married Queen-Dowager
Catherine, the last wife of Henry VIII.; she was
said to have died the next year of poison. But
ignorant and excited people, even in these days,
are apt to imagine such things without reason, as
we have heard some few years ago in the case of
the series of royal deaths in Portugal. Elizabeth
is thought to have liked Seymour, but his treasonable practices sadly interfered with his love
affairs, and, in fact, brought him to the block. The
house was bought by the Earl of Arundel, and
passed in succession to Thomas Howard, who
adorned it with works of art, both of sculpture and
painting, willing, according to Clarendon, " to be
thought a scholar; whereas to all parts of learning
he was almost illiterate, and much disposed to
levity and delights which, indeed, were very
despicable and childish." He made a magnificent
collection of marbles, however; and Clarendon
had the happy faculty of saying very unpleasant
things about people he disliked, and he disliked a
good many people.

At the house of Lady Primrose, in Essex Street,
the Young Pretender paid his secret visit to
London, in 1750; and Flora Macdonald found
refuge there. At the Essex Head Dr. Johnson

established a club, which Boswell and others continued eight years after the doctor's death.

In Norfolk Street lodged Peter the Great when visited by King William, and Peter returned the

THE STRAND, LONDON, FROM ARUNDEL HOUSE, 1700.

visit, going in a hackney-coach, and probably having a brandy-bottle with him. Peter was a great man, and a great savage. You may place to

which side of the account you like his disgust at
the number of lawyers in Westminster Hall, and
his statement that in Russia he had but two, and
meant to hang one of them when he got back.

In Norfolk Street lived Mr. Shippen, the Jacobite,
who was sent to the Tower by George I. for
saying "the only infelicity of his Majesty's reign
is his ignorance of our language and constitution"
—rather serious deficiencies. Walpole said of him:
"I will not say who are corrupt; but I will say
who was not corruptible—that man was Shippen."

Old Somerset House was built by Protector
Somerset, brother of Queen Jane Seymour, and
uncle to Edward VI. The great cloister on the
north side of Old St. Paul's, and which contained
the grim and celebrated "Dance of Death," was
demolished to find stone for the building, and
besides the Bishop's Inn, the church of St. John of
Jerusalem at Clerkenwell was pulled down to
make space for it and its gardens. The Protector
was beheaded in 1552, and did not see the completion of the building on which he had expended
about 50,000*l.* of our money.

Queen Elizabeth granted the keeping of Somerset
House to her cousin, honest Lord Hunsdon, to
whom she offered on his death-bed what she had
before refused, the Earldom of Wiltshire. "Madam,"

OLD SOMERSET HOUSE, LONDON.

said he, "seeing you counted me not worthy of
this honour while I was living, I count myself
unworthy of it now I am dying." Elizabeth went
hence to open the Royal Exchange. Charles I.
assigned Somerset House to Henrietta Maria, and
Inigo Jones erected a chapel for her. A few
tombs of her Roman Catholic attendants are built
into the cellars under the great square of the
present building. During the Christmas festivities
the Queen took part in a masque, and a new impression of Prynne's "Histriomastix" appeared
the next day with a marginal note (too coarse to
repeat, and which was improperly declared to reflect
on her Majesty), for which he, Prynne, lost his
ears. From Somerset House Charles I. expelled
Henrietta's foreign courtiers and household, after
the Queen had torn the hair from her head in a rage,
and cut her hands by dashing them through glass
windows. It required four days and nearly forty
carriages to transport the expelled foreigners to
Dover.

Oliver Cromwell's body here lay in state, and
which "folly and profusion so far provoked the
people, that they threw dirt on the escutcheon
placed over the gate of Somerset House." The
funeral cost about 28,000*l.*, but with this Cromwell
could have had nothing to do, and so the live asses

kicked at the dead lion. It was once said that
Cromwell's final resting-place was in Red Lion
Square, under a stone obelisk which formerly stood
in the centre of that out-of-the-world place.

When Henrietta Maria bade farewell to England,
Catherine of Braganza succeeded her. Poets
welcomed her, but we do not know whether any
of them equalled an Irish poet of our own age, who,
saluting a Portuguese visitor, began,

> " Princely offspring of Braganza,
> Erin greets thee with a stanza."

Here Monk lay in state, and here the Protestan
martyr, Sir Edmund Berry Godfrey, is said to
have been murdered, and his body afterwards
taken to a field near Primrose Hill.

From the time of Catherine of Braganza,
Somerset House was the nominal jointure of our
queens, and many of the apartments were given to
the poorer nobility. Walpole and Mrs. Montague
have left accounts of an entertainment given here
to George II. and the Princess Augusta. The
King wore an old-fashioned habit, and was so well
disguised that " some one asked him to hold their
cup," no doubt taking him for a greengrocer of the
period. The Duke of Cumberland looked like
Cockofogo, the drunken captain in " Rule a Wife
and Have a Wife." The Duchess of Richmond

was a **Lady Mayoress,** Lord Delaware Queen Elizabeth's **Porter, Mr.** Conway Don Quixote ; his sister,

> " Poor Jenny Conway,
> She drank lemonade
> At this masquerade,"

and was killed by the draught. **The beautiful** Miss Chudleigh, afterwards the **notorious Duchess** of Kingston, appeared in such **a remarkable "no-** costume," that the **Princess of Wales publicly** threw a veil over her.

When **these apartments** were visited by Sir William **Chambers, preparatory to** the erection of the **present building,** he walked through rooms **where foot had not** intruded for nearly a hundred years, amid mouldering walls, broken **casements,** crumbling **roofs,** and decaying furniture. **In** one the chandelier **still** depended from the ceiling, and velvet curtains, tawny with age, fringed with a few shreds of gold and spangles, hung in tatters. **In** another were articles of different ages—broken couches and tattered hangings, screens, sconces, and fire-dogs, and the vestiges of a throne. What a bogified place **it must have** been ! Quite **a** Valhalla **for the Spirit-rappers.**

Old Somerset **House was** pulled down, and **the** present building erected **in** its place. The terrace elevation was made in expectation of **the embank-**

ment of the Thames—not more than eighty years ago! Mr. Smiles narrates that Telford, the great engineer, passing over Waterloo Bridge with a friend, pointed to some finely-cut stones on the corner nearest the bridge. " You see those stones there. Forty years since I hewed and laid them, when working on that building as a common mason."

The Royal Academy Exhibition was held here until its removal to the National Gallery —with which, as the late Sir Robert Peel said, we had helped to spoil the finest square in Europe. Many of you (gentlemen, of course) must remember the old Torus and the big Farnese Hercules in the wire cage at the bottom of the stairs.

In Craven Street lived James Smith, one of the authors of " Rejected Addresses."

In James I.'s time London had grown great westward; and on the site of the present Adelphi a New Exchange or Britain's Burse was opened, but failed to rival its royal namesake in the old London city. The new Exchange became a Bazaar and the most fashionable lounge in Westminster, after the Restoration, and many of the dramatists of the day have laid scenes of intrigue in the galleries of the New Exchange. The city merchants' wives and daughters came hither to ape the manners of

the quality, and country ladies eagerly sought for
lodgings near it, that they might " stand glaring
in balconies, and staring out of window." The
walks formed a favourite promenade with the fops
about town, and who came here to show their
clothes and chat with the stall-keepers.

The Duchess of Albemarle, when the wife of
Thomas Radford, here sold wash-balls, powder,
and gloves, and when touting her wares—" Choice
of fine essences, sir. Very good wash-balls, sir "
(as was the custom)—no doubt attracted the attention of General Monk.

The Duchess of Tyrconnel, known as the
" White Widow," hired a stall and sold haberdashery. She wore a white dress, wrapping her
whole person, and a white mask, which she never
removed, and excited much interest and curiosity
(Walpole).

Some twenty years ago, a lady clothed entirely
in white, shoes and all, used to walk the streets of
London. We never could learn her story. The
black lady, whom many may remember haunting
the Bank of England, was said to have been the
sister of a clerk hung for forgery, and that she
always carried the fatal pen with which the crime
had been committed in her girdle.

The old Savoy Palace was named after its

founder, Peter, Earl of Savoy, and John, King of France, was confined there after the battle of Poictiers; and there he died, when he honourably returned from France, unable to procure his ransom. Old John of Gaunt, " time-honoured Lancaster," held possession when Wat Tyler's mob burnt the Savoy about his ears; and the palace remained in partial ruins until Henry VII. endowed it as a hospital for one hundred poor persons, and dedicated it to St. John the Baptist. At the suppression of the hospital, its beds and furniture were given to St. Thomas and Bridewell hospitals. The Savoy fell into disrepute ; and Queen Elizabeth, when taking the air, was assailed by its evil people. Warrants were issued in vain . against these rogues; and a person demanding a debt due to him of another in the Savoy sanctuary was dipped in tar, rolled in feathers, carried in a wheelbarrow, and bound to the May-pole in the Strand—rather a bold plea to an action for debt, and worthy of the Kentucky man, whose answer to a dishonoured bill was that he was a citizen of the wilds, and his home was in the setting sun. Samuel Foote considered " tar and feathers a very genteel dress, as it fitted close to the skin and kept out the rain." After the Restoration, the Commissioners for the Revision of the Liturgy

met here, and were called the Savoy Conference.
That eminent religionist, Charles II., established a
French church here. The Great Hall was, after
a while, divided into several apartments, and
deserters, men pressed for military service, Dutch
recruits, and the sick and wounded, were lodged in
the Savoy. Marriages were advertised to be performed here, and a true register kept, for a guinea,
stamp included. But time and neglect swept down
what remained of the old Palace, and the builders
of Waterloo Bridge carried away the rubbish.
The little chapel, built in 1505, remained until
destroyed by fire in 1864—its churchyard a model
of tidiness and reverent care. It had a most interesting monument within, that of Anne Kille-
grew, the painter and poet :—

> "Such noble vigour did her verse adorn,
> That it seemed borrowed where 'twas only born,
> Unmixed with foreign filth and undefiled,
> Her worth was more than man—her innocence a child."

The great Lord Burleigh, and his son after him,
had a house in the Strand, where we dare say the
former often shook his paternal head at the latter,
after the manner of his representative in the
"Critic." Elizabeth paid him a visit, and when
entering, the Chamberlain pointed out the lowness
of the threshold. "For your master's sake," she

said, " I will stoop, though I would not for the King of Spain." The Royal lady once told Burleigh, when he apologised for not rising to receive her, " My lord, we make use of you not for the badness of your legs, but for the goodness of your head."

A house belonging to the see of Carlisle stood on the site of Beaufort Buildings, and, passing at the Reformation to the Bedford family, became Russell House, until the building of Bedford House on the site of the present Southampton Street. The Chancellor Clarendon occupied this house until the completion of his new house in Piccadilly; and here, on the 3rd of September, 1660, between eleven and two at night, the Duke of York married Anne Hyde, the Chancellor's daughter.

Salisbury House stood on the site of Salisbury and Cecil Streets, and was built by Sir R. Cecil. Queen Elizabeth was present at the house-warming.

York House belonged to the Archbishop of York in the time of Queen Mary. Here the great Lord Bacon was born, and when a boy played in St. James's Fields, where the echo of a brick conduit attracted the infant philosopher, and made him seek out the cause. At York House he kept his sixtieth birthday, and there desired to die; "for York House," he said, "is the house where

my father died, and where I first breathed, and
where I will yield my last breath, if it so please
God and the king." But the Great Seal was
taken from him, and he returned to York House
no more, being forbidden to come within the verge
of the court. The Duke of Buckingham obtained
the grant of York House from James I., and
erected the rustic water-gate still standing. The
house was leased to the Duke of Northumberland
in 1628, and contained a fine collection of pictures
and sculptures. The " superstitious " pictures were
sold by order of Parliament, and the house given
by Cromwell to General Fairfax, whose daughter
married George Villiers, Duke of Buckingham,

> " Who, in the course of one revolving moon,
>   Was chemist, fiddler, statesman, and buffoon;
>   Then all for women, painting, rhyming, drinking,
>   Besides ten thousand freaks that died in thinking."

The duke resided here after the Restoration, and
subsequently sold the mansion for 3000l., when it
was pulled down, and George Street, Villiers
Street, Duke Street, Off Alley, and Buckingham
Street, were erected.

Suffolk House—known to us as Northumberland
House—named after the Earl of Suffolk (father of
the memorable Frances, Countess of Essex and
Somerset), was so called until it passed by mar-

riage to the tenth Earl of Northumberland. At
his death it devolved on Elizabeth Percy, whose
first husband, Henry Cavendish, Earl of Ogle, died
when she was very young. Her second husband,
Mr. Thomas Thynne, was shot in his coach in Pall
Mall one Sunday, in 1682, and in Westminster is
a ludicrously accurate group in marble, representing the deed. Her third husband—married in
the May of the following year—was the proud
Duke of Somerset. The fortunate lady, therefore,
had three husbands before she was eighteen. The
house was formerly three sides of a quadrangle;
the principal front was to the Strand, with gardens
and water-gate towards the Thames.

In Northumberland Court Nelson lodged; and
if his gallant spirit ever visits the glimpses of the
moon, we wonder what he thinks of Trafalgar
Square, with his own unfinished column, and the
ridiculous water-squirts called fountains.

In Hartshorne Lane Ben Jonson lived, when he
went to a private school in St. Martin's Church,
before he became a Westminster boy, under Camden, to whom he addresses a grateful and graceful
epigram.*

* As the workmen in September, 1823, were excavating a vault to
receive the remains of the lady of Sir Robert Wilson, in the north
aisle of Westminster Abbey, they discovered, at the head of it, a
leaden coffin placed in the ground perpendicularly, with the head

Let us now return to Temple Bar, in order to notice the right-hand side of the Strand. We will not say anything about the barber's shop in that side of the Bar, except that it used to excite the loyal animadversion of our friend the late Mr. Gilbert A'Beckett, who would always affect apprehensions lest the gates of Temple Bar should prove ineffective at keeping out an invading army, because the army might bolt in through the barber's. The London barbers, by-the-by, were a very important body at one time, when they were designated barber-surgeons, and when close shaving was the fashion with others than the cheap haberdashers (who only tried to "shave the ladies"), and the barber's pole indicated that you could be bled with the lancet as well as the razor. This privilege was taken away in 1745 by Act of Parliament. To attract customers, one exhibited a short-bladed instrument as the dagger with

---

downwards in a hole about two feet square. At the top of the hole was a square stone about eighteen inches wide, on which were the initials " B. J.," cut in characters rather illegible. On inquiry amongst the old men of the Abbey, they stated that the tradition is, that when Ben Jonson was seriously ill, he was asked where he would be buried. He said, " If I can get foot ground in Westminster Abbey I will be interred there:" and on the Dean of Westminster being applied to, he gave sufficient ground to admit the corpse in a perpendicular position, as it was found. The skeleton of the deceased was entire, and in a singular state of preservation.

which **Walworth** killed Wat **Tyler,** and another
wrote over his door—

" Rove not from *pole* to *pole,* but here turn in,
Where naught exceeds the shaving but the gin."

On our right hand stood, until very lately, the last
of the Bulk Shops of the Strand, and forming part
of Butchers' Row.   In this house had resided
generations of fishmongers, the last being Crockford—or Old Crocky—the notorious gambling-
house keeper.   We were told by one who knew
him that it was his custom to risk the loss only of
a certain sum ; when that was gone, he would
leave the table and go home.   If he won a certain
amount he would retire from the play, go home,
drop his winnings down his own **area, and then**
return to see what more Fortune had in store for
him.   When he became rich he would not allow
the old shop to be altered, possibly that it might
remind him of the days of his innocency, when he
sold other fish than flat fish.   Butchers' Row ran
from Temple Bar to St. Clement's, and was granted
by Edward I. as shambles for " foreign " (*i. e.*
country) butchers.   Houses of wood and plaster
succeeded, and one was inhabited, in James I.'s
time, by the French ambassador, and for one
night by the Duc de Sully.   Catesby, Wright,
Winter, and Guy Fawkes met at a house in

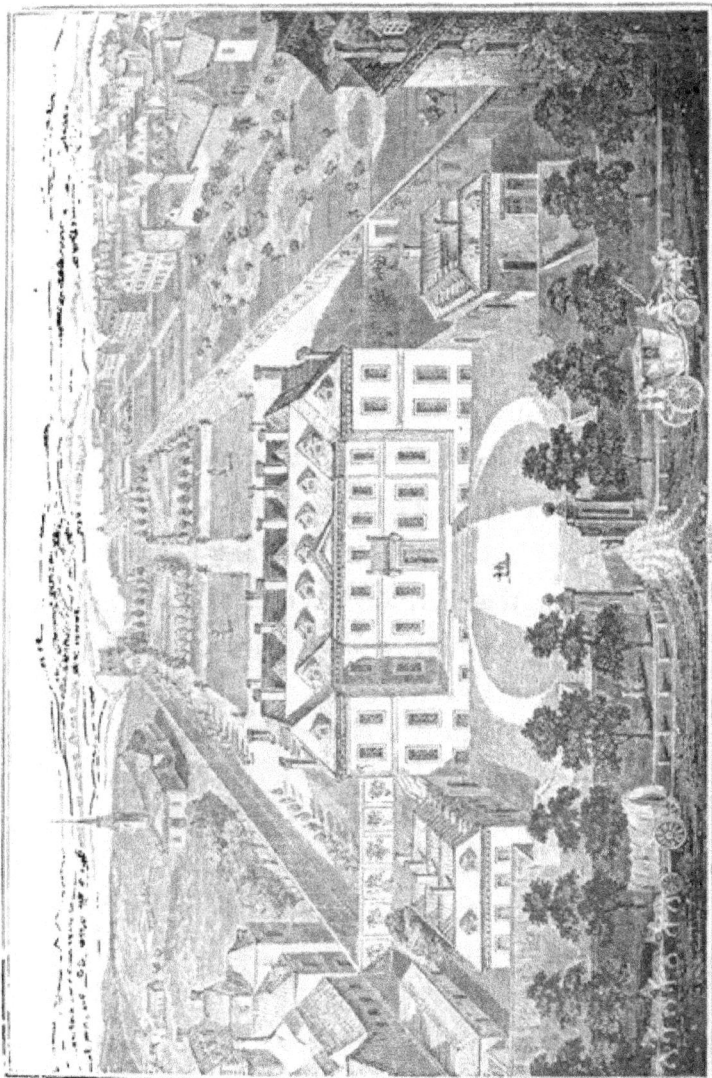

BURLINGTON HOUSE, PICCADILLY, LONDON, IN 1700.

Butchers' Row, and administered the oath of
secrecy to the conspirators, and afterwards received the sacrament in the next room, although
the plot is said to have been concocted at the Old
King's Head, in Leadenhall Street. Guy Fawkes
has been lately said to be the first person who
missed a Parliamentary *train*. Doctor Johnson
" used" a dining-house in this row—Clifton's.
Butchers' Row is now Pickett Street and Pickett
Place.

Clement's Inn, where Justice Shallow—

" No such swinge-buckler in the halls of court again "—

ate his terms and heard the chimes at midnight
with Jack Falstaff, is here at hand. The Inn is
named from the well of St. Clement's; and St.
Clement's Danes was a burial-place of Harold's
followers, it is said.

In Clement's Inn is a blackamoor, supporting a
dial, presented by Clare, Lord of the adjoining
market. We are almost ashamed to quote anything more against the lawyers, for all whom we
have known have been very good fellows; but
the lines once attached to Blackey are worth recalling :—

" From cannibals thou fledst in vain :
    Lawyers less quarter give.
The first won't eat you when you're slain,
    The last will while you live."

In the church in the Strand Dr. Johnson was a constant attendant, and a brass tablet recording the fact is attached to the pillar beside which he sat. The old Angel Inn—now St. Clement's Chambers—existed a very few years ago, and had its galleries and gable-ends and large court-yard. There, when the Angel Inn stood in the Fields, was Bishop Hooper, the Protestant martyr, taken before it was light, on his way to Gloucester, where he was burnt.

Let us pass on to the *via de Alwych*, or Wych Street, where some of the oldest houses in London are to be seen. New Inn, on the right, was the site of a guest inn about Henry VII.'s time, and had as a sign the Virgin Mary, and hence was called Our Lady's Inn, until it went into the law. In Edward VI.'s time it became a resort for law-students, and Sir Thomas More studied there before he was entered at Lincoln's Inn. It is said to be haunted, but the only spirits we have ever seen there were raised by the hospitality of literary friends. Drury House stood on its own grounds in Drury Lane in Elizabeth's time, and Lord Craven, the hero of Creutznach, built Craven House, the site of which was bought by Philip Astley, in 1803, for his Olympic pavilion, constructed principally of old ship-timber, given to

him by favour of the Duke of York; and we remember two topmasts supporting the proscenium
of the old theatre, when Liston, Farren, Keeley,
and Vestris trod the deck, and until it was
destroyed by fire in 1859.

In Craven Buildings lived Mrs. Bracegirdle
and Mrs. Pritchard, the celebrated actresses, and
Dr. Arne composed the music to " Comus " in the
back parlour of No. 17; and opposite Craven
Buildings is one of the few panelled houses still
existing. The Cock and Magpie is next door, and
Turpin is said to have there shot Tom King,
when endeavouring to rescue him, as you may
read in Mr. Harrison Ainsworth. It was also
patronized, according to that celebrated biography
of elevated characters, the " Newgate Calendar,"
by the notorious Sixteen-stringed Jack, so named
from wearing that number of strings to the knees
of his breeches.

Drury Lane was nobly tenanted until late in
the seventeenth century. Pit Place was the site
of the Cockpit, and afterwards of the first Drury
Lane Theatre.

In the Coal Yard, at Drury Lane end, was born
Nell Gwynn. She lodged afterwards at Maypole
Lane (now Little Drury Lane), and there on the
1st of May, 1667, when Mr. Pepys was on his

way to Westminster, "meeting many milkmaids with garlands upon their pails, dancing with a fiddler before them, did he see pretty Nelly standing at her lodging door, in her smock sleeves and bodice, looking upon one." She seemed a mighty pretty creature to the susceptible Samuel.

This celebrated woman possessed great interest with Charles II., and used it generously. Her origin and progress is sufficiently known; but the English people have always entertained a peculiar liking for Nell Gwynn, as they have for Robin Hood and Maid Marian, and one or two other questionable moralists. She is said to have suggested the foundation of Chelsea Hospital, and the benevolence of her character makes the story probable. Lord Buckhurst, who knew her well, says: "All hearts fall a leaping wherever she comes." The good Archbishop Tenison preached her funeral sermon, and Mr. Peter Cunningham has written her story.

At the corner of Maypole Lane and the Strand was the blacksmith's forge of the father of Nan Clarges, afterwards Duchess of Albemarle. Opposite was the maypole, said to have been set up by the old blacksmith to celebrate his daughter's good fortune.

The famous Maypole in the Strand was returned

to its place with great pomp and rejoicing, the former one having been removed by order of the Parliamentarians, in 1644. In a rare tract, called "The Citie's Loyaltie Displayed," published at the time, it appears the new pole was two pieces of cedar, and when united one hundred and thirty feet long. It was conveyed from Scotland Yard (so called because the Scotch kings lodged there) to the Strand, with the beating of drums and the sound of merry music. The Duke of York sent twelve seamen with cables and pulleys, and six great anchors to assist in raising it; and after them came three men, bareheaded, carrying three crowns. The pieces were then joined together, and hooped with bands of iron, with crowns and the King's arms richly gilt. A party of morris dancers in half shirts, with a pipe and tabor, danced round the pole; then the drums beat and the trumpets sounded, and the Strand resounded with the shouts of the assembled multitude. In 1713, however, it became decayed, and a new one was set up, richly decorated. This was taken down when the new church was built, and the parish presented the maypole to Sir Isaac Newton, who gave it to the Rector of Wanstead, to support the then largest telescope in Europe.

Here was the first stand for hackney-coaches,

in 1634. One **Captain** Bailey having appointed four **to stand there, others** soon joined them, until there **were** actually **as** many as twenty. They were not called so from Hackney, but from **a** French word, *coche-à-la-haquenée*. **Dreadful** things they were, and, O young ladies, **whose** mammas do not keep carriages, be thankful that you have not to go to parties—or to improving lectures—in such vehicles. Sheridan was very right when he paid the driver **of one** with a bad shilling. " Sir, this here's **a bad shilling,"** said the man. " All right, **this here's a bad coach,"** said Sheridan.

The **cabriolet (or** *vulgo*, **cab)** was introduced in 1823, **and** has driven the poor old " Jarvey " (also *vulgo* for hackney-coach) from the streets. We believe there is a No. One " left blooming alone," but the cabs now amount to above 6000.

The Holy **Well** in the Strand was once frequented for its sweet waters, which **still** flowed as bright and pure, when covered **over by** the Old Dog Tavern and surrounded **by some of the** worst dens of London, stored **with the** foulest moral pollution, happily removed very **recently. There** **was** once an hostelry with the **sign of a Lyon,** until Henry VIII., when it **became an Inn of** Chancery **and an** entrance to Lyon's Inn, **itself the** dreariest place we knew, long haunted, **no doubt,** by the ghost of Mr. William Ware, who left there with Thurtell to be murdered at Elstree.

Passing onward, we should have found Wimbledon House, on the site of which stood Doyley's warehouse, where Steele and Gay had their Doyley suits, and the little wine-glass napkins had their origin and name. Without Mr. Doyley's ingenious invention of cheap stuffs, Mr. Spectator thinks we should not have been able to have carried on the war.

In Exeter Street, Dr. Johnson, when he first came to London, lodged and dined for $4\frac{1}{2}d$. a day at a staymaker's, he and Garrick having borrowed five pounds on their joint note from Mr. Wilcox, the bookseller. Is it wonderful that the sturdy old Sam had little sympathy for the distresses of affectation?

In 1670 Exeter Change was built, and a Dr. Burbon, a little later, opened a sort of bazaar. We remember the common footway through it, and the milliners', hosiers', cutlers', and toy shops there on each side. One Thomas Clarke began business with a hundred pounds, and realized a fortune of nearly half a million; and had his portrait, looking out of the window of a cottage, painted on the wall. His daughter married Mr. Hamlet, the celebrated jeweller. Mr. Clarke once gave the writer a glass of wine, and did not leave him a legacy. Over the bazaar was the world-famous wild-beast show, with a big beefeater at the door, and against the wall a great picture of all the animals. It was the

EXETER CHANGE, STRAND, LONDON, 1829.

grand joy of a boy's holiday to go there and see the elephant stamp the mangel-wurzel to pieces, and take a halfpenny out of an iron box. The animals at the Zoological are too genteel for such practices. One distinguished individual created a great noise at his death, for he was shot by a file

s

of soldiers. That was Chunee, the great elephant.
His death is a most affecting story, and his
skeleton is now at the College of Surgeons.

Chunee once appeared at Drury Lane in a
pantomime, to the great disgust of the property-
man of the rival theatre, who said :

" I should be very sorry if I couldn't make a
better elephant than *that*."

COVENT GARDEN, LONDON. (From a Print by Hollar.)

The map of 1563 shows how thinly scattered
were the houses along the Strand of Elizabeth ;
there appears to have been one continuous row of
houses and gardens from Drury Lane on to

St. Martin's Lane, leaving Covent Garden quite
an open space, with a residence possibly for the
Sumpnour of Westminster Abbey, whose garden it
was. At present our destination is old Whitehall
and Westminster, merely looking up St. Martin's

COVENT GARDEN MARKET, LONDON. (From an Old Print.)

Lane as we pass. It was first named Westchurch
Lane, and among its distinguished inhabitants
were Suckling, the poet, and Sir Kenelm Digby,
the gentleman who had a naughty but beautiful
wife, for whom he was always inventing cosmetics
—one of them was viper-soup. Later, the great
Lord Shaftesbury, Dr. Tenison (he that preached
Nell Gwynn's funeral sermon), and Ambrose
Phillips. Sir Joshua Reynolds lived opposite

s 2

May's Buildings, as did Sir James Thornhill, when he created the Artists' School, in St. Peter's Court, and which Hogarth afterwards established as the Society of Incorporated Artists—the origin of the Royal Academy. Roubiliac and Fuseli lived in St. Martin's Lane ; and the Old Slaughter's Coffee House (now pulled down) was long the resort of artists.

Between St. Martin's Lane and Hedge Lane stood the Royal Mews, where the falcons of the sovereigns were kept as early as 1319, and Chaucer was one of the clerks thereof. When the royal stables at Lomesbury, or Bloomsbury, were destroyed, the hawks were removed from Charing Cross, and new stabling built for the king's horses. Most London stables are called *mews*—from this cause, and not, as generally supposed, from stable-yards being favourite promenades of musical cats. There really have been musical cats—in Paris, where trained cats were placed in a row, and, according as a monkey beat time, they mewed ; and it is recounted that " the diversity of tones produced a very ludicrous effect."

So much for the Strand ; and we hope that the progress we have made in a liberal education affords us satisfaction.

STRAND CROSS, COVENT GARDEN, ETC. LONDON, 1547.

CHAPTER VIII.

AT the village of Charing was formerly a hermit-
age. A hermit of Charing Cross would now
have abundant opportunity of meditating on the
vanities of mankind, and the electric time-ball
might call him to his dish of herbs and cold water,

unless he preferred lunch among the ladies at
Farrance's. Charing Cross was erected to mark
the last spot at which the body of Eleanor rested,
on its way to Westminster; and hence the
archæologists, who seem to us to delight in the
most impossible puns, venture to suggest came the
name of Chère Reine. The Cross was built of
Caen stone, with Dorset marble steps, and destroyed by order of the Long Parliament; part of
the stone was used to pave Whitehall. The Cross
appears to have been of considerable dimensions,
and was used as a place of execution; and on its site
several of the regicides suffered. Proclamations
for ages have been read at Charing Cross; and
our own gracious Queen was proclaimed there.
We need not remind you, with Tom Hood, that
here King Charles rides on "*in statu quo*," but
we may notice that this is one of the few London
statues that does not appear to have been erected
in honour of the late Mr. Guy Fawkes. It is not
a Guy, but a beautiful work of art.

The space extending from Charing Cross to
Westminster Hall, or Thorney Island, and from
the river to St. James's Park, formerly purchased
from the monks of Westminster, belonged to the
Archbishops of York, and received the name of
York Place. There was a public road to West-

minster through it, with a gate at either end.
Wolsey resided here in great state until his fall,
when he, brokenhearted, quitted its water-gate in
his barge for Esher.

Wolsey's residence was characterized by a
luxury and magnificence unequalled by any subject,
and scarcely surpassed by any king. His copes and
robes were the richest ever seen. He maintained a
train of eight hundred persons, among whom were
nine or ten lords, fifteen knights, and forty squires.
His domestics were persons of consequence, for
his cook wore a jerkin of satin or velvet, with a
gold chain round his neck. When Wolsey rode
forth, his comely figure was decked in silk or satin
of the finest texture, and of the richest scarlet or
crimson dye. His hat and gloves of scarlet, and
his shoes silver gilt, inlaid with pearls and
diamonds. His mule was trapped with crimson
velvet, and his stirrups were of solid silver. And
when it pleased the king's majesty for his recrea-
tion to visit him, "the banquets were set forth
with masks and mummeries in so gorgeous a sort
and costly manner that it was heaven to behold,"
writes his secretary, Cavendish. There were
numerous dames and damsels meet or apt to dance
with the gentlemen, and the whole night passed
in banqueting, dancing, and other triumphant

devices, to the great comfort of the king, if not
to the credit of the cardinal.

A few years later the Dukes of Suffolk and Norfolk waited upon Wolsey in those very chambers
to demand the Great Seal, and drive Wolsey from
his house, which his royal master coveted.

Henry appropriated York Place, or, as it was
then named, Whitehall, probably from the white-
ness of the stone of which it was constructed, the
usual building materials at that time being red
brick and timber. The king added many beautiful
and pleasant lodgings, buildings, and mansions,
together with a tennis-court, bowling-alleys, and a
cockpit, for his pastime and solace. From a stone
gallery in front he reviewed fifteen thousand armed
citizens in the Tilt Yard (now the Horse Guards),
where jousts and tournaments were of constant
occurrence. The Palace of Whitehall was seven
years in building; and the old palace at Westminster being in utter ruin and decay after the
fire, it was decreed that Whitehall and its per-
tainings should be called the Royal Palace at
Westminster. Here Henry and Anne Boleyn
were secretly married in a garret of the palace
by Dr. Lee, Mrs. Savage, Anne's trainbearer,
and two grooms of the chamber only being
present,—the shabbiest royal wedding on record.

Holbein, **whom the** king had taken into **the** palace, designed a gatehouse for the Tilt Yard, and **it** remained (used sometimes as a State Paper Office) until 1750, being then known as the Cockpit Gate. It is told of Holbein, that having been annoyed by the continual intrusion **of a** nobleman, who we suppose favoured him with amateur advice about "repainting that background and producing **tone," he** knocked his admirer, or critic, down stairs, and then sought the king's protection, **telling** him the whole story. The noble followed, **but found the** king defended the **painter,** and said, "You have not to deal with Holbein **now,** but with me. Remember, of seven peasants I can make seven lords, but not one Holbein." Henry collected many fine pictures, and made also munificent proposals to Raphael and Titian, but they were declined.

At Whitehall Henry VIII. was seized with his last sickness. So great was his fear of death, that several persons had been executed for saying he was dying; even his physicians would not tell him of his approaching end; nor would his courtiers, until **Sir** Anthony Denny undertook the task. Cranmer **was** sent for, but the king was speechless, and **a** grasp of the hand was the only answer to the archbishop's exhortation. Henry

died on Thursday, January 28, 1546. Thursday
was a fatal day to Henry and his posterity, as
Edward, Mary, and Elizabeth all died on a
Thursday.

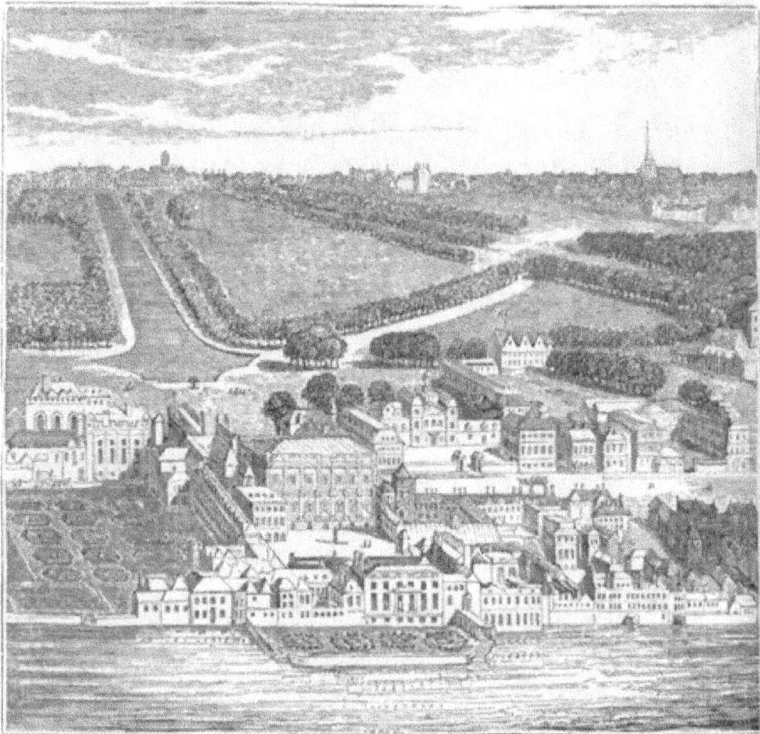

WHITEHALL IN THE REIGN OF JAMES I.

Edward VI. held a parliament here; and
Elizabeth was taken thence on Palm Sunday a
prisoner to the Tower; and when queen, here
occurred much of her flirtation with the ill-used

Duke of Anjou; and after they had parted at Canterbury, the queen taking a weeping farewell, she would not return to Whitehall for some time, because "the place should not give cause of remembrance of him from whom she so unwillingly parted." It was evidently "a case" with the gentle Eliza; and had the duke lived, there might have been another royal wedding at Whitehall. Hentzer, who visited England in 1598, has left an interesting account of his visit. He describes the queen (and in no spirit of detraction) as having a wrinkled face, red periwig, little eyes, hooked nose, skinny lips, and black teeth, yet listening still to the flattery of her courtiers concerning her beauty. We don't believe it—quite. Her books, he says, were in the Greek, Latin, French, and Italian languages, and bound in velvet, with pearls and precious stones set on the binding, and with gold and silver clasps. Her writing materials were kept in two little silver cabinets; she wrote a beautiful hand, unlike Sydney Smith's, which was, he said, "as if a swarm of ants, escaping from an ink bottle, had walked over a sheet of paper without wiping their legs." Her bed—Paul Hentzer was evidently a little of an Iachimo, or shall we say a Paul Pry?—her bedstead was of woods of divers colours, with quilts of gold, silver, silk, velvet, and embroidery. She had a little chest all over pearls, wherein she kept her most valuable jewels, and a piece of clock-work—an Ethiop riding a rhinoceros, with four attendants, who all made a bow when it struck the hour! In the Conduit Court, a Frenchman—the M. Blondin of the period—did feats upon a rope, and bears, bulls, and apes were baited before her in the Tilt Yard. On Wednesdays she had solemn dancing, Sir Christopher Hatton leading off, no doubt, as he had often done in the Temple Hall.

" But all that's bright must fade,"

and Whitehall was not exempt from change. On March 24, 1603, all that remained of our true English Elizabeth was brought here from Richmond, on its way to Westminster Abbey.

In the gardens of Whitehall James I. knighted three hundred or four hundred judges, serjeants, and doctors of law, Francis Bacon among the number. Here Lord Monteagle told Salisbury of the warning letter he had received of the Gunpowder Plot. Guy Fawkes was examined at Whitehall, in the king's bedchamber, and answered one of James's inquiries by saying, "One of my objects was to blow Scotchmen back to Scotland." Old Guy paid dearly for the jest.

Inigo Jones built the present Banqueting House, commenced in 1691, and completed in about two years. It cost seventeen thousand pounds, his own charges being 8s. 4d. a day as surveyor, and forty-six pounds a year for house rent, clerk, and incidental expenses : so at those rates Inigo could hardly have been the architect of his own fortune. What would Sir Charles Barry have said to that ? Nicholas Stone, the master mason, was paid 4s. 10d. a day. The Banqueting House is now a chapel; and here, on Maundy Thursday, the royal eleemosynary money—those pretty silver pennies and twopences—is distributed to poor and aged men and women This fine building was only a part of Inigo's grand design for a palace, which was to have covered twenty-four acres, or nearly twelve times the space of Buckingham Palace. The drawings are preserved at Worcester College, Oxford.

Many most glorious masques by Inigo Jones and Ben Jonson were performed at Whitehall— one cost three thousand pounds.

Charles I. added to Henry's collection other pictures of immense value ; but on the Civil War, Parliament seized on Whitehall (1645), and sold great part of the paintings and statues, and burnt others.

Here, in the Cabinet Room, Charles I. prayed
his last prayer in Whitehall. In the Horn
Chamber he was delivered to the officers, and
through an opening, broken in the wall at the
north end, he was led to the scaffold in front of the
Banqueting House, and at two o'clock in the afternoon beheaded. Lilly the astrologer asserts, on the
authority of Richard Spavin, one of Cromwell's
secretaries, that Colonel Joyce was the executioner.

Cromwell had the use of the Cockpit as a
lodging for some time, and to Whitehall he went
with the keys of the House of Commons in his
pocket, after dissolving the Long Parliament.
When he was settled at Whitehall, he repurchased
the cartoons, and many other pictures, which had
been dispersed, and Evelyn found the palace very
glorious, and well furnished. Cromwell's own
diet was spare, and not curious, except on public
treatments, which were given on every Monday
to all officers not below a captain, when he used to
dine with them, and a table was spread every day
in the week for each officer who should casually
come to court. He was a great lover of music,
and respected all persons examinous (or eminent)
in art. He was often jocund, and would order the
drum to beat before dinner was half over, and call
in his foot-guards to finish it ; and a capital joke

it was—for the foot-guards.   Milton was then his
secretary, and Andrew Marvel, and Waller, his
friend and kinsman, were his constant guests, as
also young Dryden.   On the anniversary of his
great victories at Worcester and Dunbar, Cromwell
died (September 3) at Whitehall, and lay in state
at Somerset House.   Richard Cromwell resided

OLIVER CROMWELL'S HOUSE, WHITEHALL.

here during his brief exercise of power, and quitted
it with only two old trunks, which contained, as
he said, the lives and fortunes of all the good
people of England — being the congratulatory
addresses which had been showered upon him nine
months before, when the good people of England

thought he deserved them. The Rump Parliament would have sold Whitehall, Hampton
Court, and Somerset House, had not General Monk
brought back Charles through the City to Whitehall, taking seven hours to perform the journey.
Charles built a stone gallery, where Prince Rupert
lodged in 1667, and in Privy Gardens, below it,
were suites of apartments for the king's beauties.
The Duchess of Portsmouth was very difficult to
please, and her lodgings were altered and re-
decorated twice or thrice.

Charles re-collected, by proclamation, the plate,
hangings, pictures, and sculpture, which had been
sold or stolen during the Commonwealth, and the
gardens were laid out in terraces and parterres,
and ornamented with bronze, marble, and dials, a
few of which are now at Hampton Court. One of
those dials was damaged by a nobleman, and
Andrew Marvel wrote—

> " This place for a dial was too insecure,
> And a guard and a garden could not defend;
> For so near to the court they will never endure
> Any witness to show how their time they misspend."

Misspent time, indeed, if we recal Evelyn's well-
known description of the last Sunday evening
Charles lived out in Whitehall. " The king," he
says, " sitting and toying with his concubines,

Portsmouth, **Cleveland,** Mazarin, &c., a French boy singing love-songs in those glorious galleries, whilst about twenty of the great courtiers and other dissolute persons were at basset round a large table, a bank of at least two thousand pounds in gold before them :—six days after, all was dust." What other History of the Court Life of Charles II. is needed?

James II. here washed the feet of the poor on Maundy Thursday, and was one day receiving Quaker Penn in his closet, and the next rebuilding the chapel for Roman worship, and adorning it with statues. Grinling Gibbons and Verrio were the artists he employed.

When James quitted Whitehall for **ever, his** palace was soon to be nothing but walls and ruins. A lazy maid-servant burning a candle from a pound, instead of cutting it (what does Mrs. Pater-familias say to *that?*), caused a fire, which destroyed a great part of the palace. Six years later the laundry took fire, and all the pictures in the palace were destroyed, and twelve persons perished. The site of the ruins was given away by the Crown—part **to the** Duke of Richmond.

On what was once Thorney Island stands West-minster Abbey, as left by the Confessor and Henry III.

T

Enter! The very walls are histories; and beneath our feet the past itself seems buried. Look around on every side until you lose the consciousness that all this solemn beauty is the work of man. Look until arise visions of kings

CHAUCER'S TOMB, WESTMINSTER ABBEY.

and queens, with crowns and sceptres, surrounded by hosts of nobles in all their state and glory. Look, until darker visions come—of kings and queens, and nobles wrapped in cere-cloths, only to be remembered by benefits conferred or crimes committed. or upon still greater men, who have left to all who follow them legacies of noble thoughts and ennobling deeds. So with a reverent bow, pass we on to the world without.

Thorney Island, on which the abbey stands, and the old palace of Westminster stood, is four hundred and seventy feet long and three hundred and seventy feet broad. It was once enclosed within lofty stone walls, having gates—one at King Street (the principal gate); a second rear New Palace Yard; a third, opening into Tothill Street; and a fourth near the mill, in College Street. The first Westminster Palace was a royal residence in the days of Canute, and was destroyed by fire in the time of Edward the Confessor, who rebuilt the palace, and died there, in an apartment known as St. Edward's Chamber, and afterwards as the Painted Chamber, when Henry III. added to the building. When the old tapestry was removed from the walls of this room, at the commencement of the present century, the original paintings were discovered, consisting of sacred subjects, with some battle-pieces, very spiritedly painted, and most valuable as specimens of early art; but the authorities, as a matter of course, had them covered with whitewash, and ought to have been soused in baths of the same mixture for their imbecility. In this chamber the death-warrant of Charles I. was signed.

The old House of Lords was another portion of the Confessor's palace, and the gunpowder treason of Guy Fawkes was concealed in the kitchen beneath. It was a kitchen, and not a cellar, for in 1828 the buttery hatch and ambry, or

GUY FAWKES'S HOUSE, LAMBETH.

cupboard, were discovered—so perhaps wicked Guy may have gained admission on pretence of seeing the cook. This portion of the building was called the Little Hall, to distinguish it from the Great Hall, built by Rufus, for grand banquetings and feastings, on high festivals and coronations,

and only ceased to be so used within our memory.
Rufus, returning from Normandy, visited the new
hall at Westminster with a large military retinue.
Some person remarked that it was too large—
larger than it should have been. The king replied,
" that it was only a bedchamber in comparison
with the building which he intended to make."
Rufus, no doubt, would have used the new clock
tower as an eight-day clock, and the York and
Nelson pillars as a pair of candlesticks. The
arrow saved some trouble to the Chancellor of the
Exchequer of the period. And here Richard II.
was at dinner when he heard that King Philip had
entered Normandy. The lion heart rose up and
swore a deep oath that he would never turn away
his face until he had met Philip ; and as his back
chanced to be to the door, they cut a hole through
the wall to let the king out, on his way to Portsmouth—a very straightforward proceeding on the
part of the king. The Little Hall was called
Whitehall—not the Whitehall—and it was a Court
of Requests in Henry VII.'s time. It was called
Poor Man's Court (says Stow), because there he
could have right without paying any money.
What a pity it was ever abolished to make a
House of Lords, where certainly justice was not to
be obtained upon such very easy terms. This

THE HOUSE OF LORDS AND THE HOUSE OF COMMONS. (Before the Fire in 1834.)

house was destroyed by fire in 1834, when the beautiful **tapestry**, representing the victories **over** the Spanish Armada, **were** burnt, and which had cost the **brave** Commander of the British fleet not less than 1,628*l.* of money in Elizabeth's time. The border was composed of the **heads of the** English commanders. The **destruction of this** remarkable piece of **work was one of the greatest** losses by the **fire.**

Here, when the **Black** Prince, and the French **king,** his prisoner, **came to** Westminster, Edward III. **sat** on his throne **to** receive the august captive. As **John** entered the hall, the king descended from **his seat** and embraced him, and led him **to** the banquet prepared for his entertainment.

In Richard II.'s time, the hall in **part was** rebuilt **as we now** see it, and the wonderful **roof** placed **on it.** It is composed of chestnut wood, and the **vulgar** believed that spiders **could** not live there, thinking it made of Irish **oak,** which is supposed to possess a property adverse to those primitive weavers. During the rebuilding, Richard built a temporary **wooden** building, which **was open on all** sides (an effective mode of ventilation worthy **the** attention of Dr. Reid), that constituents might **see** what **was** going on, **and,** as Pennant remarks, "to **secure** freedom **of debate,** he **sur-**

rounded the house with four thousand Cheshire
archers, with bows bent and arrows notched ready
to shoot." The votes of supply must have passed
with a rapidity which a modern Chancellor of the

THE STAR CHAMBER AND EXCHEQUER BUILDINGS AT WESTMINSTER.
(Destroyed by Fire, 1834.)

Exchequer must envy. When Richard II. re-
nounced his crown in this hall, Henry IV. stood
forward and claimed succession as descended from
the third Harry.

St. Stephen's Chapel was built by the king of
that name, and twice rebuilt, the last time by the
Second and Third Edwards. When the chapel
was fitted up for the Commons, in Edward VI.'s
time, the walls were wainscoted, a new floor raised
above, and a new ceiling placed below the original
one, so that the beautiful paintings—and they
were beautiful—and other artistic embellishments,
of what are called the dark ages, were preserved,
and revealed in 1800, when the side walls of the
chapel were taken down to make room for the
Commons at the time of the Union. Many of the
paintings were in oil, and, of course, representing
scriptural subjects. There exists a royal order,
dated 1350, for impressment of painters and others
for these very works. The walls, as was seen, had
been originally adorned with sculpture, richly
decorated in colour and gilding, and the windows
had been filled with stained glass, thus showing a
high development of art. The cloisters were
added by Henry VIII., and vied in splendour with
the neighbouring mausoleum of Henry VII. The
poet Chaucer was appointed Clerk of the Works,
and resided in the precincts and on the very site
of Henry VII.'s Chapel.

Thrice had fire vanquished the old palace, the
last being when Henry VIII. was driven to seek

shelter in York Place (*the* Whitehall), and from
that time the old palace ceased to be a royal residence, remaining for a long time in utter ruin
and decay, the Great Hall with the courts of law
and some other offices excepted.   The courts of
law were, as you know, originally, in fact, the

INTERIOR OF THE STAR CHAMBER, WESTMINSTER.   (Before the Fire, 1834.)

" King's Court," and the king presided in person,
the bench being his seat, until the inconvenience of
the judges following the Court became so great,
they were permanently settled at the king's chief
residence, the Palace of Westminster.   That
terrible institution, the Star Chamber, the terror

and abhorrence of the people of England, as its decrees over-rode law and liberty, and for whose destruction we owe the Commonwealth a deep debt of gratitude, was at Westminster : the building so named, erected in Elizabeth's time on the site of an older one, was pulled down in the present century. Its name is thought by Sir Thomas Smith to have come either because it was full of windows, or because the first roof was decked with images of stars gilded—Blackstone says from its being a place of deposit for contracts of the Jews, called *starra*, or stars, from the Hebrew *shetar*.

How many changes of scenes and actors have occurred in old Westminster Hall besides those already named! Here Sir William Wallace was tried and condemned ; Sir Thomas More and Protector Somerset were doomed to the scaffold ; the murderers of Sir Thomas Overbury, the notorious Earl and Countess of Somerset, were tried here, and here also the great Earl of Strafford was condemned, when " none was more a looker-on than he," the king being present and the Commons sitting bareheaded : and here Charles I. sat covered, the colours taken at Naseby above his head, arraigned for treason to his people, before the counsellors of the Commonwealth, and Lilly, the astrologer, saw the golden top fall from the king's staff—an omen of what followed. Here, on June **26th,** 1653 (to the Naseby banners were added **those** taken at Worcester, Preston, and Dunbar), Oliver Cromwell came—the Lord Mayor bearing **the** City sword—and was inaugurated Protector under a prince-like canopy of state, with the Bible, sword, and sceptre of the Commonwealth before him. Seven years later, at that hall-gate, Charles II. was proclaimed, **and upon** the south gable were set up the heads of Cromwell, Ireton, and Bradshaw—Cromwell's remained there twenty years. Here **James** II.'s seven bishops were acquitted, and in 1745 Kilmarnock, Balmerino, and Lovat were condemned.

Here Warren Hastings was impeached, and the **last** public trial in the hall itself was Lord Melville's, in 1806.

Booksellers, who were first migratory, like hawkers, and then became known as *stationarii*, from having booths **or** stalls at the corners of streets, in market and other public places exposed **their** wares, as did sempstresses and milliners, in Westminster Hall, and the revenues were received by the Warden of the Fleet Prison ; but the poor scholars of Westminster **were** allowed to sell books here without charge. Not many years ago, **fellows** frequented the courts to be hired as witnesses, and carried straws in their shoes to show their infamous profession.

Old Palace Yard has been the scene of many popular executions. The front of the scaffold was usually towards the hall. Among others, Guy Fawkes, Winter, Rookwood, and Keyes, for the Gunpowder Plot; Lord Sanquar, for procuring the assassination of Turner, a fencing-master, in Fleet Street, and whose hanging Lord Bacon declared to be the most exemplary piece of justice in any king's reign. Here, in 1618, the gallant, noble, brave Sir Walter Raleigh was executed, on a sentence found fourteen years before. " What dost thou fear? Strike, man!" were his last words to the executioner. Here Prynne, Bastwick, and Burton stood, one June day (30th, 1637), in the pillory, when Bastwick's wife received his ears in her apron and kissed them. And here the Duke of Hamilton, Lord Holland, and Lord Capel lost their heads.

In New Palace Yard, the open space before the north entrance of the hall, were two interesting structures—the conduit which flowed with wine for all comers, on occasions of great festivities— something like a drinking-fountain! and the lofty clock-tower, erected out of a fine inflicted on one of the Chief Justices of the King's Bench, for making a rasure of a court-roll, and reducing a poor man's fine from 13s. 4d. to 6s. 8d. The clock struck hourly, and was intended to remind the

OLD CLOCK HOUSE, WESTMINSTER.   (From a Print by Hollar.)

judges of the fate of their brother, and teach lawyers the difference of value between 13s. 4d. and 6s. 8d.

In the Chapter-house of the Abbey, on the right, the Commons of England first sat as a separate body from the Lords; and, upon one occasion, when they became riotous, and created a turmoil (a Congress in fact), the abbot waxed wroth, and turned out the legislative wisdom bodily, and vowed the place should not be again defiled with such rabble.

The last coronation procession that passed through Palace Yard to banquet in the Great Hall, was George IV.'s. We knew a little boy—for there were little boys when we were young, though now-a-days, we believe, there are only children and "young fellahs"—who was sent to bed at seven o'clock on the eve of that ceremony, 1821, and who scarcely slept a wink until he was waited upon at twelve o'clock, and then dressed in a plum-coloured suit, and the collar of his shirt turned back over his shoulders. This little boy was taken in a coach to Palace Yard; deposited in a house with scaffolding in front, and shown afterwards into a room, dimly lighted by candles. He was told to keep himself quiet; but the glimpses he had of a platform stretching from the hall to the abbey, whose fretted work was all a-glow in the light of many fires, round which were seated soldiers in their greatcoats, their arms piled and glittering in the fire-light also, kept the little boy wide awake and in considerable excitement. At

the early hour of five he took in the dim room, on
the recommendation of another little boy, what the
late Mr. Robson called "a glass of very excellent
sherry," and found, on emerging into daylight,
that his head had been converted into a humming-
top, and only returned again to its natural state in
the dim room, so that our little friend came to the
conclusion, that when the ceremony of the day
took place, he should not be able to see it. The
fates were more propitious; and he saw twenty
Lifeguardsmen, with laurel in the scales of their
breastplates, and with swords drawn, ride around
an open carriage, in which sat Queen Caroline and
Alderman Wood! A surging mob was in the
distance, shouting and groaning alternately, and
the little boy thought that a civil war had broken
out, and was coming into Palace Yard. He saw
the queen go away as she had come, having been
refused admission to the old hall, and felt very
much relieved by the proceedings. After a while,
red lines of soldiers took their stand beside the
platform, and real officers on horseback rode about
doing an immensity of nothing. Trumpets and
drums! Trumpets and drums! began braying
and bumping on all sides, and beefeaters and
heralds, and other splendid beings connected with
the court, marched past, preceding the "first

gentleman in Europe," with a crown of diamonds
on his head, and a golden canopy over that, and
a velvet train, gold-embroidered, supported by
noble young pages with feathers in their caps.
That was King George IV. on the **way to** take
dinner in the hall, after he had been crowned in
the abbey. Then came Lord Castlereagh, with
such a plume of feathers in his hat, that forty
years have not removed them from the mental
eyes of the little boy, they were so tremendous!
Then there was the Champion of England, Mr.
Dymock, in real armour, and mounted on a
beautiful white charger, and he rode into the hall
to challenge all the king's enemies, so the **little**
boy was told, and he wished at that moment **that**
he could have been his second. And **then** the
little boy and his tempter went back **into the** dim
room, and drank the king's health with **three** times
three, and that is all the little boy remembers of
the last coronation procession that passed into old
Westminster Hall, little thinking that he should
live to tell the little story here to-day.

We will pass at once through the beautiful gate
of small square stone and flint boulder, glazed and
tessellated—with its terra-cotta busts, naturally
coloured, and gilt—designed by Holbein, and used
until 1750 as a State-paper Office, until it was

pulled down to widen the **street,** and so enter St.
James's Park. **It** may not be amiss to pause a
minute at the Admiralty,* considered to be,
without flattery, **the** ugliest building in Her
Majesty's service—and that is saying a great deal
—the site of Wallingford House, from whose roof
Bishop Usher saw King Charles led to the scaffold,
and swooned at the sight. Most of our kings, save
the Conqueror, had vessels of war; and as early as
1297 the records speak of a William de Laybourn
as *Amiral de la Mer,* or First Lord of the Admiralty. **It is** usual to suppose that Henry VII.
provided our first State Navy, but he did little
more than build the Great Harry. It was his son,
Harry VIII., who perfected the designs of his
father. He instituted **the** Navy Offices and the
Trinity House, and made the sea service a distinct
profession, leaving at **his** death **a** navy of twelve
thousand tons, including the Henri Grace de Dieu,
of a thousand and more. These ships were high,
unwieldy, and narrow, with lofty poops and prows;
and one, the Mary Rose, " a goodly ship of the
largest size," Raleigh says, her ports being within
sixteen inches of **the water,** capsized at Spithead

---

* The present screen was erected **by** the Brothers Adams to
conceal the ugliness of **the** building. **Lord** Nelson lay in state in
one of the apartments, Jan. 8, 1806.

in swinging **in presence** of the king. Most of the **officers and crew were** drowned. In Elizabeth's **reign** such lubberly craft as the Mary Rose received but little improvement; but the pay of the seamen was increased from five shillings to ten shillings per month; and the London merchants encouraged to build ships convertible into men-of-war on emergency. Of the one hundred and **seventy-six** ships and fifteen thousand men which met **the** Spanish Armada, a considerable number were **not** " shippes royal." The first **great** impulse given towards making us a nation **of** mariners was when Frobisher departed for the Northern Seas, and Queen Bess, **the** prototype of Black-eyed Susan, bade " Adieu! Adieu!" and waved her lily hand **to** him and his gallant crew—their example to be followed by other enterprising men, and hardy as the oak which bore them. Frobisher was the first Englishman who tried to find a north-west passage to China (1576). Frobisher's Straits are named after him. He returned to England, bringing with him a quantity of black ore supposed to contain gold, and this circumstance induced money-loving Elizabeth to fit out a second expedition, which proved unsuccessful. Frobisher was killed at the taking of Brest, 1594. James I. made a considerable **advance in** the construction of vessels, and employed Phineas Pett, the scientific ship-builder, who relieved the vessels of much of their top hamper.

But avast!—we believe that is the proper word —or we shall drift out to sea, instead of taking a peep at the Horse Guards, on the site of the old Tilt Yard, and then away to St. James's Park, originally a swampy field belonging to St. James's Hospital, and which Henry VIII. attached to the buildings of Whitehall, when he took up his abode at the Hospital, and converted it into a royal palace, of which only the old gate remains. During the reigns of Elizabeth and the two first Stuarts little was done for the Park. It was merely a nursery for deer; and at one time a small royal menagerie (Evelyn), containing, amongst other animals, two Balearian cranes, one with a wooden leg, made by a soldier, occupied the inward Park. From St. James's Palace to Whitehall walked Charles I. (Jan. 30, 1648-9) on the way to death, and is said to have pointed to a tree planted by his brother Henry, near Spring Gardens. The Council of the Commonwealth once proposed to cut down the living gallery of aged trees in St. James's Park, and sell them, so that no footsteps of monarchy might remain unviolated. They were spared, however; and beneath them Cromwell asked Whitelock, " What if a man should take upon him to be king?" and was told, in reply, "That the remedy would be worse than the disease." The answer, no doubt, closed the conversation.

Charles II. added thirty-six acres to the Park, and had it greatly improved and ornamented by Le Nôtre. Evelyn and Pepys have left many records of the alterations then effected, and tell how there, for a wager, before the king, Lords Castlehaven and Arran run down and killed a stout buck : how, for a thousand pounds, the Western and Northern men wrestled before his Majesty, and large sums were betted, the Western men winning. " In a smooth hollow walk, covered with powdered cockle shells, to make it bind, planted with trees on both sides, having at each end an iron hoop depending from an arm of a long pole, through which a ball was struck," the game of Pall Mall was played by king and nobles. Here Cibber saw King Charles caressing his dogs and feeding his ducks, to the delight of his loving people ; and virtuous Evelyn was shocked to note " familiar discourse between the king and Mistress Nelly, as they called an impudent comedian, she looking out of her garden on the top, and the king standing on the green walk beneath," part of which remains by the wall of Marlborough House ;

and amongst the list of Nelly's debts was the account
for making this green mound, and also her sedan
chair, and her silver bedstead, which cost over
eleven hundred pounds.

Here, in Birdcage Walk, was a pleasant aviary,
the keeper, Edward Storey, living at Storey's
Gate; and here, in the inward Park, was the Decoy,
or Duck Island, with withy pots for the wild fowl
to lay their eggs in. Here, in winter, Pepys, for
the first time in his life, saw the people sliding with
the skates, and which he thought a very pretty art
—the King and Court looking on, no doubt as they
did when Evelyn was a spectator also.

The Park was a sanctuary from arrest, and
traitorous expressions used there were severely
punished. One Francis Head was whipped from
Charing Cross to the Haymarket, fined, and imprisoned, for wishing James III. a long and prosperous reign; and a soldier, for drinking the Duke
of Ormond's health, and hoping soon to wear his
right master's cloth, was whipped in the Park.
The Duke of Wharton was seized by a guard for
singing a Jacobite song—

"The king shall have his own again;"

and Richard Harris, for throwing an orange at the
king, was sent to Bedlam—a proper punishment

for the "man's first disobedience, and the fruit."
Aubrey tells a rather uncomfortable story of one
Evans, who had a fungous nose. One day, he
seized the king's hand, rubbed his nose with it, and
was cured—having previously kissed his royal
pocket handkerchief. "The king was disturbed."
We should fancy so!

At the death of Charles, the Park was deserted
by royalty, but continued to be frequented by the
people; and here, in summer, the fashion of the
day walked for two hours after dinner. Tom
Browne mentions: "Bareheaded beaux, French
fops, clusters of senators, belles in sacks and
powder; whilst the milkwomen cried, 'A can of
fresh milk, ladies. A can of red cow's milk, sir, if
you please.'" We have often tasted it when a
boy, and a cow or two still stand near Spring
Gardens.

Spring Gardens was a place of entertainment in
Charles I.'s and Charles II.'s time. It had its
pheasantry, bowling-green, boxes, bathing-pond,
dark alleys, and derived its name from a concealed
spring to a jet of water which wetted whoever
trod upon it. There was a six-shilling ordinary—
though the king's proclamation allowed but two
shillings to be charged elsewhere,—with continual
bibbing and drinking all day, and two or three

quarrels a week.   It was more than once suppressed for its irregularities, and New Spring
Gardens, or Vauxhall, opened in its stead.

> " Now Drummond's stands where gardens once did spring,
> And wild ducks quack where grasshoppers did sing."

The Mulberry Gardens were planted by James I.,
and were originally intended to breed silkworms.
It became a place of pleasant entertainment, and
occupied the site of Buckingham Palace.

> " A princely palace on that space doth rise,
> Where Sedley's noble muse found mulberries."

On the south-east side, from Henry VIII.'s time,
was Rosamond's Pond, a place of assignation, according to the old comedies of Congreve, Farquhar,
and Colley Cibber.   It derived its name, it is
said, from the number of silly boys and girls
who drowned themselves for love—cold water
being a capital extinguisher of flames, either of
fire or love. Hogarth painted a picture of this pond
for the small charge of 1*l*. 7*s*., the receipt for the
same existing in Mrs. Hogarth's handwriting. The
pond was filled up in 1770. George Colman the
younger was born at the south-eastern corner of
Rosamond's Pond ; and near it, in Petty France,
was Milton's Garden House, when he was Cromwell's secretary, and before his blindness. Hazlitt

lived there, and entertained Haydon, Charles Lamb, and his poor sister, and all sorts of odd people, in a large room, wainscoted.

Beneath a tent on the Parade of St. James's Park was placed the funeral car of Arthur Duke of Wellington, and down the Mall and past Buckingham Palace, and then on to St. Paul's went a procession of solemn grandeur, never to be forgotten by those who witnessed it.

The space between Charing Cross and St. James's appears to have been fields about 1560, and down this road Sir Thomas Wyatt marched, hard by the Court-gate of St. James's to Whitehall. Where Carlton House stood were, in Henry VI.'s time, some monastic buildings belonging to the monks of Westminster, and called " The Rookery ;" and there, when the buildings were demolished at the Reformation, a secret smithy was discovered, used by Henry VI. for the practice of alchemy. Near there Erasmus lived.

Carlton House, with its gardens, wood-work, and wilderness, which extended from the open space in Regent Street, where stands the York Column, to Marlborough House, belonged to Frederick Prince of Wales, father of George III., and he added a bowling-green, grottoes, and statuary to the garden. The Prince died at Kew in 1751, and the Princess at Carlton House in 1772. The first house was red brick, but George IV. cased it with stone, and added an Ionic screen and a Corinthian portico, the pillars of which were transferred to the National Gallery when Carlton House was pulled down.*

We remember the admiration excited by the tall porter of George IV., who allowed himself to be looked at—framed in the lodge doorway—once a day ; he was the most tremendous " proud young porter" we have ever seen.

The street which now bears the name of Pall Mall was occasionally called Catherine Street in Charles II.'s time. The houses on the south side had gardens looking to the Park, and divided from it by the mound on which Mistress Nelly Gwynne stood to talk to the king. Her house was on the site of No. 79, and when first presented to her was only a leasehold. The *conveyance* of a *free* message from Nelly to the king, however, procured it to be a freehold, and it is now the only one on the south, or park-side, of Pall Mall. The looking-glass

---

* The first purchase of pictures by the Government for the National Gallery was Mr. Angerstein's collections for fifty-seven thousand pounds—about forty in number. The collection has been greatly increased, since 1822, by gifts from Sir G. Beaumont, Mr. Holwell Carr, the British Institution, and other donors. The edifice in Trafalgar Square, designed by Mr. Wilkins, **was** opened in 1838.

which has often reflected Nelly's pretty face now hangs in the visitors' dining-room of the Army and Navy Club. On the north side was a row of trees, one hundred and forty in number. Bubb Doddington and Lady Griffin—terrible name!—who was seized for putting treasonable letters into the false bottoms of two large brandy-bottles—filled with a treasonable spirit no doubt—lived here. At Marlborough House—built by Wren for the great Duke of Marlborough, upon part of the pheasantry of St. James's, at a cost, the duchess says, of forty or fifty thousand pounds — the great warrior died. The duchess intended to have made a grand entrance into Pall Mall, but Walpole, to annoy her, bought the requisite houses in Pall Mall, and shut her grace in. The duchess delighted to call the king "Neighbour George," and once received the Lord Mayor and Sheriffs sitting up in bed. Marlborough House was bought for Prince Leopold on his union with the Princess Charlotte, who, it may be remembered, escaped before her marriage from a house in Warwick Street, Cockspur Street (a gloomy place, we remember it), and went in a hackney coach to her mother. Marlborough House is now settled on the Prince of Wales.

George IV. proposed to connect Carlton House, Marlborough House, and St. James's by a gallery of National Portraits, but Mr. Nash built out the idea, and Carlton House was deserted.

Schomberg House, built in 1650, and enlarged and beautified by the son of the Duke of Schomberg (killed at the battle of the Boyne, 1690), is still preserved, though divided into two or three tenements. Formerly it was a fair mansion enclosed with a garden, and at the Restoration was inhabited by several Court favourites. The Duke of Cumberland—he of Culloden—died here (1760); Astley, the artist and "beau," and Cosway, the miniature painter, lived in Pall Mall, as did also Gainsborough, who died in a second-floor room, having been reconciled to Sir Joshua Reynolds. His last words were, "We are all going to heaven, and Vandyke is of the party."

There is a story told of the celebrated Dr. Sydenham, which it is now difficult to realize. He was sitting at his window smoking his pipe, and with a silver pot before him. A thief seized the pot and ran into Bond Street, and was lost amongst the *bushes*—the thief, no doubt, rejoicing at his pot-luck.

An impostor named Psalmanazar also lived in Pall Mall, and invented a language which he said was that of Formosa, and deceived many of the wise men of the east and of the west, who, by-the-by, are generally to be bought very great bargains, and would possibly have reviewed a Grammar of the Gorillas.

At the King's Arms, in Pall Mall, the Liberty or Rump Steak Club (not to be confounded with the existing club of that name established by Rich and his scene-painter Lambert, 1735), was held, every member a peer, and in opposition to Walpole.

The Haymarket, when it was opened in Elizabeth's time, comprised only a few houses and hedge-rows, and where—since 1791, when the present Opera House was opened, " Semiramide," " Lucrezia Borgia," and " Norma" have held sway —" washing was taken in."   We shall return to this locality presently.

CHAPTER IX.

St. James's was made a royal palace by Henry VIII., as we have said, and little remains of it but the red-brick gateway, around which chairmen and flunkies have fought many a battle for precedence in days gone by. What is called the Chapel Royal was also part of the old building, and for which our great-grandmothers were wont to dress with as much care as for the Opera, and by their ogling and sighing aroused the anger of Bishop Burnet:

> " When Burnet perceived that the beautiful dames,
> Who flocked to the chapel of holy St. James,
> On their lovers the kindest of looks did bestow,
> And smiled not on him while he bellowed below,
>   To the Princess he went
>   With pious intent,
>   The dangerous ill in the Church to prevent;"

and was laughed at for his pains.

The great Duke of Wellington was a constant attendant at the Chapel Royal when in town.

There are few historical associations (except drawing-rooms, levées, and state-balls) associated

with St. James's Palace ; and some of those we do
not care to mention. Queen Mary died here, as
did Caroline, George II.'s queen. Charles II. and
the Old Pretender were born at St. James's ; and
here Charles I. passed the night before his execution. St. James's Street, in Strype's time, was a
spacious street, some of the houses having a terrace
walk, ascended by steps in front of them, and was
well inhabited by gentry, when on Tuesday evening, December 6th, 1670, Colonel Blood made his
desperate attack on the Duke of Ormond, whilst on
his way to Clarendon House, and, in spite of the
six walking footmen, dragged the duke from his
coach, and carried his grace towards Tyburn,
where he intended to have hanged him. The
villains were pursued, and the duke discovered
struggling in the mud in Piccadilly and rescued.
Blood and his party escaped.

Edmund Waller, the poet, lived in St. James's
Street, as did Gibbon the historian ; and in St.
James's Place, opposite, lived Addison in 1710.
It was long the rage to frequent

> " The Campus Martius of St. James's Street,
> Where the beau's cavalery pass to and fro
> Before they take the field in Rotten Row ;
> Where Brookes's Blues and Walter's light dragoons
> Dismount in files and ogle in platoons."

Gilray, the great caricaturist, when insane, threw

himself from the window of his lodging at No. 20,
and was killed.

Lord Byron lived in lodgings in St. James's, at
a time when it was necessary to carry pistols in his
carriage on a visit to Tom Campbell at Sydenham;
and amongst other distinguished residents was
Samuel Rogers, who lived at No. 22. Lord Byron
has recorded the impression produced upon him by
the almost fastidious elegance of the apartments.

Perhaps you would like to be introduced to
Lord Byron as he appeared about 1809. "His
face was void of colour and he wore no whiskers.
His eyes were grey, fringed with long black lashes,
and his air was imposing but rather supercilious.
He wore a very narrow cravat of white sarsenet,
with the shirt collar falling over it, then in
remarkable contrast to the stiff starched cravats
generally in vogue. A black coat and waistcoat
and very broad white trousers of Russia duck in
the morning, and of jean in the evening. His
watch-chain had a number of small gold seals
appended to it, and was looped up to a button of
his waistcoat."

St. James's Street has long been a favourite
locality for clubs, and (as it is no longer) for
gaming-houses, or hells, as they were most appropriately called from the misery they occasioned,

and after **a dark room in** St. James's Palace where hazard **was played.** *

Brookes's Club is probably the most aristocratic club in London, and had formerly amongst its members the Prince of Wales, **and** other royal personages. It was a great betting **club ; and the** old betting-book, still preserved, is a great curiosity from the oddity of some of **the** bets it contains. The club was formed by **Brookes,** a wine merchant, described as **one** who

> " Nursed in clubs, disdains a vulgar trade,
> *Exults* in trust, and blushes to **be** *paid*."

At one time an introduction to Almack's **in** King Street, St. James's, was a passport to **the** world of fashion, and coveted accordingly ; **but the** glory has departed, and the exclusive character of the assemblies at " Willis's Rooms," very greatly declined. Almack was a Scotchman, and opened his assembly under high patronage, Feb. 12, 1765. His real name is said to have been Macall.

Let us now enter the Green **Park** (formerly Little St. James's Park), and away by Constitution

* **The** internal decorations of Crockford's cost over ninety-four thousand pounds, and everything that any member had to lose, and chose to risk, was swallowed up. " The Pluto became Plutus, and retired," says **a** writer of the time, " much as an Indian chief from a hunting-ground, when there is not game enough left for his tribe." Crockford's ceased as a club, and became elevated into the Wellington Dining-rooms in 1862.

Hill (memorable for three outrages against the
dearest life in Great Britain, and the accident
which ended the career of one of England's
greatest statesmen, Sir Robert Peel) to Hyde Park
Corner, where Charles II., crossing the road almost
unattended, met the Duke of York, and said to

TYBURN TURNPIKE.—THE ROAD ON THE LEFT LED TO TYBURN TREE.

him, in reply to an expression of brotherly alarm,
" I am in no danger, James, for no man in England
will take my life to make you king." The arch
now at the entrance of the Green Park is a poor
adaptation from the Arch of Titus, and on the top of

it is the **arch-absurdity** of London, the Duke **of** Wellington's statue. It was originally put up there **for** the benefit of " Punch," who certainly pulled it to pieces, although he could not pull it down.

Let us pause for a moment **at the site** of old Tattersall's, or the Corner, **as it was called.** Richard Tattersall, the founder, was training groom to the **Duke of Kingston,** brother **of** Lady Mary Wortley **Montagu, and** after the death of the duke, **took no other service.** He purchased the **celebrated** racehorse Highflyer for 2500*l.* The **horse was** the foundation of Tattersall's fortune, **and he** gave the name of Highflyer Hall to a house he **built at** Ely. Tattersall's was opened as an auction mart about 1795, when it stood on the verge of the " five fields " which sloped down to the stream which carried off the superfluous water of Hyde Park. The five fields were celebrated for nightingales and footpads. What a change in less than a hundred years ! **Belgravia,** a new London, **grew** round Tattersall's, **and has at** last squeezed it **out of its long-known** corner. Charles Mathews the **elder,** and celebrated mimic, often accompanied one of the Mr. Tattersalls to Newmarket races, and upon **a certain** occasion took it into his head to imitate **his friend the** auctioneer when selling the

blood stock usually offered **for sale** there. Tattersall bore this very well for some time. " No. 44,"
said Mr. Tattersall. " No. 44," said Mathews. " A
brown filly, by Smolensko—what shall we say to
begin ?" said Mr. T. " A brown filly, by Smolensko
—what shall we say to begin ?" echoed Mathews.
" One hundred guineas, to begin ?" asks Mr. Tattersall.   " One hundred guineas," answered Mathews.
" It's yours, Mr. Mathews, and thank you," said Mr.
Tattersall, knocking down a very weedy affair, to
the astonishment of his tormentor.

So far westward, we must take a peep at
Ranelagh, and the merry ghosts of those who
crowded its rotunda, which stood on the site of
Ranelagh House, built in 1691 by Charles II.'s
favourite earl of that name.

The older gardens of Vauxhall, however, claim
precedence, although not in Westminster.

Fulkes Hall was called after one of King John's
Norman warriors, and the name corrupted into
Fauxes-hall, Foxhall, and Vauxhall, and Guy
Fawkes appears to have had some connection with
it. It has been the prison of Lady Arabella Stuart,
and the refuge of the gay and gallant Duke of
Monmouth after Sedgmoor fight, and the home of
Ambrose Philips, the pastoral poet. When **it**
became a place of entertainment it was called **New**

OLD VAUXHALL GARDENS, LONDON (1740).

Spring Gardens. **Pepys went there** " by water, **to**
observe the humours of **the** citizens pulling of
cherries, and to see the fine people walking, hear
the nightingales and other birds, and the fiddles,
and the harp, and the Jews' trump." He fell
in with Harry Killigrew and young **Newport,**
and **their** mad talk **and** other improprieties made
his heart ache.

Who has not been to Vauxhall with the " Spectator" as Sir Roger de Coverley ? If you have not
prithee turn to No. 383 in those enchanting volumes,
and join that pleasant party ; and there are other
happy ghosts with whom old Vauxhall might be
revisited, and not only **at** the " witching hour of
night." In later **times** some of our best singers
took the place of **the** nightingales ; and Braham,
Incledon, Storace, **Mrs.** Billington, and choirs of
others were wont to charm the ear of our grand-
fathers. What a fairy **place** it seemed to us !—we
won't say how many years ago—and how one
walked and walked, and gaped, **and** stood in
breathless wonder **as** Madame Saqui climbed up
that dark thread **to** a blazing temple high up
amongst the clouds : **or** with what zest one ate
those **wafers of** ham **and** Lilliputian chickens which
cost so much, but for which **we** paid cheerfully in
compliment to the affable and graceful Mr. Simp-

son's bow and welcome to the "Royal Property."
We are glad that there is nothing of Vauxhall
Gardens remaining — that they are entirely
and utterly effaced, affectionately buried in the
past!

In 1742 the gardens of Ranelagh House were
opened to the public under the direction of Lacy, the
Drury Lane manager, as a winter Vauxhall, and
were frequented by princes, princesses, dukes, and
nobility, and much mob besides (says Walpole), and
my Lord Chesterfield was so fond of it that he had
all his letters addressed there. The rotunda was
one hundred and eighty feet in diameter, warmed by
a centre apparatus and the promenade matted. The
interior was fitted with boxes for refreshments, and
lighted by chandeliers hanging from the highly-
painted ceiling. There was a Venetian pavilion in
the centre of a lake in the garden to which visitors
were rowed in boats, and the grounds were laid
out in green alleys and dark walks. Concerts
were given, the music composed by Dr. Arne,
and here the first compositions of the Catch Club
were performed. The admission was a shilling;
and there Sunday tea-drinking, masquerades, and
ridottes were held at intervals, to which the admission was a guinea. Masquerades are said to
have been in fashion at the Court of Edward III.

(1340), and in the reign of Charles II. masquerades were common among the citizens. They were suppressed in the reign of George I., as the bishops and clergy preached against them—no less than six masquerades being subscribed for in a month. They were revived and carried to a shameful excess (according to Mortimer) by the connivance of the Government, and a ticket for one or two at Ranelagh were subscribed at twenty-five guineas each (1776). Of late years masquerades have been only scenes of senseless noise and debauchery, including supper and a first-rate headache in the morning. The downfall of Ranelagh was the French Revolution. Until then the tradesman, in his sober suit, never thought of mixing with swords and bag-wigs, the hoops and satin trains of his superiors in rank, even at Ranelagh, although the price of admission was low and the same to all. But the Revolution swept away such invidious distinctions. Maid-servants acquired rights which now exhibit our cooks in crinoline : dress ceased to be distinctive of a class, and so Ranelagh and Vauxhall faded away, and Cremorne flourishes in its stead. In 1802 the installation ball of the Knights of the Bath was held here, and the Peace fête in 1803. Next year Ranelagh was deserted and pulled down, and part of the grounds included in the old men's garden of Chelsea Hospital.

OLD CHELSEA BUN HOUSE.

At the bottom of Jews Row, and near the Compasses, was Richard Hand's old Chelsea Bun House, where royalty and every one pretending to fashion made a small investment. Queen Charlotte presented Mr. Hand with a silver half-gallon mug with five guineas in it.   On Good Friday morning upwards of fifty thousand persons have assembled here, and in one day more than two hundred and

CHELSEA BUN HOUSE.

fifty pounds have been taken for buns.   When Ranelagh declined the Bun House languished also.

Its last day of glory was Good Friday, 1839, when two hundred and forty thousand buns were sold ; and next day black draughts and Dover's powders were in universal demand, no doubt.

Hot cross-buns were the ecclesiastical *Eulogiæ* or consecrated wafer bestowed as alms on those who, from any impediment, could not receive the host.

We may as well remind you that the earliest manufactories of porcelain in England were at Bow and Chelsea; and at Chelsea China Works Dr. Johnson made his experiments on tea-cups. The works were in Justice Walk, and subsequently became a stained-paper manufactory. A pair of rare old Chelsea vases, painted with Roman triumphs, brought 23*l.* 10*s.* at the Stowe sale.

Kensington Palace was Lord Chancellor Finch's house at Kensington, and which his second son sold to William III., who added to the old building another story, designed by Wren. George II. added a royal nursery, destined, at a later date, to cradle our gracious sovereign Queen Victoria. In Kensington Palace died William and Mary, Queen Anne, and George, Prince of Denmark, King George II., and the late Duke of Sussex. The gardens attached were at first nothing but gravel-pits; but Wise and Loudon, whom Addison dignifies as the heroic poets of gardening, produced the

fine effects we now witness, although marred by
the formal alterations of Bridgeman, the Dutch
gardener.   And here—

> "The dames of Britain oft in crowds repair
> To gravelled walks and unpolluted air ;
> Here, while the town in damp and darkness lies,
> They breathe in sunshine and see azure skies.
> Each walk with robes of various dyes bespread,
> Seem from afar a moving tulip bed,
> Where rich brocades and blooming damasks glow,
> And chintz the rival of the showery bow."—TICKELL.

These gardens are **now** much frequented by nurse-
maids **and** children, converting **them** literally into
nursery gardens; and we are of opinion that our little
men and women possess the strongest claims to have
their rights considered, knowing, as we do, the value
of fresh air to children, especially London children.

The manor of Hyde belonged to the monks at
Westminster until exchanged with the adjoining
manor of Neyte and the advowson of Chelsea for
the priory of Hurley, in Berkshire.   Henry VIII.,
no doubt, had the best of the bargain.   It was
surrounded with a deer-fence at a very **early**
period, and, in 1550, the French ambassador
hunted here with the king.   In Charles II.'s time,
foot and horse races took place round the ring,
then a fashionable ride and promenade, none more
so—not even Gray's Inn Gardens and Lamb's
Conduit Fields—but partly destroyed by the for-

mation of the Serpentine. Nearly a thousand coaches have been seen there of an evening (Oldys), and amongst them the Duchess of Cleveland's, when she abused Wycherley. It was the place of flirtations, except on a windy day, when a well-dressed gentleman could not stir abroad but had to seek shelter in the playhouse (Colley Cibber). To be the envy of the ring "was held out as a temptation" to hesitating Mirandas ("The Busy-Body," Centlivre). Poets and play writers have kept its memory green.

During the Commonwealth the Park was sold, and the sordid fellow who had purchased it of the State charged, to Evelyn's great disgust, one shilling for every coach and sixpence for every horse. Oliver Cromwell, who really seems to have been "fast" for a Puritan, came as he would say, perhaps, were he living now,—came to grief, in attempting to drive six-in-hand in Hyde Park. The horses had been given to him by the Earl of Oldenburg. Oliver drove pretty handsomely for some time, but provoking the horses too much with the whip, the animals bolted, and his highness was thrown off the box on to the pole, where he lay upon his body until he rolled on to the ground. His foot caught in the tackle, and his pistol went off in his pocket. The report was favourable. He was not much hurt, and was **soon** about again. Here Sydenham **and** Cecil laid wait to assassinate Oliver, the hinges of the park gates being filed off to secure their escape, but a divinity hedged a Protector for once.

In Charles II.'s time Hyde Park was, as De Grammont says, the promenade **of** London. Nothing was so much the fashion during the fine weather ; every one, therefore, who had sparkling eyes or splendid equipage repaired thither to see the **king, who** seemed **pleased** with the place. Evelyn went to see a coach-race in Hyde Park, having collationed in Spring Gardens ; and Pepys carried his wife in a coach of his own, and ate a cheesecake and drank a tankard of milk.

George II. granted the privilege to sell victuals to a pilot who saved him from wreck, and also gave his deliverer a silver-gilt ring, still preserved, of course. The curds and whey sold in the Park, fifty years ago, were really delicious ! From the time of Henry VIII. duels were—until common-sense would tolerate them no longer—of frequent occurrence in the Park. Lord Mohun here fought **the Duke of** Hamilton, when the former **was killed, and the** latter supposed to have been stabbed over Colonel Hamilton's shoulder by Macartney, Mohun's second. Hamilton died before he could leave the Park, and Macartney fled to Hanover, when a reward of eight hundred pounds was offered for his apprehension. He was afterwards employed by George I. to bring over six thousand Dutch troops at the Preston rebellion. He then surrendered, was tried, and found guilty of manslaughter. Here Wilkes and Martin fought on account of a passage in the "North Briton," and Wilkes was wounded (1763). Many other encounters took place here, the last in 1822, between the Duke of Bedford and the Duke of Buckingham.

The Wellington statue is at the east end of Rotten Row, so called from *rotteran*, "to muster," and it might have been a muster-ground during the civil war, when there was a breastwork at Park Lane. A very pleasant muster-ground is Rotten Row still of a summer's evening, and where horse and foot practise what we believe is called "the art of killing," and it seems to have been frequented for that purpose by the swell of the past, who—

> " Anxious yet timorous his steed to show
> To hack Bucephalus of Rotten Row;
> Careless he seems, yet vigilantly shy,
> Woos the stray glance of ladies passing by ;
> While his off heel insidiously aside
> Provokes the caper which he seems to chide."

The statue of Achilles was cast by Westmacott,

from **twelve** twenty-four pounders, weighing up-
wards of twenty tons, taken at Salamanca, Vittoria,
Toulouse, and Waterloo, and is eighteen feet high.

George II. recognizing an old soldier, named
Allen, who had fought under him at Dettingen, in-
quired what he could do for him. **Allen, after**
some hesitation, asked for a permanent apple-stall
at Hyde Park Corner. The grant was made, and
Allen's stall—a poor tenement—stood there until
purchased by Apsley, Lord Bathurst; and so the
apple-stall of the old Dettingen soldier grew to be
the mansion of Arthur, Duke of Wellington.

One Higgins, a tailor, residing in the western
suburbs of Westminster, invented **a** stiff collar
with a round hem, and as the folds resembled
spear heads, he called it Piccadilly. Investing his
fortune in houses, he built many **in** the street
which bears the name of his handicraft, so says
Blount, in 1656; but sixty years before, Gerard
speaks in his "Herbal" of the small wild buglosse
which grows on the drie banks of Piccadilly. So
Higgins seems to have cabbaged the name for his
collars.

Mr. Peter Cunningham, who devoted much
pains **to** searching the rate-books of the metropolis,
and **to** whose labours we have been frequently
indebted, discovered that one Richard Baker,

devised to his wife Mary, Piccadilly Hall, which
stood at the now corners of Windmill Street and
Coventry Street, when all the intervening space
round about, and to St. Martin's Lane, behind the
King's Mews, was open fields, over which, after
Lammas, the parishioners had a right of common.
Piccadilly Hall became a house of entertainment
and gaming, with handsome gravel walks and an
upper and lower bowling green. It was pulled
down in 1685, but the Fives Court remained to
my time; and there "the noble art of self-defence"
was practised before the high-born, the gentle, and
the blackguard.

> " But the club pugilistic,
> Which held the art fistic
> In such estimation at last has gone dead."

About the middle of the Haymarket was a windmill then at the Cawsey Head, and over against
the street which preserves its name stood Shaver's
Hall, a gaming-house, built by the barber of the
Earl of Pembroke, after Spring Gardens was put
down.

Its Tennis Court remains in James Street, Haymarket, and where the door is shown through
which Charles II. and Mistress " Moll " Davis used
to enter from the King's Mews.

OLD VIEW OF PICCADILLY.   FROM HYDE PARK CORNER TURNPIKE.

CHAPTER X.

PICCADILLY originally was not one-fourth its present length, extending only to Sackville Street, and appears in the rate-books of St. Martin's for the first time in 1673.   The history of Piccadilly may be read in the names of its streets.   From Sackville Street to Burlington Street was originally called Portugal Street, after Charles II.'s queen ; and all beyond "The Great Bath Road," or "The Way to Reading."   As late as 1734, Piccadilly, from Devonshire House, formerly Berkeley House,

to Hyde Park Corner, was occupied by the shops
and stoneyards of statuaries, and cottages, as
shown in engravings of the time. The road was
unpaved, and coaches were frequently overturned.
Remembering what a family coach was, one
wonders how they managed to get them up again.
Lord Clarendon's house, which he built at great
cost during a time of great public calamity
[Burnet], excited the people, who cut down, says
Pepys, the trees before the house, and broke the
windows, and set up or painted a gibbet on his
gates, and these words writ :

> " Three sights to be seen—
> Dunkirk, Tangier, and a barren queen."

The populace called it Dunkirk House, believing
that Clarendon had feathered his nest out of the
sale of Dunkirk. After Clarendon's flight and
death the house was sold to the Earl of Albemarle,
who again sold it to Sir Thomas Bond, of Peckham.
Two Corinthian pillars at the Three Kings' Gateway (formerly No. 75) are believed to have
belonged to Clarendon House. Burlington House
was named after its builder; the Gardens were
called the Ten Acres. Devonshire House was the
site of Berkeley House, built about 1665, on the
site of Hay Hill Farm. On Hay Hill the head of

Wyatt was set upon a gallows, and the late Duke
of York and the Prince of Wales were stopped and
robbed there. Coventry House was built on the site
of an old inn, and sold by Sir Hugh Hemlock (1704)
for ten thousand guineas to the Earl of Coventry.

More notabilities than we have space to enu-
merate, or you patience to read about, have occupied
Piccadilly.   John Evelyn lived on the east side of
Dover Street, and where he " had been sometimes
so cheerful and sometimes so sad" with Chancellor
Hyde.   On the west side lived Arbuthnot, the
friend of Pope, and Swift, Gay, and Prior all had
met here, and perhaps concocted the " Beggar's
Opera" for Manager Rich—a work that was said
to have made " Rich Gay and Gay Rich."*   From

---

* It was Dean Swift who first suggested the idea of the " Beggar's
Opera," by observing what an odd pretty sort of thing a Newgate
pastoral might make.   " Gay," says Pope, " was inclined to try at
such a thing for some time; but afterwards thought it would be
better to write a comedy on the same plan.   This was what gave
rise to the ' Beggar's Opera.'   He began on it, and when first he
mentioned it to Swift, the doctor did not like the project.   As he
carried it on, he showed what he wrote to both of us; and we, now
and then, gave a correction or a word or two of advice, but it was
wholly of his own writing.   When it was done, neither of us
thought it would succeed.   We showed it to Congreve, who, after
reading it over, said, 'It would either take greatly, or be damned
confoundedly.'   We were all, at the first night of it, in great uncer-
tainty of the event, till we were very much encouraged by our
hearing the Duke of Argyle, who sat in the next box to us, say, 'It
will do,—it must do.   I see it in the eyes of them.'   This was a
good while before the first act was over, and so gave us ease soon;
for the duke (beside his own good taste) has as particular a knack

No. 80 Sir Francis Burdett was taken to the Tower—the street filled with the Horse Guards—the officers scaled the windows, and found Sir Francis instructing his son in Magna Charta. At the old Pulteney Hotel stayed the Emperor of Russia in 1814, and there the Princess Charlotte was introduced to Prince Leopold. At No. 23 lived Lord Nelson's Lady Hamilton, and opposite the opening into the Park the Duke of Queensberry, or " Old Q.," as he was called. He was a thin, withered old man with one eye, and used on fine days to sit on his balcony, which was nearly level with the street, winking at all the females who passed. We have often seen Old Q., as Leigh Hunt describes him, " sunning himself in Huncamunca's eyes," and wondered at the longevity of his dissipation and the prosperity of his wickedness. His dying bed was covered with billet-doux addressed to the " sweet eyes of his money-box." At the corner of Whitehorse Street Sir Walter Scott used to stay when in town; and Lord Byron brought Lady Byron when they were married to No. 139. There was a Whitehorse Cellar as early

---

as any one living in discovering the taste of the public. He was quite right in this as usual; the good nature of the audience appeared stronger and stronger in every act, and ended in a clamour of applause."

as 1720, and the mail coaches were a sight worth seeing in our young days starting on their course to the West. The White Bear existed in 1685, and the Hercules Pillars, where Squire Western stopped when in pursuit of Tom Jones, and where the brave old Marquis of Granby spent many a pleasant hour, were close to Apsley House.

St. James's Market and Market Street are contiguous to Piccadilly. Over a room of the Market House, Richard Baxter, the celebrated Nonconformist, used to preach. On the first occasion, the main beam of the building cracked with the weight of his congregation. And here, behind the bar of the Mitre, Farquhar found the celebrated Mrs. Oldfield, then only sixteen, rehearsing Beaumont and Fletcher's "Scornful Lady." In Market Street lived George III.'s fair Quakeress, Hannah Lightfoot.

Hard by, in Jermyn Street, lived many distinguished people—the great Marlborough, when Colonel Churchill; La Belle Stuart, who figured as the Britannia of our old coinage; Sir Isaac Newton, and Secretary Craggs, the friend of Pope and Addison; and at the St. James's Hotel was the last lodging in London of Sir Walter Scott. "He lay here three weeks, either in a stupor or a waking dream," says Mr. Cunningham, "and when he left, and the assembled populace saw the vacant eye and prostrate figure of the illustrious poet, there was not a covered head, and hardly a dry eye."

HOUSE OF SIR ISAAC NEWTON, NEAR LEICESTER SQUARE, LONDON.

Let us return to Leicester Fields, or Leicester Square—now surrendered to our friendly French invaders. It has fallen sadly from its high estate since the Earl of Leicester built Leicester House

about Charles I.'s time, and paid three pounds for
Lammas dues to St. Martin's parish for house and
gardens, the field before the house, and Swan Close.
His lordship used to let his mansion to people of
fashion ; and here died the unfortunate Queen of
Bohemia.   A great many modern Bohemians are

HOGARTH'S HOUSE, LEICESTER SQUARE, LONDON.

still to be found in that neighbourhood.   Colbert,
the French ambassador, and other notabilities,
lived here.   Pennant called it " Pouting Place," as
the Prince of Wales, afterwards George II., bought
it when he quarrelled with his father; and here
the hero of Culloden was born.   When George II.
quarrelled with his son, Prince Frederick, he came

also to Pouting Place; and, to annoy the king, had " Cato " played, the future George III. enacting Portius. The Duke of Gloucester also lived here.

In " the Fields," when converted into a square, Hogarth (1764) resided at the sign of the Golden Head, made by himself out of pieces of cork glued together and painted. In the enclosure of the

HOGARTH'S CARD.

square he was often seen in his scarlet roquelaur and cocked hat. John Hunter's Museum was next door to the house Hogarth had occupied, and Sir Joshua Reynolds lived at No. 47.

New Street, Covent Garden, was fashionably inhabited in Charles II.'s time, and Vandyke's love,

the Countess of Chesterfield, lived there. At the
Pine Apple, Dr. Johnson dined very well for 8d.
—a cut of meat 6d., bread 1d., waiter 1d., which
gratuity "those who paid a shilling and had worse,
did not give"—so the Doctor was as well served as
they. And there, in King Street, lived Lenthall,
the Speaker, in the time of the Commonwealth;
and Dr. Arne and his sister, Mrs. Colley Cibber,
were born there; as was Quin, the actor. Nicholas
Rowe, the poet, died there; and Garrick lived
there in 1745.

It was not until Henry VIII.'s time that any
salads, carrots, cabbage, or other edible roots were
produced in England (Butler). Beneath a small
grotto of trees, under the north side of the garden
wall of Bedford House (1656), was the first Covent
Garden Market for the sale of fruits, herbs, flowers,
and roots. It derives its name from there having
been formerly a convent garden and burial ground,
belonging to Westminster, on its site. The wine
cellars of the Tavistock Hotel were formerly convent cells, and never better occupied than at present.
After the Dissolution, the grounds were granted
by Edward VI. to the Duke of Somerset; and, on
his attainder, having reverted to the Crown, they
were then granted to John, Earl of Bedford, and
seven acres, called Long Acre, of the yearly value

of 6*l*. 6*s*. 8*d*. **John of** Bedford builded a town residence, principally of wood, on the site of Southampton Street, where it remained until 1704.

In 1679 there were twenty-three salesmen severally rated at two shillings and one shilling to the poor. In 1704 Tavistock Row was built, **and the** market people **forced into** the centre of the square, where **a column with** steps of black marble, and a dial, formerly **stood.** On these steps old women sold rice-milk and barley-broth; and we remember when the bird-fanciers **made a** great show in the centre of the market.

The Piazzas were built from designs by Inigo Jones, and were very fashionable when first erected. The north side was called the Great Piazza, **the** eastern the Little Piazza, half of which, where the Hummums stand, was destroyed **by fire.** The fronts of the houses were originally **of** red brick, and had balconies. It appears from **the** baptismal registers, that Piazza was a favourite name for parish children, and Peter Piazza and Mary Piazza are of constant occurrence. On the same authority it appears also that almost all the foundlings of the parish were laid at the door of the Bishop of Durham. [Wycherley's " Country Wife."]

St. Paul's Church was called by its founder " the handsomest barn in England." In the churchyard lie Carre, Earl of Somerset, father of Lady Rachel Russell; "Hudibras" Butler; Sir Peter Lely—he who

> " On animated canvas stole
> The sleepy eye that spoke the melting soul ;"

Wycherley; Joe Haines; Estcourt, the caterer of a Beefsteak Club—

> "Gay Bacchus, liking Estcourt's wine,
> A noble meal bespoke us;
> And for the guests that were to dine
> Brought Comus, Love, and Jocus ;"

Sir Robert Strange, the celebrated engraver of Titian's pictures; Macklin, the great actor, who for thirty years "balmed his stomach with a pint of stout sweetened to a syrup ;" Peter Pindar Walcot; and others. Upon the site of Sir Kenelm Digby's laboratory, and where he made his sympathetic powder, a house was built for Lord Oxford, the victor of the Hague in 1692. It is now Evans's Hotel, better known, perhaps, as Paddy Green's, the name of the most courteous of hosts, and who is deservedly respected for having reformed the character of London supper-rooms.

We should fill a large volume did we attempt to introduce you to one half of the other noted taverns and coffee-houses of Covent Garden, and there tell you a tithe of their stories.

The Rose Tavern was in Brydges Street in Charles II.'s time; part pulled down when Garrick made a new front to the theatre. " On May 18, 1668 [Master Samuel Pepys], it being almost twelve o'clock, went to the King's playhouse to see Sedley's ' Mulberry Garden.' " He was there a little before the doors opened, and found, when he did get in, many people already come by private ways into the pit; but, after a while, having **eat** nothing —Sedley's wit had no chance against the stomachic vacuum—Pepys did slip out, leaving a boy to keep **his** place, and got half a breast of mutton off the **spit,** and dined all alone at the Rose. The Rose **was the** fashion in its day, and figures largely **in** the *Ana* of a hundred years ago.

Will's Coffee House, Tom's Coffee House, and Button's—who has not read of those famous resorts of Dryden, Addison, Pope, Cibber—nay, all the **wits and** men of note in days gone by?

Will's was at **the** corner of Bow **Street,** then a **fashionable locality,** long frequented by **those** who **sought**

" For **new lampoons,** fresh cant, and modish air."

An evening in Bow Street has a very suspicious **signification now** a days; but Wycherley lived **there when King** Charles paid him a visit; and,

in after time, Henry Fielding, the great English
novelist. Will's was named after William Unwin,
and made famous by Dryden, who was there the
arbiter of critical disputes. He had a particular
chair by the fire in winter, and in summer it was
carried into the balcony. It was probably returning from Will's to his house in Long Acre, that
Dryden was waylaid in Rose Street by Rochester's
bully, Black Will, with a cudgel. So famous was
this ambuscade, that many allusions are made to it in
old state poems, and Mulgrave's " Essay on Satire,"
which occasioned it, was called " The Rose Alley
Satire."

Tom's, kept by one Thomas West, was of the
same character as Will's and Button's, but in 1704
assumed the form of a club, having seven hundred
members, and its suite of card, conversation, and
coffee-rooms, extending from No. 17 to the adjoining
house. Here met Johnson, Garrick, Murphy, Goldsmith, Dr. Dodd, Reynolds, Foote, Moody, George
Colman the elder, and many others, including some
of the principal nobility. The subscriptions were
kept up till 1814.

There was another Tom's, kept by an old
Etonian, who, fearing to be plucked at college,
went away and kept a coffee-house in Covent
Garden Market.

Moll King's was frequently the scene of midnight brawls, and a favourite studio of Hogarth, who has preserved it in his "Frosty Morning."

Here, in front of the church, in former days, took place the elections for Westminster, and many an election row, the Garden supplying striking arguments more irresistible than the eloquence of the hustings. No end of smart things are recorded about them, some very abusive. Horne Tooke said a good one to a rough fellow in the crowd, who cried out, "Well, Mr. Tooke, you will have all the blackguards with you to-day!"—"I am delighted to hear it," said Tooke; "and from such good authority as you are."

CHAPTER XI.

THE Shakespeare Tavern, when the Lion's Head **was removed** from Button's, must not be passed by, as it **was the** first tavern opened in Covent Garden, and Tomkins, its proprietor, had never less than a hundred pipes of wine in his cellar. He kept seven waiters, all neatly dressed with ruffles, and died worth forty thousand pounds.

Honest Jack Stacie, his apprentice, kept the Bedford Coffee House when Henry Fielding, **Hogarth**, Churchill, Goldsmith, and others had their gossiping shilling rubber club. Fielding was a very merry fellow, but Churchill and Hogarth quarrelled with each other. Here the celebrated Beefsteak Club, founded by Lambert, Rich's scene-painter, in the scene room of **the** theatre, was held, after migrating to the Shakespeare and back again to the theatre. Among the members of the steaks were some of the most distinguished noblemen and gentlemen of their time. Steaks, fried onions, and port wine constituted the bill of fare, and the first toast was, "Success to the Ten Acres" on which Covent Garden stands, completely surrounded by St. Martin's parish.

Addison, after a time, patronized Button, formerly a servant to the Countess of Warwick. And his coffee-house continued in vogue until Addison's death and Steele's retirement into Wales. The literature of the time, as you are aware, abounds with allusions to Button's. Steele, Budgell, Phillips, Carey, Davenant, and Colonel Brett were Addison's chief companions at Button's. Addison usually studied all the morning, dined at Button's, and stayed there some hours, and at times far into the night. Pope was of the company for about a year, but it hurt his health, and so he quitted it. It is possible that a rod, which Ambrose Phillips hung up at the bar for Pope's especial comfort, might have had something to do with the retirement of the satirist.

Here you remember the Guardian had his Lion's Head in imitation of its Venetian prototype. This leonine letter-box was removed to the Shakespeare Tavern under the Piazza, then to the Bedford Hotel, then sold by Mr. Robins to Mr. Richardson,

who had Evans's Hotel. The Head is now preserved at the Duke of Bedford's, at Woburn.

SERVANTUR MAGNIS
ISTI CERVICIBUS UNGUES;
NON NISI DELECTÂ PASCITUR
ILLE FERA.

LETTER-BOX AT BUTTON'S COFFEE-HOUSE.   (Designed by Hogarth.)

Long Acre was formerly called the Elms.   Here
Captain Oliver Cromwell resided in a fair house in
1643, and John Dryden, in a house on the north
side, facing Rose Alley.   In a shoemaker's shop
Richard Wilson's early landscapes were exhibited
for sale, and Thomas Stothard, the painter, was
born here.   Defoe describes a celebrated Mug
House, where persons met for vocal harmony—
a harp playing at one end of the room.   Ale only
was drunk out of mugs, each toper chalking his

score on the table.   On King George's ascension the friends of the Protestant cause, to oppose the Tory mobs, opened Mug Houses in various parts of London, and where they assembled their adherents. Many violent encounters ensued, until an Act of Parliament put an end to the city strife and these political Muggletonians.

Partridge, the almanack-maker, whom Swift killed and buried many years before his death, and Mrs. Clive, the favourite Nell (in "The Devil to Pay") of her day, lived in Henrietta Street, Covent Garden, when Tavistock Street was the fashionable emporium for millinery; and here Lord Sandwich first met Miss Ray, whom Parson Hackman shot from the window of the Bedford Hotel.   At the White Peruke, in Maiden Lane, lived Voltaire ; and Turner, the painter, was born in the same locality.

Covent Garden, "for cabbages and comedians famed in story," and its adjacent coffee-houses, are so intimately associated with the theatres, that we will very briefly recall some of the records of those popular places of amusement.   The first playhouse erected purposely for scenic representation was called the Theatre in Holywell Lane, Shoreditch, built by John Brayne, the father-in-law of Burbidge, the actor, and by trade a joiner.   Paris Gardens existed still earlier—in 1560—for bull and bear-baiting only; and there plays were also performed subsequently. The Globe, Hope, Rose, Blackfriars, Whitefriars, and other theatres have been already spoken of. The Cockpit, or Phœnix Theatre, occupied the site of Pitt Place, in Drury Lane, and was twice nearly destroyed by the London apprentices, and pulled down in 1649 by sectarian soldiers.

When the stage revived, after the Restoration, the king, however, patronising only two theatres —the King's and the Duke's—little attention was paid to correctness of costume, but the dresses were magnificent and costly—mostly left-off suits of royalty and the nobility; and these continued to be presented to the theatres as late as George II. The scenery improved, and some attempt was made to realise the incidents described, as in before time Desdemona had been frequently smothered on a deal table, and the gorgeous Henry VIII. listened to Catherine's appeal when seated in great state on a three-legged stool. The only female sovereign who had visited a public theatre was Henrietta Maria, until Charles II.'s time, as the plays of Shakespeare—

"Which so did take Eliza and our James "—

were always played in the halls, banqueting houses, or cockpits attached to the Court. Charles made

the theatre the fashion, and the queen and ladies
of the Court attended, generally wearing masks.
For

> "The wits of Charles found easier way to fame,
> Nor wished for Jonson's art nor Shakespeare's flame;
> Themselves they studied, as they felt they writ—
> Intrigue was plot, obscenity was wit."

Women's parts had hitherto been played only
by men — Kynaston was very celebrated — but
actresses now appeared upon the stage, and many
have become closely associated with the licentious
history of the time. The first female actress
was said to have been a Mrs. Saunderson, who
belonged to Davenant's company, and performed
the part of Ianthe in the "Siege of Rhodes."
Malone, however, disputes this lady's questionable
distinction. The play began at three, and so
allowed a visit to the Mulberry Garden or Vauxhall after. The prices were somewhat less than
at present; and servants in livery were admitted
free to the upper gallery after the fifth act had
commenced. The orange girls were an impudent
set, who stood in the pit with their backs to the
stage, and chatted with the beaux, who paid, like
Mr. Pepys, sixpence apiece for their oranges. Their
mistress, or superior, was called Orange Moll, and
found a capital representative in Mr. Keeley, when
the writer's late most valued friend, Douglas

Jerrold, produced his " Nell Gwynn." The ladies in
the pit wore vizards or masks; and Mr. and Mrs.
Pepys long affected the middle gallery, price
eighteenpence.

It was customary (we quote Ryan's "Dramatic
Table Talk") to admit that class of spectators who
frequented the boxes on to the stage, and to
accommodate them with stools, for the use of
which they paid sixpence or a shilling, according
to circumstances. It would seem, however, that
this absurd custom was confined to the smaller
houses, or private theatres, as they were termed,
where the company was less numerous and more
select. Here the fastidious critic, the wit, ambitious
of distinction, and the gallant, studious of the
display of his apparel or of his person, were to be
seen seated upon stools, or reclining upon the
rushes with which the stage was strewn, and
regaling themselves with pipes of tobacco, supplied either by their own pages or by the boys
of the house. Amidst such "most admired con-
fusion" and indecency were the dramatic works of
Shakespeare and his contemporaries produced,
works which we,

"With all appliances and means to boot,"

with everything that can promote the reality of

the scene, have **never** seen equalled, and very
seldom, indeed, approached. The following quotation, from the introduction to " Cynthia's Revels,"
is quite in point :

> And here, I enter.
> 1st CHILD. What! upon the stage, too ?
> 2nd CHILD. Yes: and I step forth **like** one of the children, and
> ask you, Would you have **a** stool, sir?
> 3rd CHILD. A stool, boy !
> 2nd CHILD. Ay, sir, if you give me sixpence, I'll find you one.
> 3rd CHILD. For what, I pray thee ? What shall I **do** with it ?
> 2nd CHILD. O lord, sir! will you betray your ignorance so much?
> Why, *throne yourself in state upon the stage,* **as** *other gentlemen use,* sir.

Seated, then, at their ease, they laughed, talked,
and cracked jokes with each other during the
performance, and had, as Decker says, " a signed
patent, to engross the whole commodity of censure ;
may lawfully presume to be a guider, **and stand** at
the helm, to steer the passage of the scenes." The
style and manner of the criticisms which they
vented between the whiffs **of their** pipes are
admirably ridiculed by Jonson.

" Now, sir, suppose that I am one of your genteel
auditors that am come in, having paid my **money**
at the door, with much ado ; and here I take **my**
place and **sit** down. I have my three sorts of
tobacco in my pocket, my light by me, and thus I
begin (*at the breaks he takes his tobacco*). By this
light! **I** wonder that any man is **so** mad to

come to see these rascally tits play ; here they do act like so many wrens or pismires; not the fifth part of a good face amongst them. And then their music is abominable ; able to stretch a man's ears worse than ten pillories ; and then their ditties—most lamentable things, like the pitiful fellows that make them. Poets ! By this vapour, an 'twere not for tobacco, I think the very stench of them would poison me—I should not dare to come in at their gates. A man were better visit fifteen jails, or a dozen or two of hospitals, than once venture to come near them." The disgust which so ridiculous and absurd a custom could not fail to excite in the audience, at length, however, banished it from the theatres, although an attempt was made, in comparatively modern times, to revive it, in favour of the Duchess of Queensbury, at the performance of the "Village Opera" at Drury Lane, in 1729. The ill success of this experiment was very elegantly alluded to by a wit of the day, in the following lines :

> " Bent on dire work, and kindly rude, the town,
> Impatient, hissed thy seat, dear duchess, down,
> Conscious, that there had thy soft form appeared,
> Lost all in gaze, no vacant ear had heard.
> Thy lambent eyes had looked their rage away,
> And the relenting hiss, and sav'd the play.
> Thus not in clouds (as father Homer sung),
> Such as fair Venus round Æneas flung,
> Had our dull bard escap'd the dreadful fright,
> But sunk, concealed, in an excess of light !"

At the Cockpit the first printed play, " Shirley's Wedding," was performed (1629). The Duke's Theatre and Opera was originally a tennis-court, and opened with Davenant's " Siege of Rhodes," and there Rich first introduced pantomimes, playing Harlequin himself. Quin played there, and from a fracas in which he was embroiled behind the scenes originated the sergeant's guard at the theatres royal. Gay's " Beggar's Opera," produced there, ran sixty-two nights the first season, the original Polly Peachum afterwards becoming the Duchess of Bolton. In 1848, during some alterations, the old stage-doors were discovered, and over them two busts, one supposed to have been Ben Jonson (unfortunately destroyed) and the other Shakespeare, presented to the Garrick Club by the late Duke of Devonshire, and now associated with the best collection of theatrical pictures in England. The College of Surgeons occupies the site of the Duke's Theatre—very appropriately, as no doubt much mangling of poets had been done at the Duke's.

The first Covent Garden Theatre was on the site of the old convent, and the second, of which Rich became manager, was opened in 1732. Garrick played there, having first appeared at Goodman's Fields, and drawn all London—horn mad, Walpole

says—to that remote region. In 1808 the theatre
was destroyed by fire, and rebuilt by Smirke, the
first stone being laid by the Prince of Wales. In
1809 it opened with new prices, which caused the
notorious O. P. or Old Price row, and which continued for seventy-seven nights, during which time
scarcely a word that was uttered on the stage was
heard for the rioting of the incensed audience. The
manager had to surrender at discretion; and eight
years after John Kemble took his farewell of the
stage, as did his brother Charles in 1840: and
here Edmund Kean acted for the last time in 1833.
With what wonderful actors is Covent Garden
Theatre associated in our memory, when the play
was indeed " the thing." This theatre was destroyed
by fire in 1856, at the conclusion of a masquerade,
one of the last, we hope, in England.

The first Drury Lane Theatre was built on the
site of the present one for Thomas Killigrew, the
company being called the King's servants; and
here Nell Gwynn first appeared. The King's
House was destroyed by fire, and was rebuilt by
Sir Christopher Wren for Killigrew, Hart, Mohun,
and (according to Mr. Collier) Dryden. Dryden
wrote the opening prologue and epilogue; and
when Garrick took the theatre, Dr. Johnson wrote
the prologue; and there Garrick, the greatest actor

perhaps that ever played, took leave of the stage. **Richard Brinsley** Sheridan then became part proprietor, and John Kemble stage-manager. The theatre was taken down and another erected, called by Mrs. Siddons "The Wilderness," as it was capable of holding from 4000 to 5000 persons. It was destroyed by fire in 1809, and rebuilt, Lord Byron writing the prologue for the opening night. James and Horace Smith's "Rejected Addresses," in imitation of the poets of the day, had their origin **in** the committee's advertisement for "an occasional prologue," that is, a prologue for the occasion. There was an iron curtain at Drury Lane, which, in case of need, was to be let down, so, as the prologue stated,

> "So, to assure their generous benefactors,
> They'd only burn the scenery and the actors."

There was also a water tank, by which the managers undertook

> "To drown the audience in a minute."

So it was out of the frying-pan into the water-butt.

We have necessarily passed over many subjects of considerable interest, but we only professed **to tell** you as much of old Westminster as could be told in a day's ramble; and now that we must part company, we are no worse friends, let us hope, than when we made acquaintance in the preface.

THE END.

LONDON : PRINTED BY WILLIAM CLOWES AND SONS, STAMFORD STREET
AND CHARING CROSS.

www.ingramcontent.com/pod-product-compliance
Lightning Source LLC
Chambersburg PA
CBHW021109270326
41929CB00009B/798